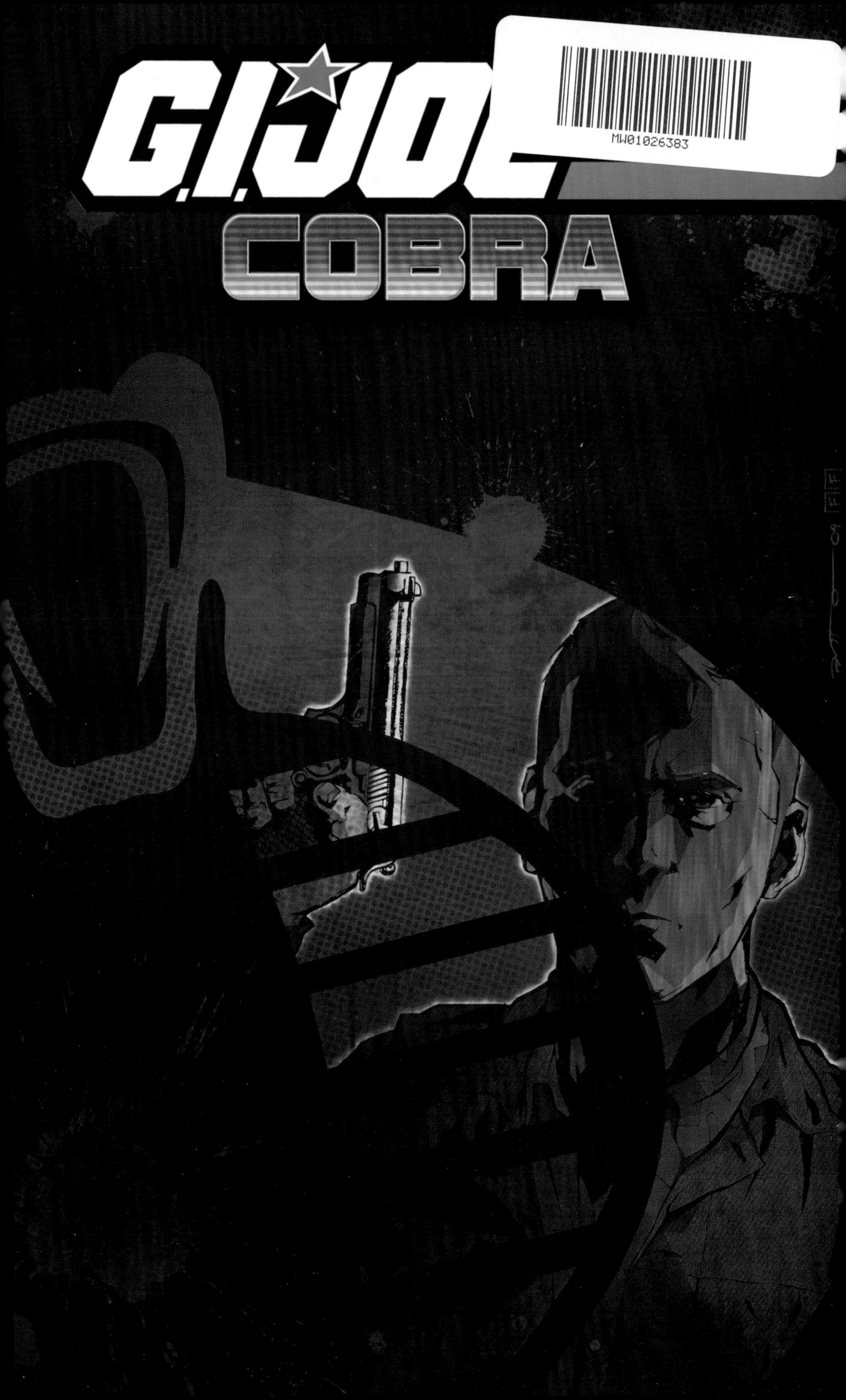
G.I. JOE
COBRA

# G.I. JOE: COBRA

Written by **Mike Costa & Christos N. Gage**
Art by **Antonio Fuso**
Colors by **Chris Chuckry & Lovern Kindzierski**
Letters by **Chris Mowry, Robbie Robbins, & Neil Uyetake**
Original Series Edits by **Andy Schmidt**
Assistant Editor **Carlos Guzman**

Collection Edits by **Justin Eisinger**
Editorial Assistance by **Mariah Huehner**
Collection Design by **Chris Mowry**

ISBN: 978-160010-535-7

12 11 10 09     1 2 3 4

www.idwpublishing.com

IDW Publishi
Operatior
Ted Adams, Chief Executive Offic
Greg Goldstein, Chief Operating Offic
Matthew Ruzicka, CPA, Chief Financial Offic
Alan Payne, VP of Sa
Lorelei Bunjes, Dir. of Digital Servic
AnnaMaria White, Marketing & PR Manac
Marci Hubbard, Executive Assista
Alonzo Simon, Shipping Manac
Angela Loggins, Staff Accounta

Editori
Chris Ryall, Publisher/Editor-in-Ch
Scott Dunbier, Editor, Special Projec
Andy Schmidt, Senior Edi
Justin Eisinger, Edi
Kris Oprisko, Editor/Foreign L
Denton J. Tipton, Edi
Tom Waltz, Edi
Mariah Huehner, Associate Edi
Carlos Guzman, Editorial Assist

Desig
Robbie Robbins, EVP/Sr. Graphic Ar
Neil Uyetake, Art Direc
Chris Mowry, Graphic Ar
Amauri Osorio, Graphic Ar
Gilberto Lazcano, Production Assist

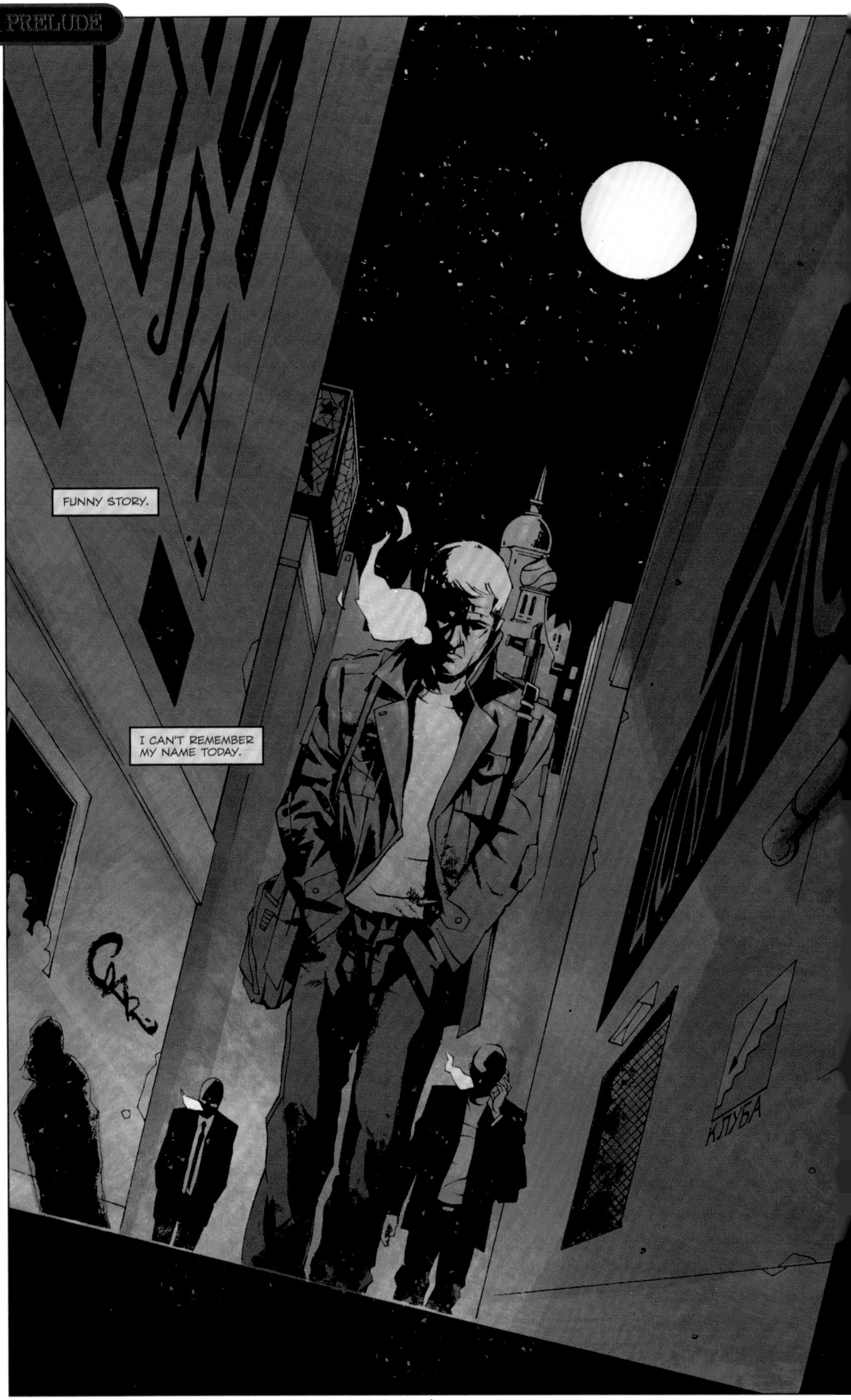
FUNNY STORY.
I CAN'T REMEMBER MY NAME TODAY.
КЛУБА

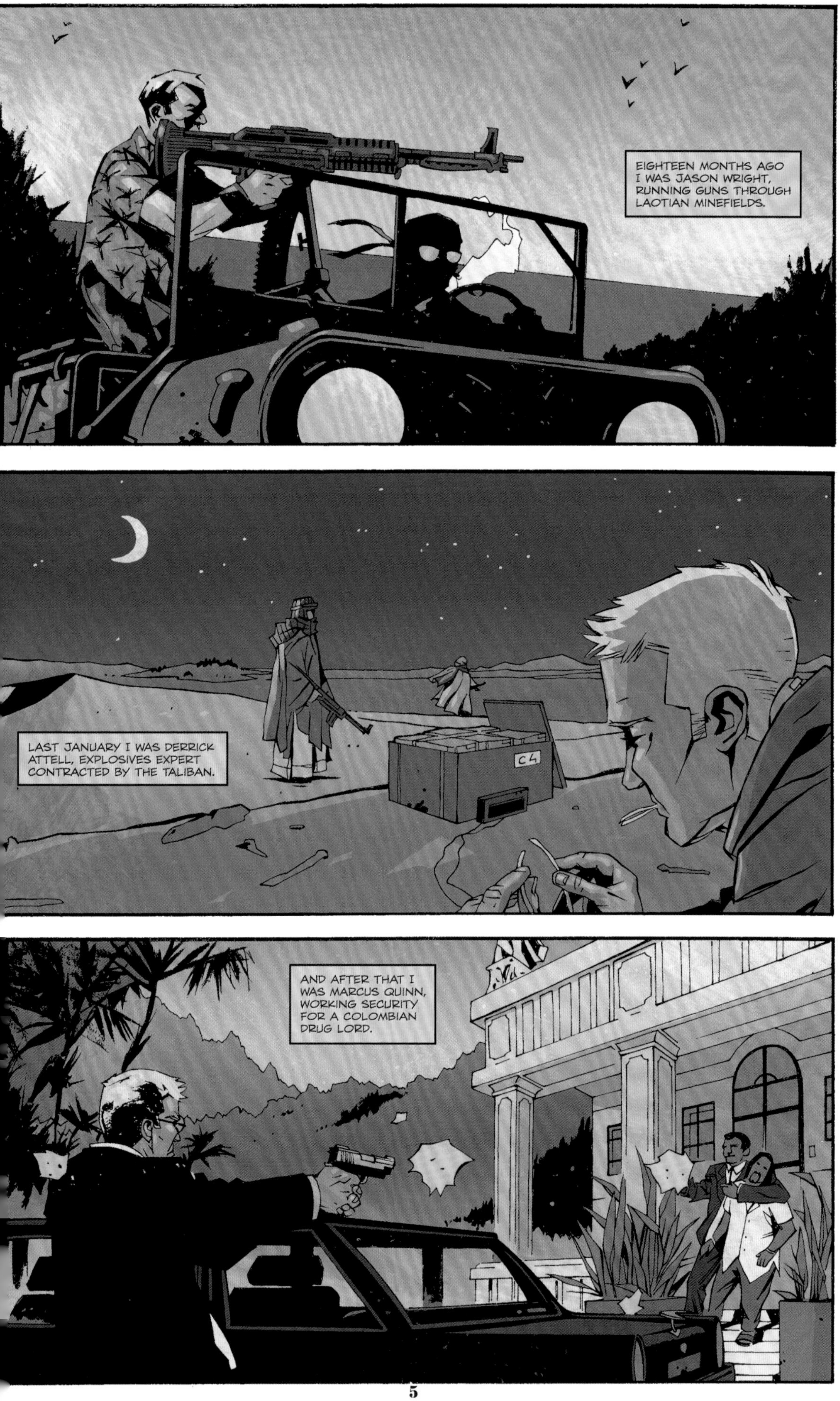
EIGHTEEN MONTHS AGO I WAS JASON WRIGHT, RUNNING GUNS THROUGH LAOTIAN MINEFIELDS.
LAST JANUARY I WAS DERRICK ATTELL, EXPLOSIVES EXPERT CONTRACTED BY THE TALIBAN.
C4
AND AFTER THAT I WAS MARCUS QUINN, WORKING SECURITY FOR A COLOMBIAN DRUG LORD.

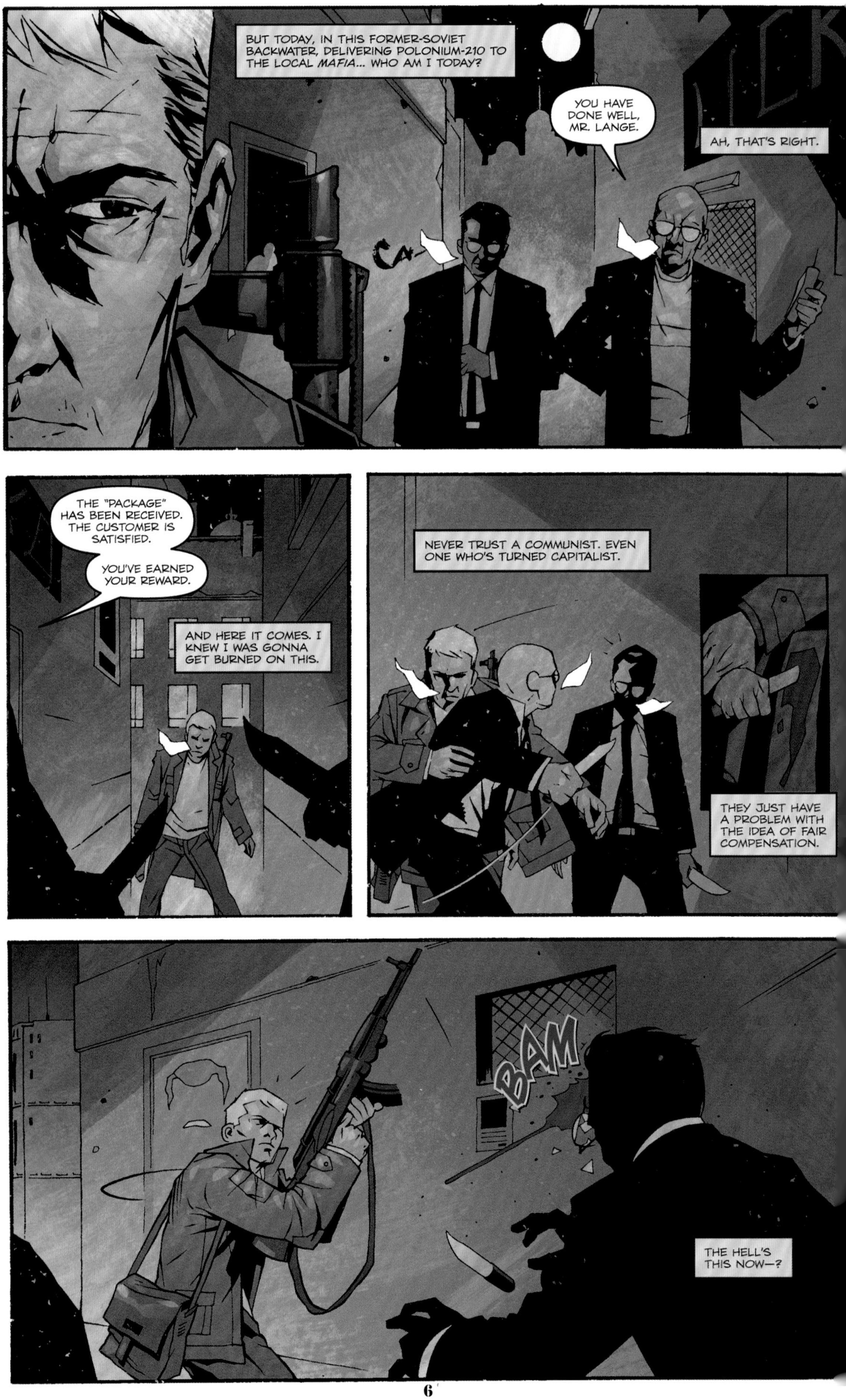
BUT TODAY, IN THIS FORMER-SOVIET BACKWATER, DELIVERING POLONIUM-210 TO THE LOCAL *MAFIA*... WHO AM I TODAY?
YOU HAVE DONE WELL, MR. LANGE.
AH, THAT'S RIGHT.
THE "PACKAGE" HAS BEEN RECEIVED. THE CUSTOMER IS SATISFIED.
YOU'VE EARNED YOUR REWARD.
AND HERE IT COMES. I KNEW I WAS GONNA GET BURNED ON THIS.
NEVER TRUST A COMMUNIST. EVEN ONE WHO'S TURNED CAPITALIST.
THEY JUST HAVE A PROBLEM WITH THE IDEA OF FAIR COMPENSATION.
BAM
THE HELL'S THIS NOW—?

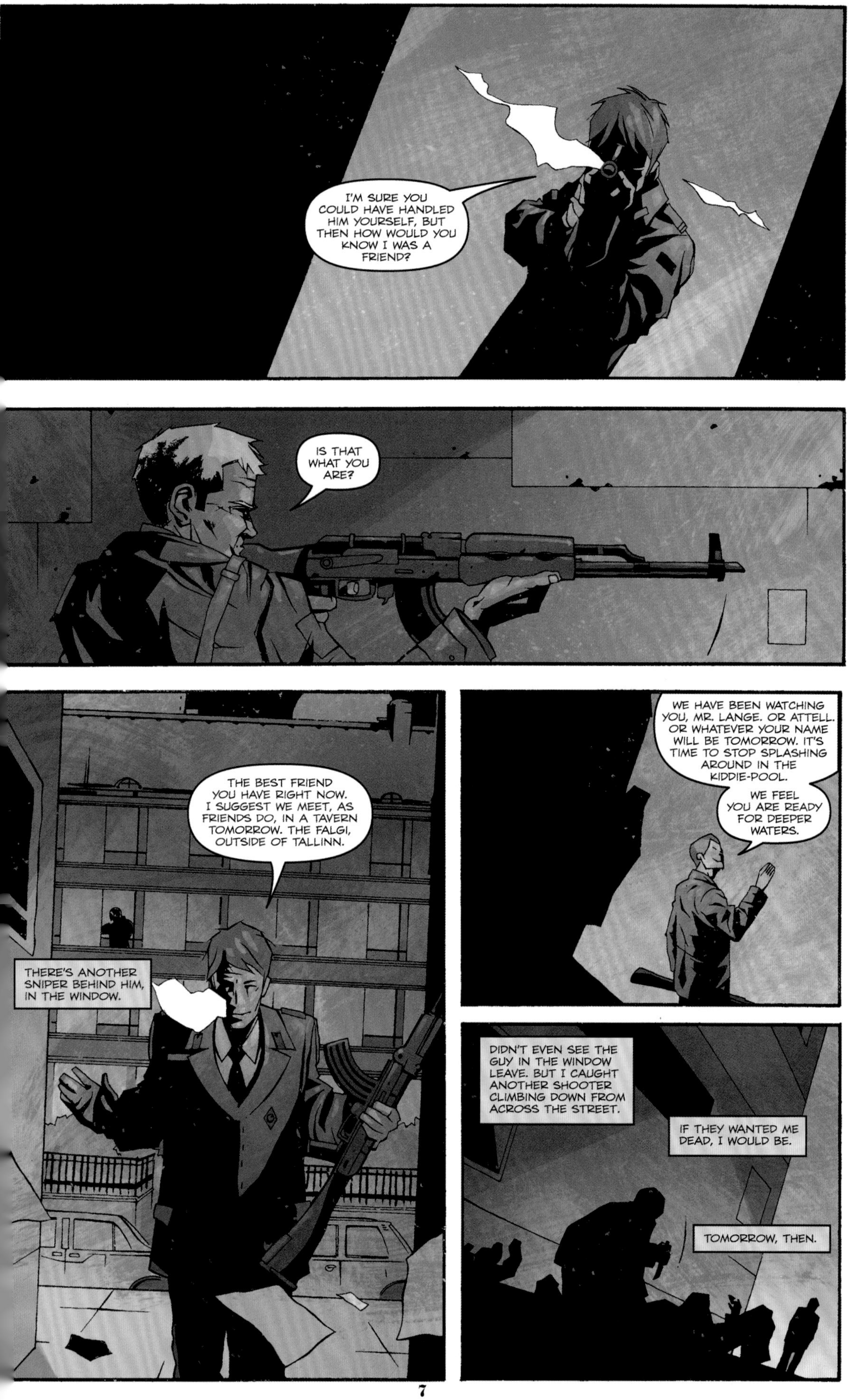
I'M SURE YOU COULD HAVE HANDLED HIM YOURSELF, BUT THEN HOW WOULD YOU KNOW I WAS A FRIEND?
IS THAT WHAT YOU ARE?
THE BEST FRIEND YOU HAVE RIGHT NOW. I SUGGEST WE MEET, AS FRIENDS DO, IN A TAVERN TOMORROW. THE FALGI, OUTSIDE OF TALLINN.
THERE'S ANOTHER SNIPER BEHIND HIM, IN THE WINDOW.
WE HAVE BEEN WATCHING YOU, MR. LANGE. OR ATTELL. OR WHATEVER YOUR NAME WILL BE TOMORROW. IT'S TIME TO STOP SPLASHING AROUND IN THE KIDDIE-POOL.
WE FEEL YOU ARE READY FOR DEEPER WATERS.
DIDN'T EVEN SEE THE GUY IN THE WINDOW LEAVE. BUT I CAUGHT ANOTHER SHOOTER CLIMBING DOWN FROM ACROSS THE STREET.
IF THEY WANTED ME DEAD, I WOULD BE.
TOMORROW, THEN.

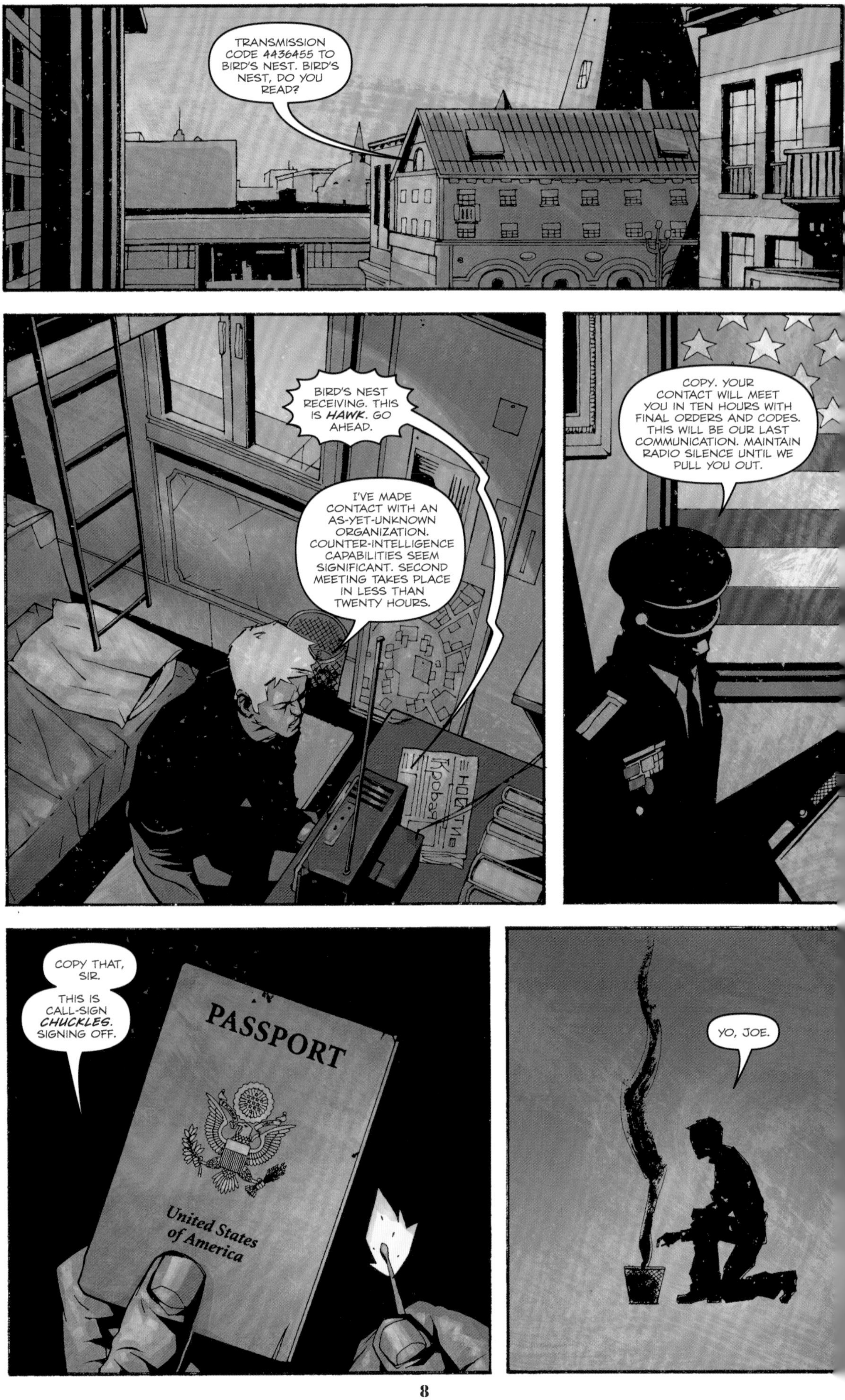
TRANSMISSION CODE 4436455 TO BIRD'S NEST. BIRD'S NEST, DO YOU READ?
BIRD'S NEST RECEIVING. THIS IS **HAWK**. GO AHEAD.
I'VE MADE CONTACT WITH AN AS-YET-UNKNOWN ORGANIZATION. COUNTER-INTELLIGENCE CAPABILITIES SEEM SIGNIFICANT. SECOND MEETING TAKES PLACE IN LESS THAN TWENTY HOURS.
COPY. YOUR CONTACT WILL MEET YOU IN TEN HOURS WITH FINAL ORDERS AND CODES. THIS WILL BE OUR LAST COMMUNICATION. MAINTAIN RADIO SILENCE UNTIL WE PULL YOU OUT.
COPY THAT, SIR.
THIS IS CALL-SIGN ***CHUCKLES***. SIGNING OFF.
PASSPORT
United States of America
YO, JOE.

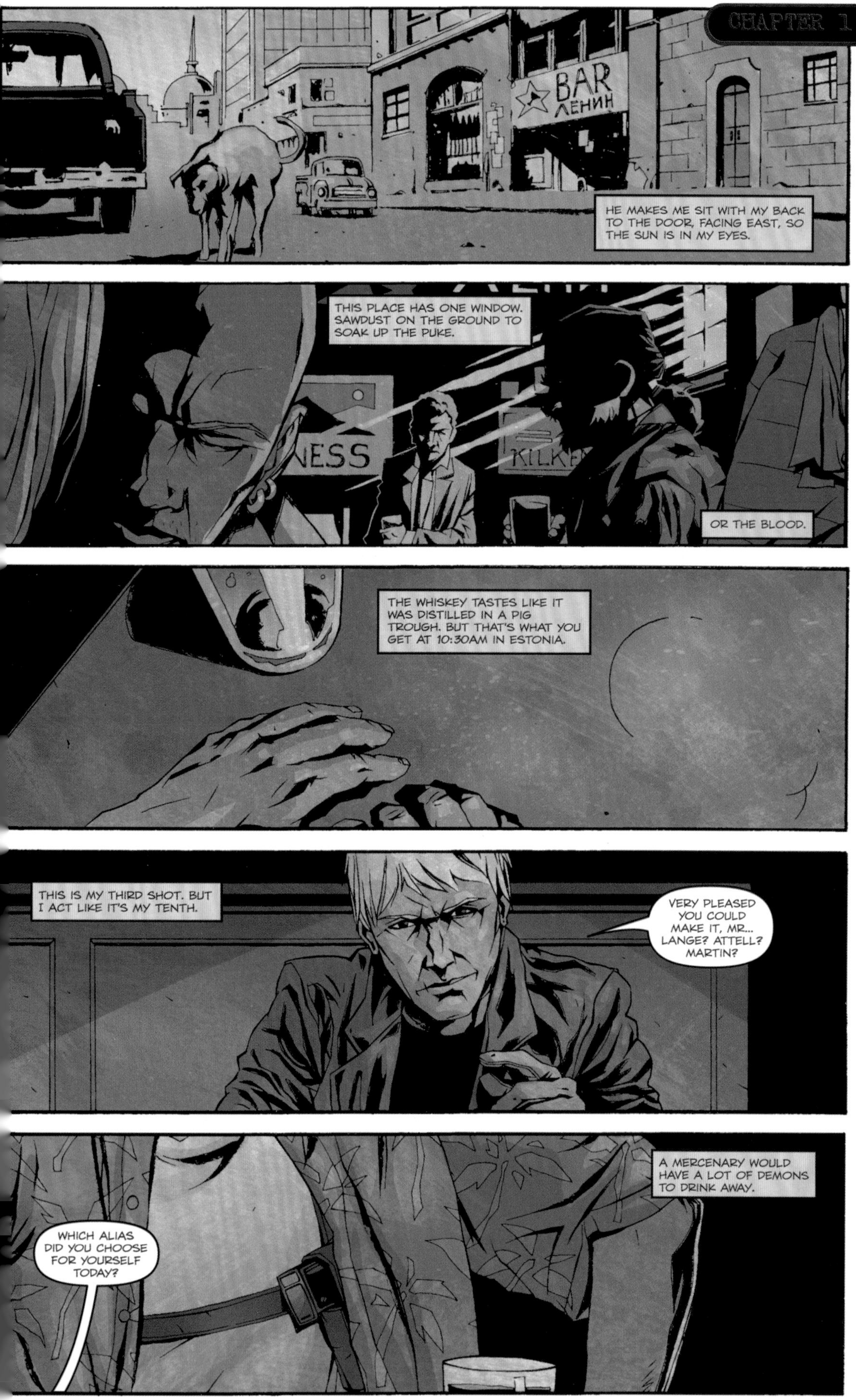
BAR
ЛЕНИН
HE MAKES ME SIT WITH MY BACK TO THE DOOR, FACING EAST, SO THE SUN IS IN MY EYES.
THIS PLACE HAS ONE WINDOW. SAWDUST ON THE GROUND TO SOAK UP THE PUKE.
OR THE BLOOD.
THE WHISKEY TASTES LIKE IT WAS DISTILLED IN A PIG TROUGH. BUT THAT'S WHAT YOU GET AT 10:30AM IN ESTONIA.
THIS IS MY THIRD SHOT. BUT I ACT LIKE IT'S MY TENTH.
VERY PLEASED YOU COULD MAKE IT, MR... LANGE? ATTELL? MARTIN?
A MERCENARY WOULD HAVE A LOT OF DEMONS TO DRINK AWAY.
WHICH ALIAS DID YOU CHOOSE FOR YOURSELF TODAY?

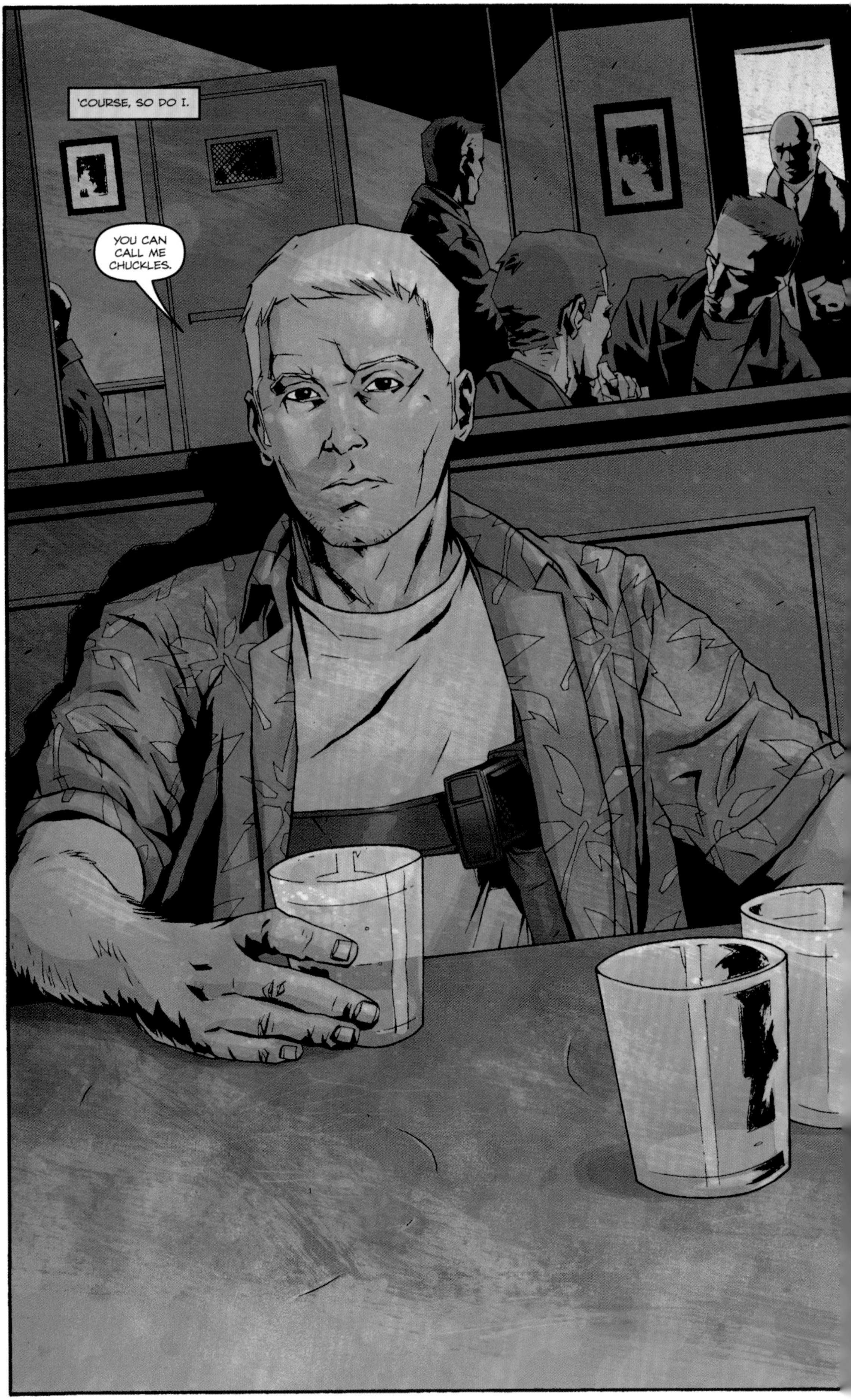
'COURSE, SO DO I.
YOU CAN CALL ME CHUCKLES.

I SEE. VERY HUMOROUS.

HE LIKED THAT. GOOD.

THE SECOND HE STOPS LIKING ME I'M DEAD.

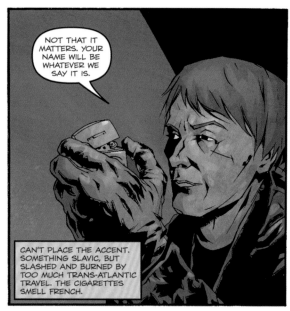

NOT THAT IT MATTERS. YOUR NAME WILL BE WHATEVER WE SAY IT IS.

CAN'T PLACE THE ACCENT. SOMETHING SLAVIC, BUT SLASHED AND BURNED BY TOO MUCH TRANS-ATLANTIC TRAVEL. THE CIGARETTES SMELL FRENCH.

OKAY. YOU TELL ME TO MEET, I MEET. BUT NOW IT'S TIME TO EXPLAIN YOURSELF.

I ONLY SLUR THE FIRST FEW WORDS. LET HIM THINK I'M PULLING MYSELF TOGETHER.

YOU ARE A MAN OF ACTION. I APPRECIATE THAT. THAT'S WHY WE WANT YOU.

HE SMILES LIKE WE'RE PALS. THE GLANCE I STOLE BEFORE WE SAT DOWN SAYS HE'S PROBABLY NOT ARMED.

YOU'RE ALSO NOT A STUPID MAN. THIS IS ANOTHER REASON.

BUT HIS PAL AT THE BAR DEFINITELY IS.

I'M HERE TO OFFER YOU A JOB.

THINK OF THIS AS YOUR INTERVIEW.

HE'S LEFT-HANDED.

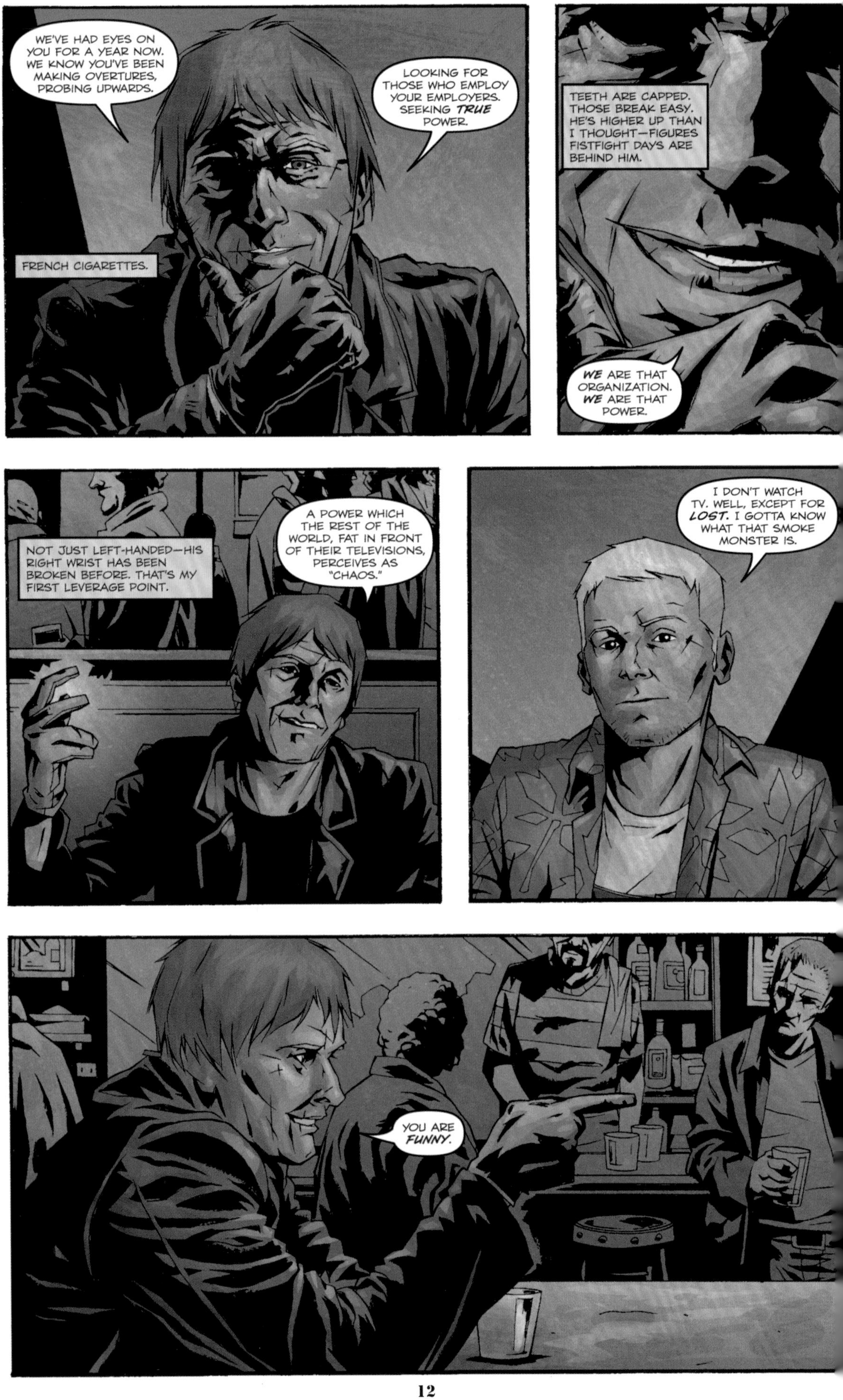
WE'VE HAD EYES ON YOU FOR A YEAR NOW. WE KNOW YOU'VE BEEN MAKING OVERTURES, PROBING UPWARDS.
LOOKING FOR THOSE WHO EMPLOY YOUR EMPLOYERS. SEEKING TRUE POWER.
FRENCH CIGARETTES.
TEETH ARE CAPPED. THOSE BREAK EASY. HE'S HIGHER UP THAN I THOUGHT—FIGURES FISTFIGHT DAYS ARE BEHIND HIM.
WE ARE THAT ORGANIZATION. WE ARE THAT POWER.
NOT JUST LEFT-HANDED—HIS RIGHT WRIST HAS BEEN BROKEN BEFORE. THAT'S MY FIRST LEVERAGE POINT.
A POWER WHICH THE REST OF THE WORLD, FAT IN FRONT OF THEIR TELEVISIONS, PERCEIVES AS "CHAOS."
I DON'T WATCH TV. WELL, EXCEPT FOR LOST. I GOTTA KNOW WHAT THAT SMOKE MONSTER IS.
YOU ARE FUNNY.

LISTEN. I'VE WORKED FOR DRUGLORDS, TERRORISTS, MILITIA... HELL, I'VE WORKED FOR THE YAKUZA. WHOEVER WAS PAYING.

SO YOU CAN'T CALL ME PICKY. BUT I HAVE NO IDEA WHO YOU PEOPLE ARE.

CAN'T SAY "YES" RIGHT AWAY. IT'S PART OF THE DANCE.

AND YOU WON'T. NOT UNTIL YOU AGREE.

WE DO NOT ADVERTISE, MR. CHUCKLES. WE SIMPLY COLLECT. AND WE ARE NOT THE ONLY ONES.

YOUR LAST THREE ENGAGEMENTS DREW THE ATTENTION OF A HIGH-LEVEL COUNTERTERROR ORGANIZATION.

WE BELIEVE THEY ARE AMERICAN. WE BELIEVE YOU'VE BECOME A HIGH-PROFILE TARGET FOR THEM. PERHAPS THAT INFLUENCES YOUR DECISION.

I DON'T KNOW WHAT THE HELL YOU'RE TALKING ABOUT.

WHAT?

THEN YOU MAY NOT BE THE MAN WE SEEK.

CRAP. I'M GONNA HAVE TO KILL THESE GUYS.

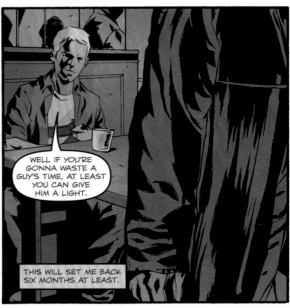

WELL IF YOU'RE GONNA WASTE A GUY'S TIME, AT LEAST YOU CAN GIVE HIM A LIGHT.

THIS WILL SET ME BACK SIX MONTHS AT LEAST.

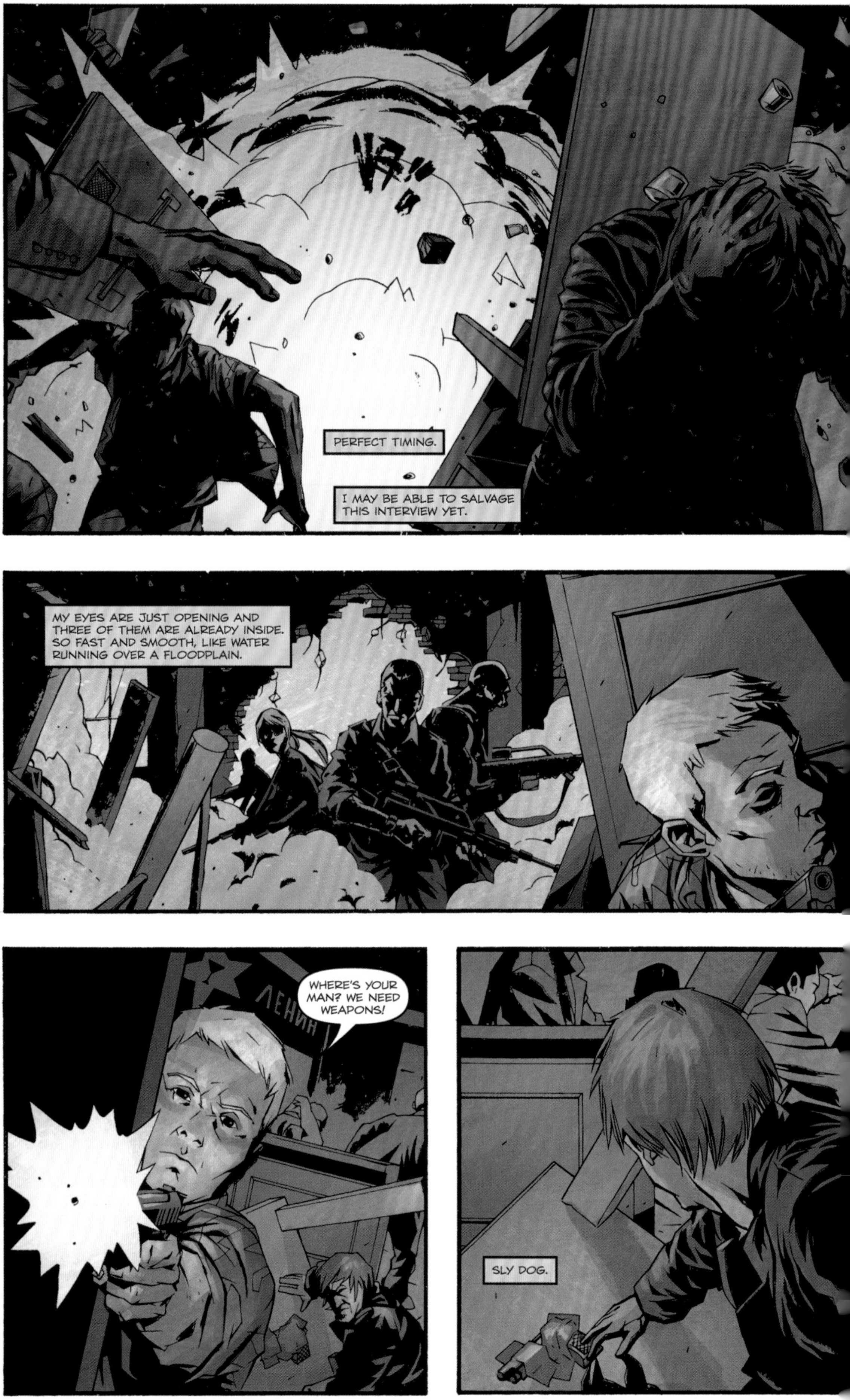
PERFECT TIMING.
I MAY BE ABLE TO SALVAGE THIS INTERVIEW YET.
MY EYES ARE JUST OPENING AND THREE OF THEM ARE ALREADY INSIDE. SO FAST AND SMOOTH, LIKE WATER RUNNING OVER A FLOODPLAIN.
ЛЕНИН
WHERE'S YOUR MAN? WE NEED WEAPONS!
SLY DOG.

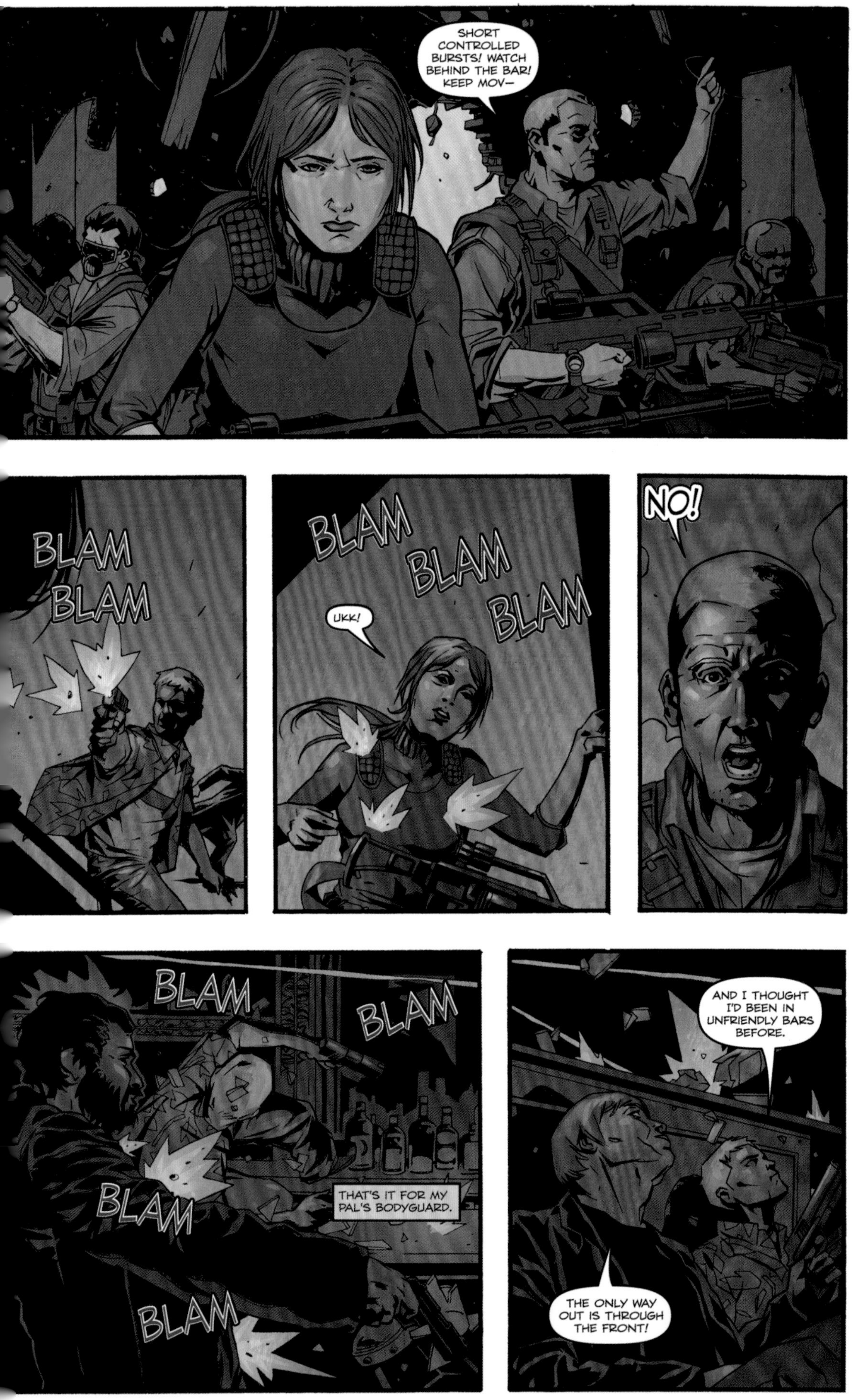
SHORT CONTROLLED BURSTS! WATCH BEHIND THE BAR! KEEP MOV—
BLAM
BLAM
BLAM
BLAM
BLAM
UKK!
NO!
BLAM
BLAM
BLAM
THAT'S IT FOR MY PAL'S BODYGUARD.
BLAM
AND I THOUGHT I'D BEEN IN UNFRIENDLY BARS BEFORE.
THE ONLY WAY OUT IS THROUGH THE FRONT!

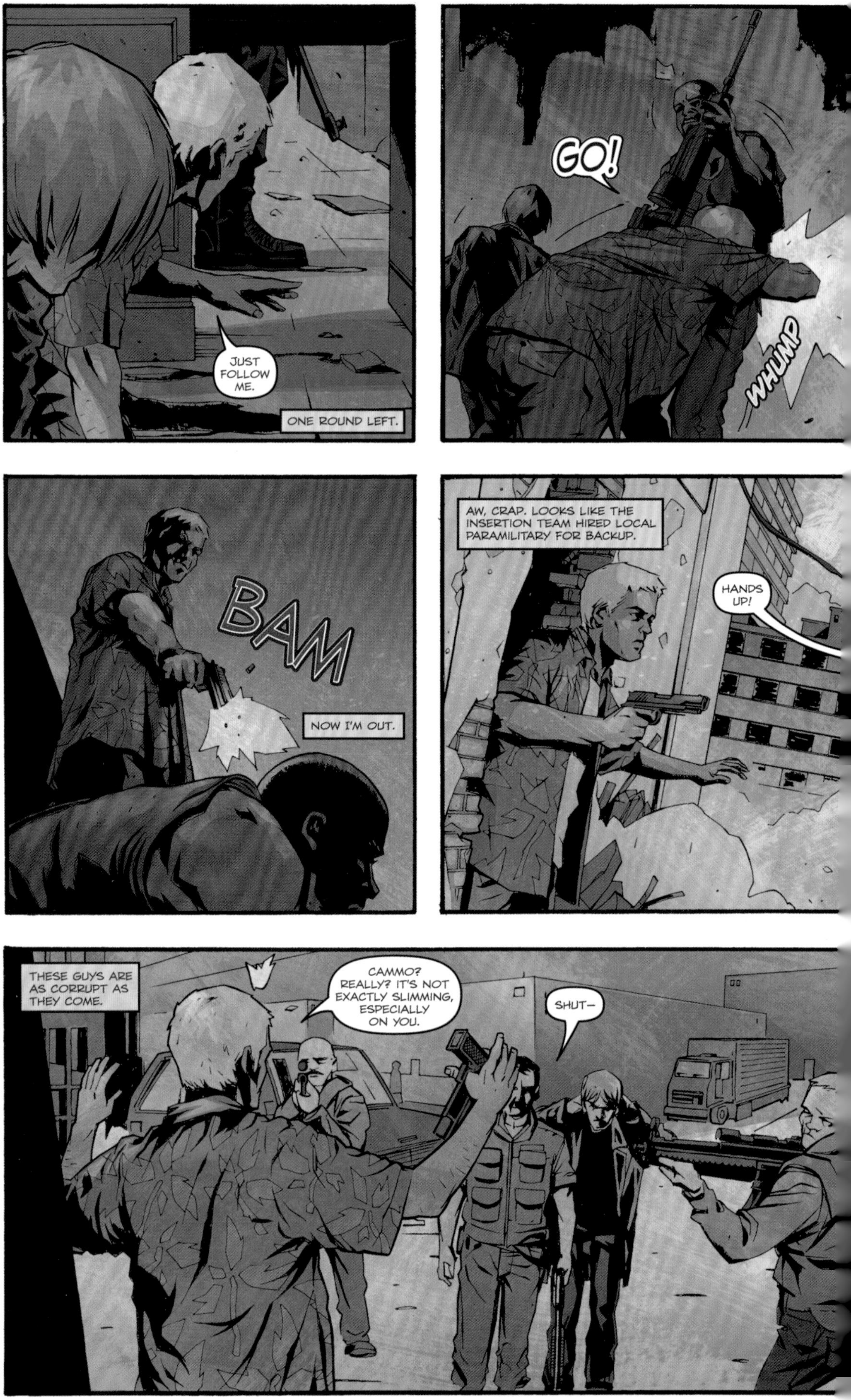
JUST FOLLOW ME.
ONE ROUND LEFT.
GO!
WHUMP
BAM
NOW I'M OUT.
AW, CRAP. LOOKS LIKE THE INSERTION TEAM HIRED LOCAL PARAMILITARY FOR BACKUP.
HANDS UP!
THESE GUYS ARE AS CORRUPT AS THEY COME.
CAMMO? REALLY? IT'S NOT EXACTLY SLIMMING, ESPECIALLY ON YOU.
SHUT–

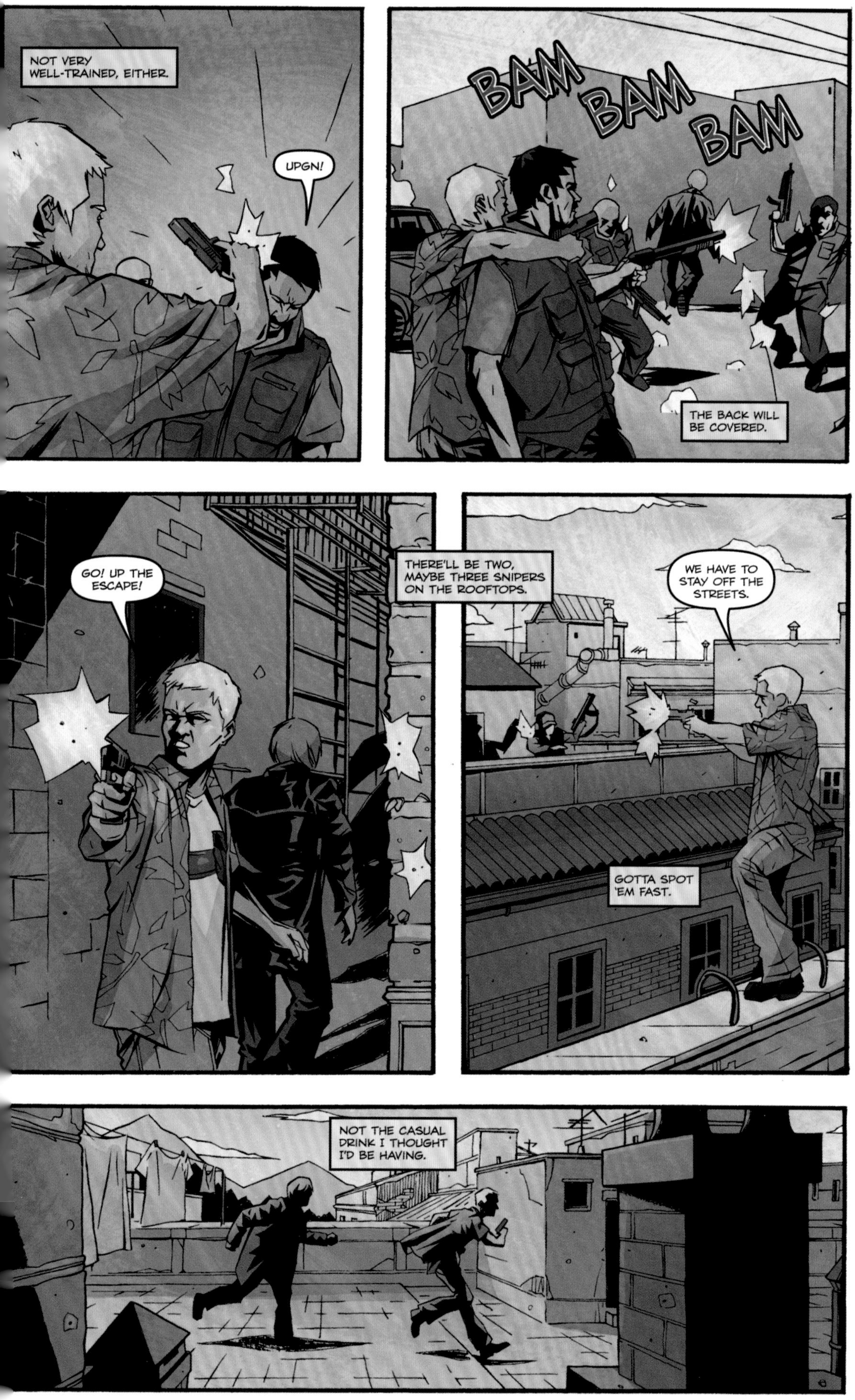
NOT VERY WELL-TRAINED, EITHER.
UPGN!
BAM BAM BAM
THE BACK WILL BE COVERED.
GO! UP THE ESCAPE!
THERE'LL BE TWO, MAYBE THREE SNIPERS ON THE ROOFTOPS.
WE HAVE TO STAY OFF THE STREETS.
GOTTA SPOT 'EM FAST.
NOT THE CASUAL DRINK I THOUGHT I'D BE HAVING.

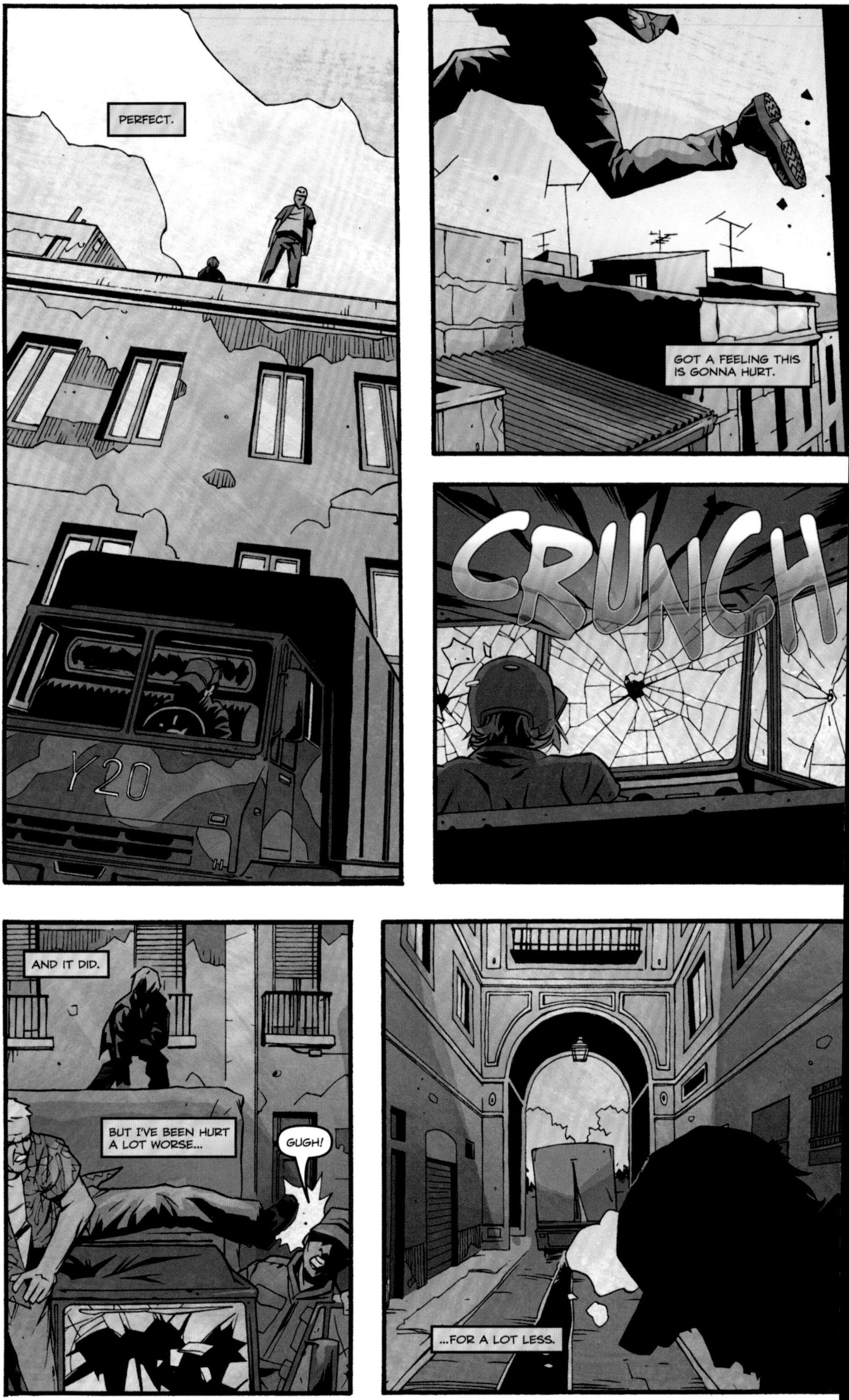
PERFECT.
GOT A FEELING THIS IS GONNA HURT.
CRUNCH
Y20
AND IT DID.
BUT I'VE BEEN HURT A LOT WORSE...
GUGH!
...FOR A LOT LESS.

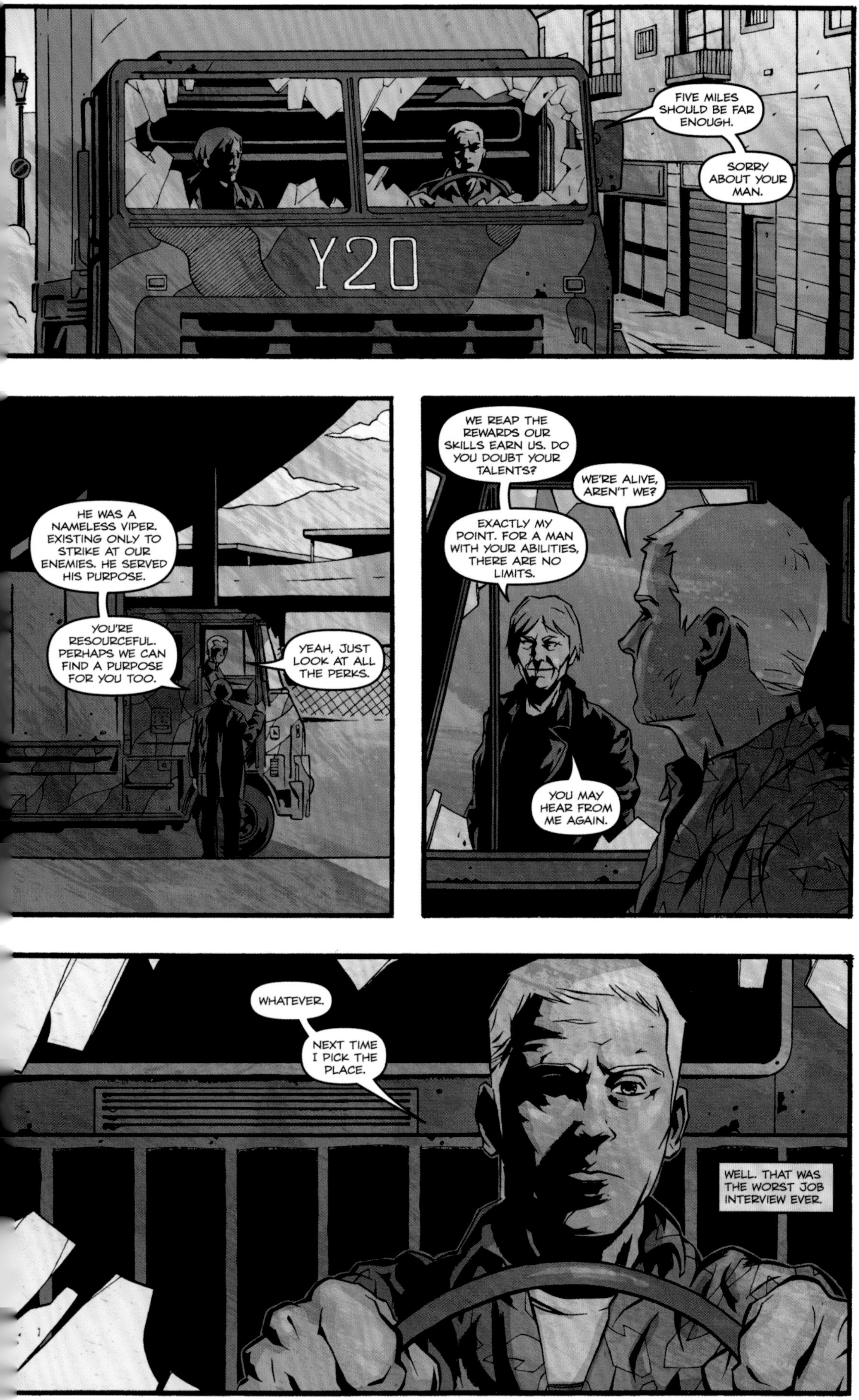
FIVE MILES SHOULD BE FAR ENOUGH.
SORRY ABOUT YOUR MAN.
Y20
HE WAS A NAMELESS VIPER. EXISTING ONLY TO STRIKE AT OUR ENEMIES. HE SERVED HIS PURPOSE.
YOU'RE RESOURCEFUL. PERHAPS WE CAN FIND A PURPOSE FOR YOU TOO.
YEAH, JUST LOOK AT ALL THE PERKS.
WE REAP THE REWARDS OUR SKILLS EARN US. DO YOU DOUBT YOUR TALENTS?
WE'RE ALIVE, AREN'T WE?
EXACTLY MY POINT. FOR A MAN WITH YOUR ABILITIES, THERE ARE NO LIMITS.
YOU MAY HEAR FROM ME AGAIN.
WHATEVER.
NEXT TIME I PICK THE PLACE.
WELL. THAT WAS THE WORST JOB INTERVIEW EVER.

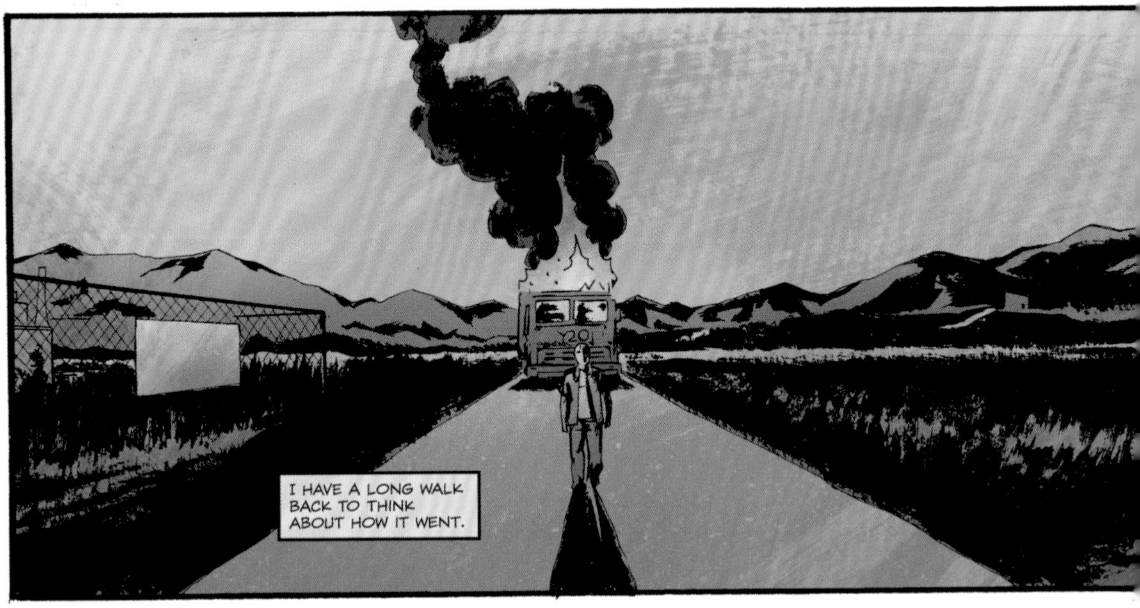
I HAVE A LONG WALK BACK TO THINK ABOUT HOW IT WENT.
Y20

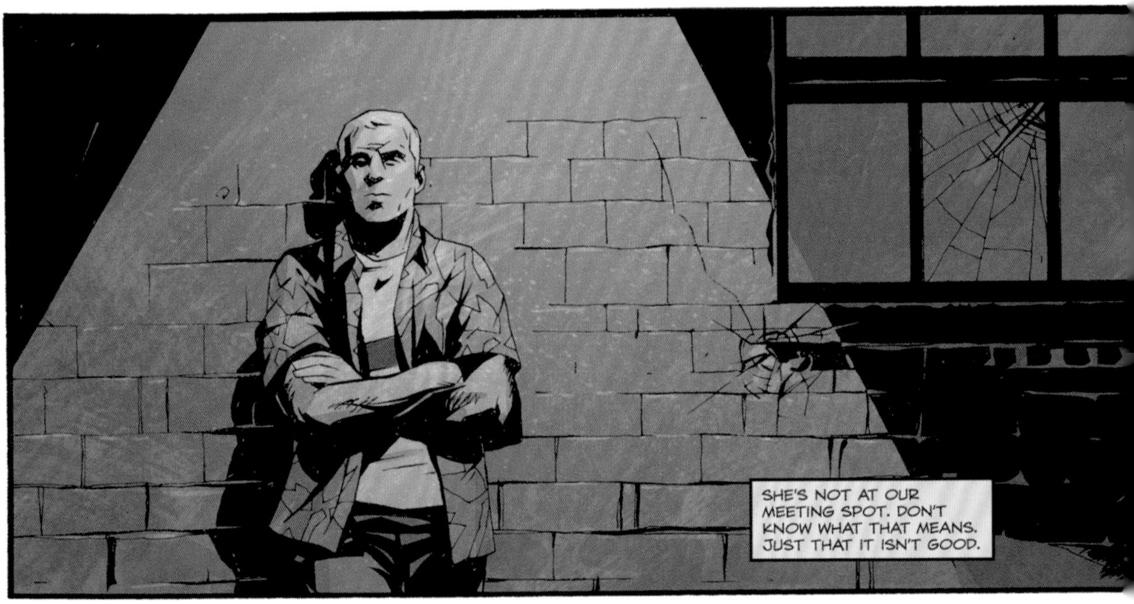
SHE'S NOT AT OUR MEETING SPOT. DON'T KNOW WHAT THAT MEANS. JUST THAT IT ISN'T GOOD.

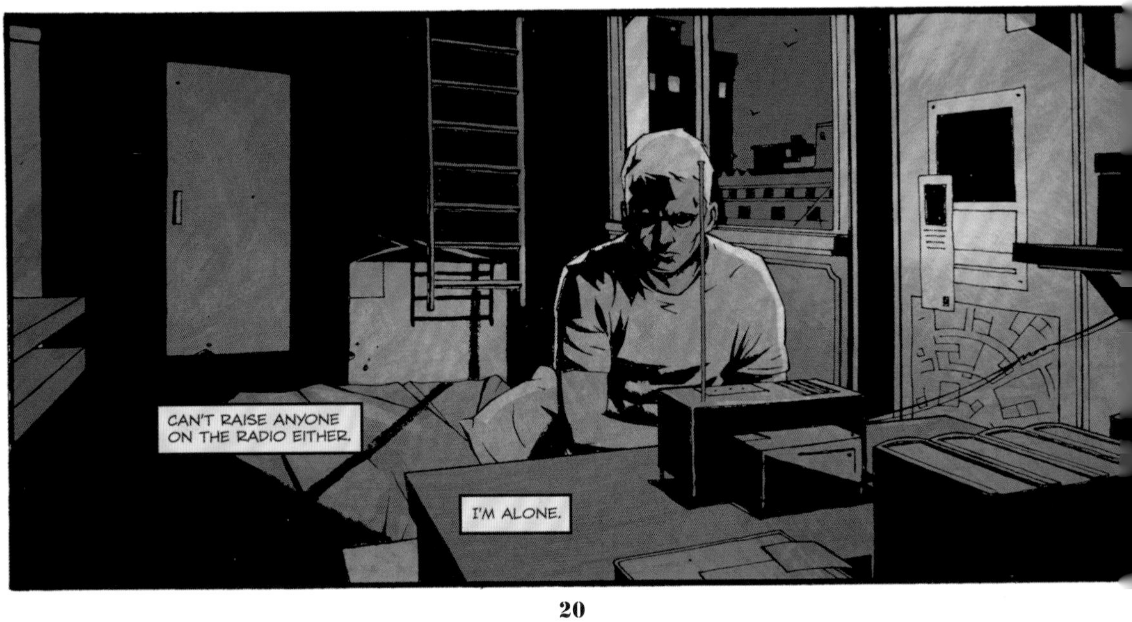
CAN'T RAISE ANYONE ON THE RADIO EITHER.
I'M ALONE.

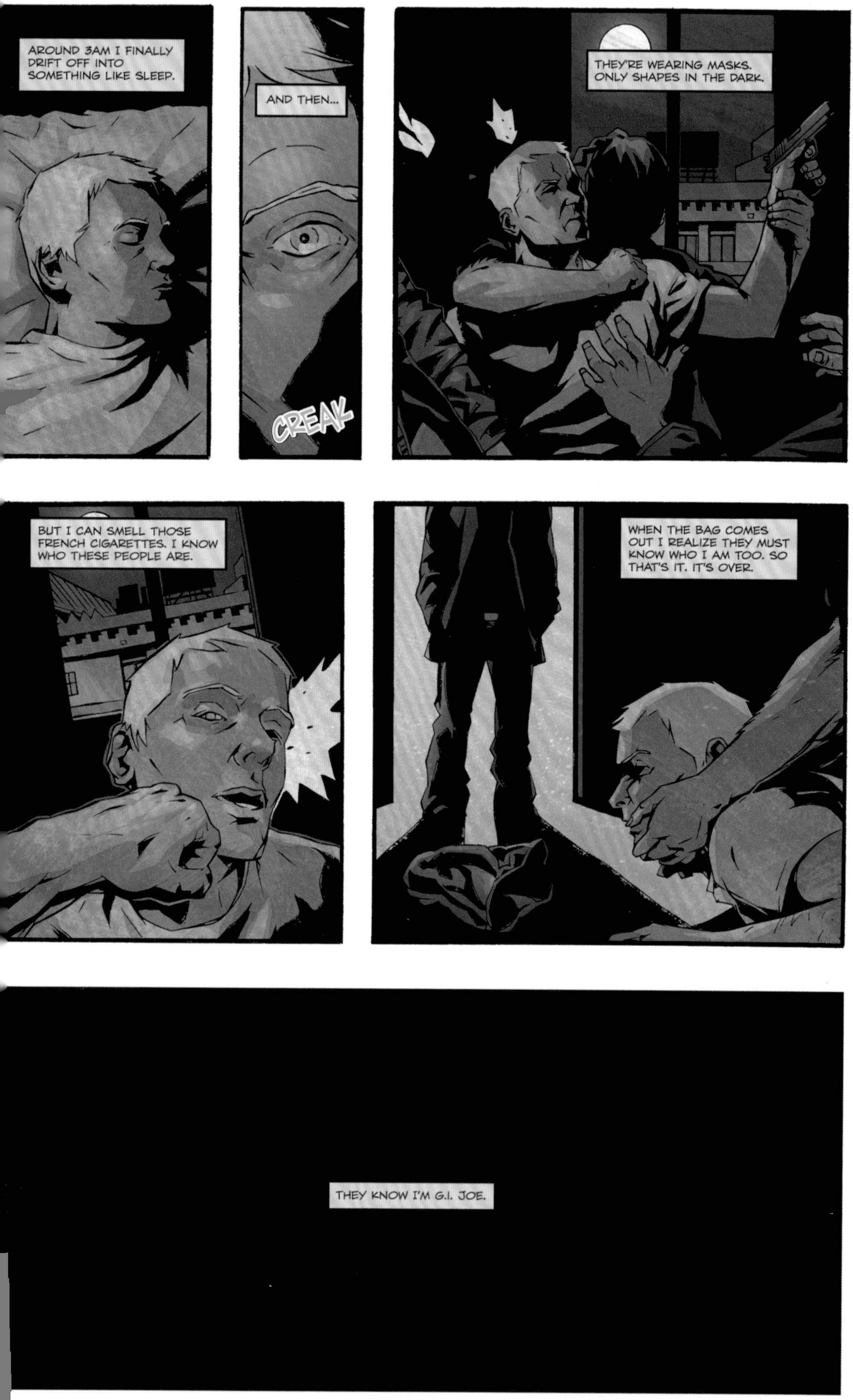
AROUND 3AM I FINALLY DRIFT OFF INTO SOMETHING LIKE SLEEP.
AND THEN...
CREAK
THEY'RE WEARING MASKS. ONLY SHAPES IN THE DARK.
BUT I CAN SMELL THOSE FRENCH CIGARETTES. I KNOW WHO THESE PEOPLE ARE.
WHEN THE BAG COMES OUT I REALIZE THEY MUST KNOW WHO I AM TOO. SO THAT'S IT. IT'S OVER.
THEY KNOW I'M G.I. JOE.

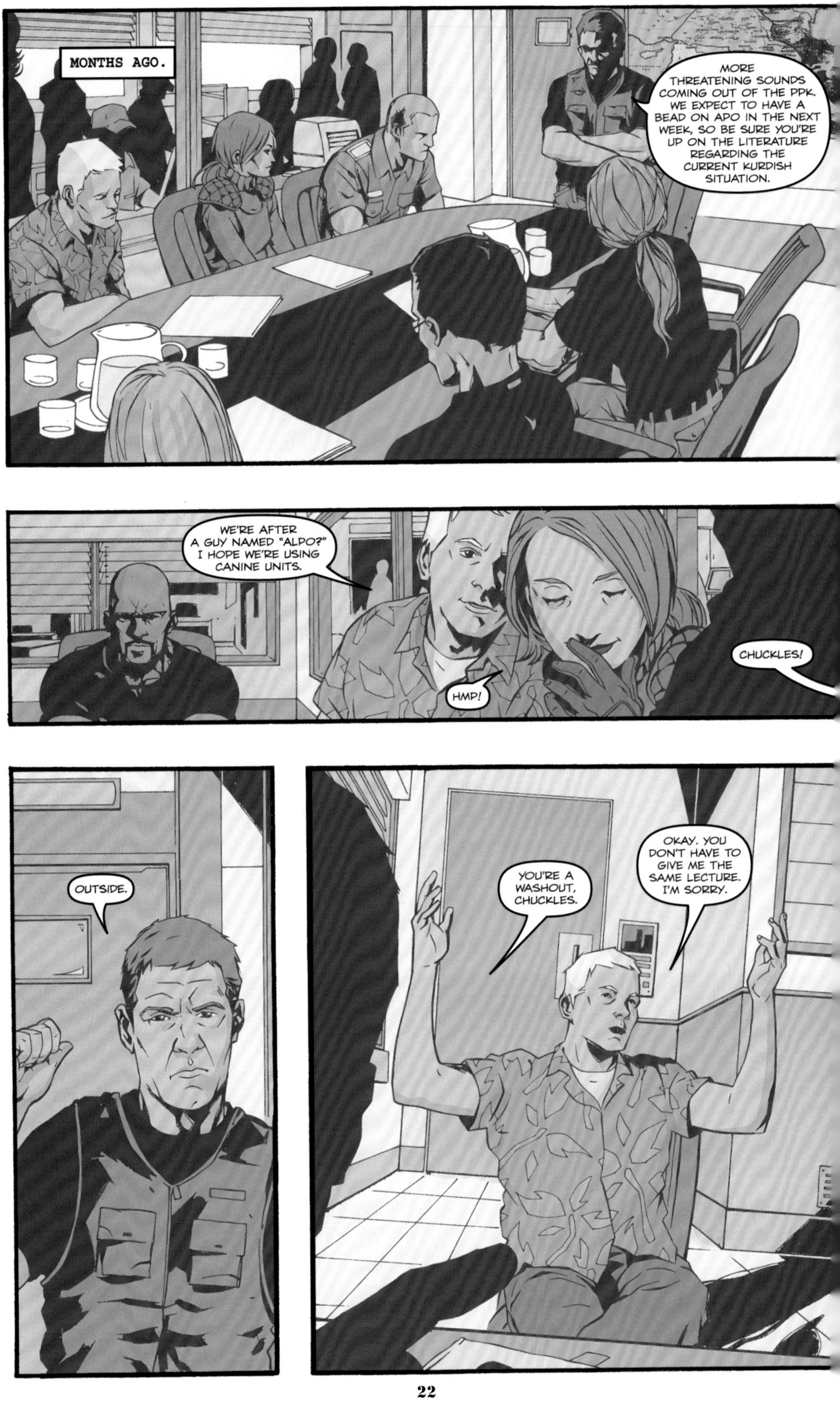
MONTHS AGO.
MORE THREATENING SOUNDS COMING OUT OF THE PPK. WE EXPECT TO HAVE A BEAD ON APO IN THE NEXT WEEK, SO BE SURE YOU'RE UP ON THE LITERATURE REGARDING THE CURRENT KURDISH SITUATION.
WE'RE AFTER A GUY NAMED "ALPO?" I HOPE WE'RE USING CANINE UNITS.
HMP!
CHUCKLES!
OUTSIDE.
OKAY. YOU DON'T HAVE TO GIVE ME THE SAME LECTURE. I'M SORRY.
YOU'RE A WASHOUT, CHUCKLES.

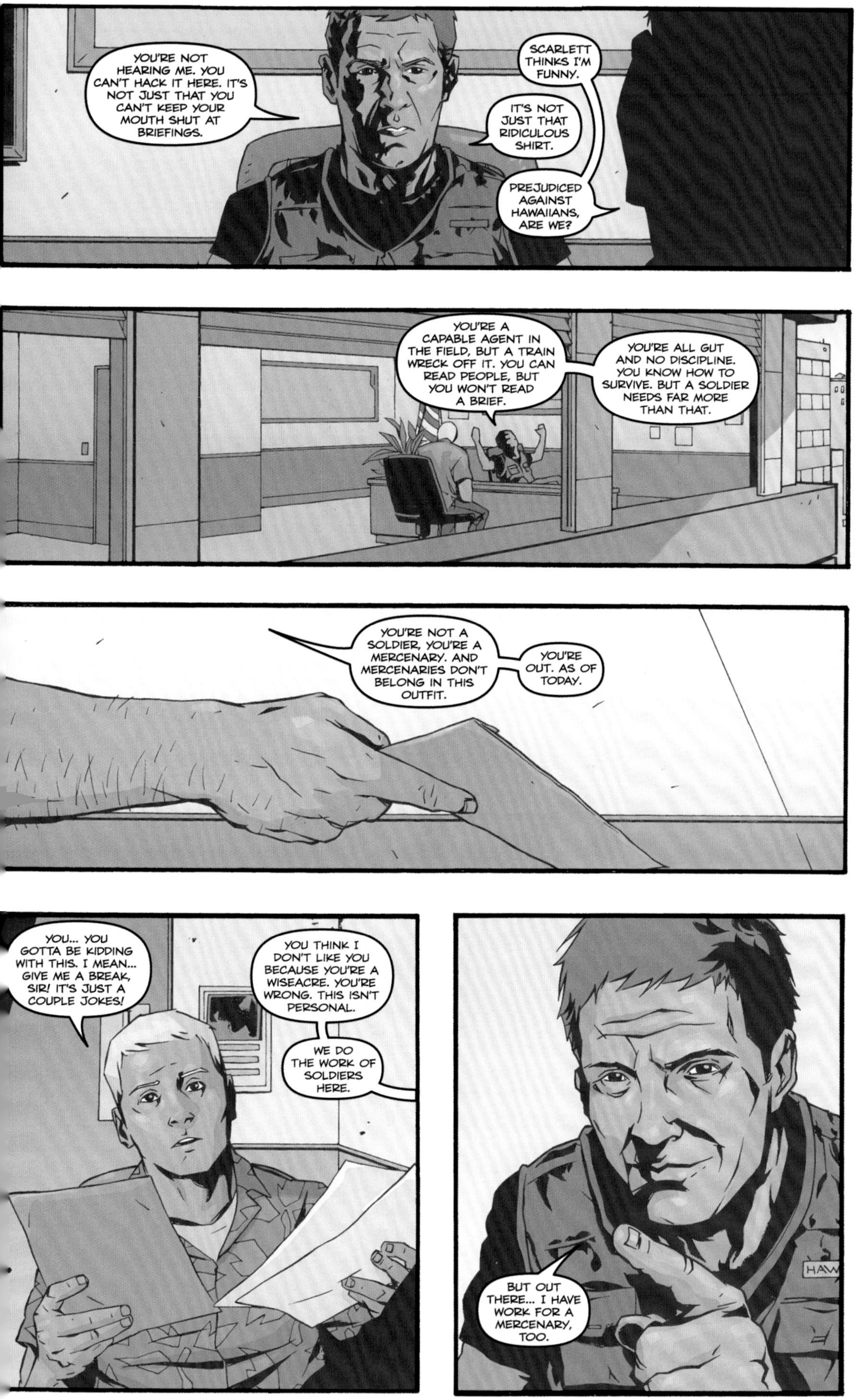
YOU'RE NOT HEARING ME. YOU CAN'T HACK IT HERE. IT'S NOT JUST THAT YOU CAN'T KEEP YOUR MOUTH SHUT AT BRIEFINGS.
SCARLETT THINKS I'M FUNNY.
IT'S NOT JUST THAT RIDICULOUS SHIRT.
PREJUDICED AGAINST HAWAIIANS, ARE WE?
YOU'RE A CAPABLE AGENT IN THE FIELD, BUT A TRAIN WRECK OFF IT. YOU CAN READ PEOPLE, BUT YOU WON'T READ A BRIEF.
YOU'RE ALL GUT AND NO DISCIPLINE. YOU KNOW HOW TO SURVIVE. BUT A SOLDIER NEEDS FAR MORE THAN THAT.
YOU'RE NOT A SOLDIER, YOU'RE A MERCENARY. AND MERCENARIES DON'T BELONG IN THIS OUTFIT.
YOU'RE OUT. AS OF TODAY.
YOU... YOU GOTTA BE KIDDING WITH THIS. I MEAN... GIVE ME A BREAK, SIR! IT'S JUST A COUPLE JOKES!
YOU THINK I DON'T LIKE YOU BECAUSE YOU'RE A WISEACRE. YOU'RE WRONG. THIS ISN'T PERSONAL.
WE DO THE WORK OF SOLDIERS HERE.
BUT OUT THERE... I HAVE WORK FOR A MERCENARY, TOO.

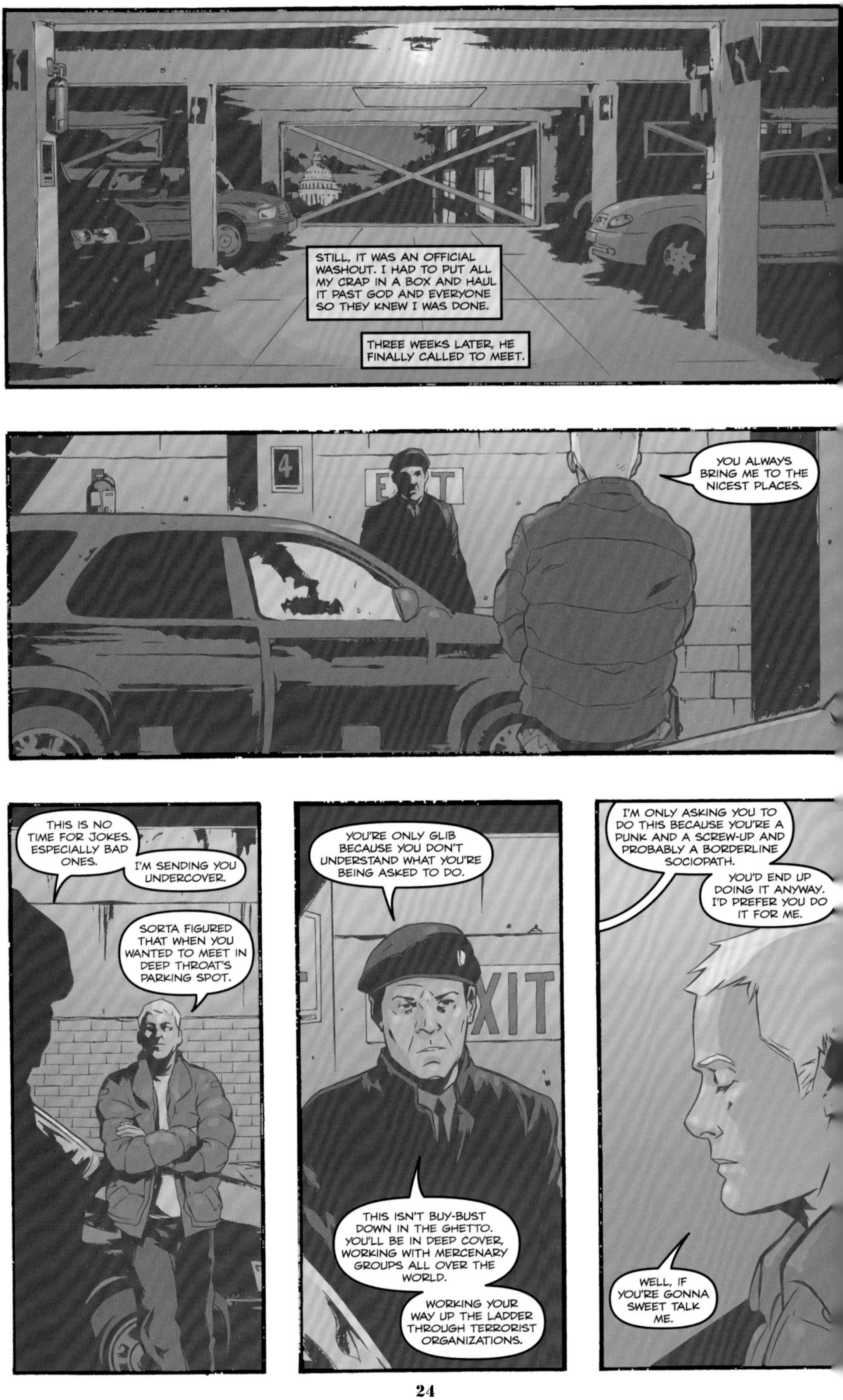
STILL, IT WAS AN OFFICIAL WASHOUT. I HAD TO PUT ALL MY CRAP IN A BOX AND HAUL IT PAST GOD AND EVERYONE SO THEY KNEW I WAS DONE.
THREE WEEKS LATER, HE FINALLY CALLED TO MEET.
4
EXIT
YOU ALWAYS BRING ME TO THE NICEST PLACES.
THIS IS NO TIME FOR JOKES. ESPECIALLY BAD ONES.
I'M SENDING YOU UNDERCOVER.
SORTA FIGURED THAT WHEN YOU WANTED TO MEET IN DEEP THROAT'S PARKING SPOT.
YOU'RE ONLY GLIB BECAUSE YOU DON'T UNDERSTAND WHAT YOU'RE BEING ASKED TO DO.
EXIT
THIS ISN'T BUY-BUST DOWN IN THE GHETTO. YOU'LL BE IN DEEP COVER, WORKING WITH MERCENARY GROUPS ALL OVER THE WORLD.
WORKING YOUR WAY UP THE LADDER THROUGH TERRORIST ORGANIZATIONS.
I'M ONLY ASKING YOU TO DO THIS BECAUSE YOU'RE A PUNK AND A SCREW-UP AND PROBABLY A BORDERLINE SOCIOPATH.
YOU'D END UP DOING IT ANYWAY. I'D PREFER YOU DO IT FOR ME.
WELL, IF YOU'RE GONNA SWEET TALK ME.

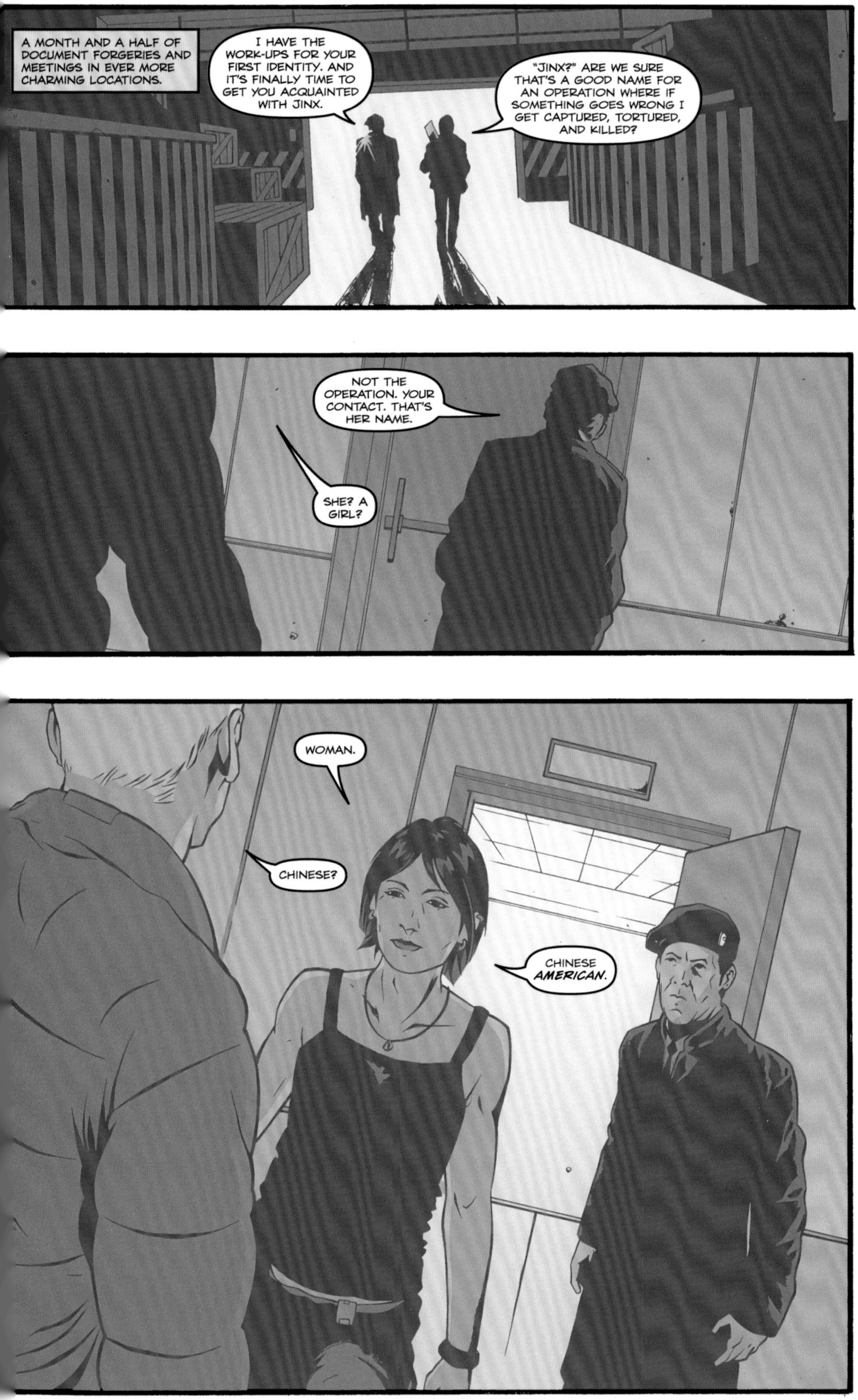
A MONTH AND A HALF OF DOCUMENT FORGERIES AND MEETINGS IN EVER MORE CHARMING LOCATIONS.
I HAVE THE WORK-UPS FOR YOUR FIRST IDENTITY. AND IT'S FINALLY TIME TO GET YOU ACQUAINTED WITH JINX.
"JINX?" ARE WE SURE THAT'S A GOOD NAME FOR AN OPERATION WHERE IF SOMETHING GOES WRONG I GET CAPTURED, TORTURED, AND KILLED?
NOT THE OPERATION. YOUR CONTACT. THAT'S HER NAME.
SHE? A GIRL?
WOMAN.
CHINESE?
CHINESE *AMERICAN*.

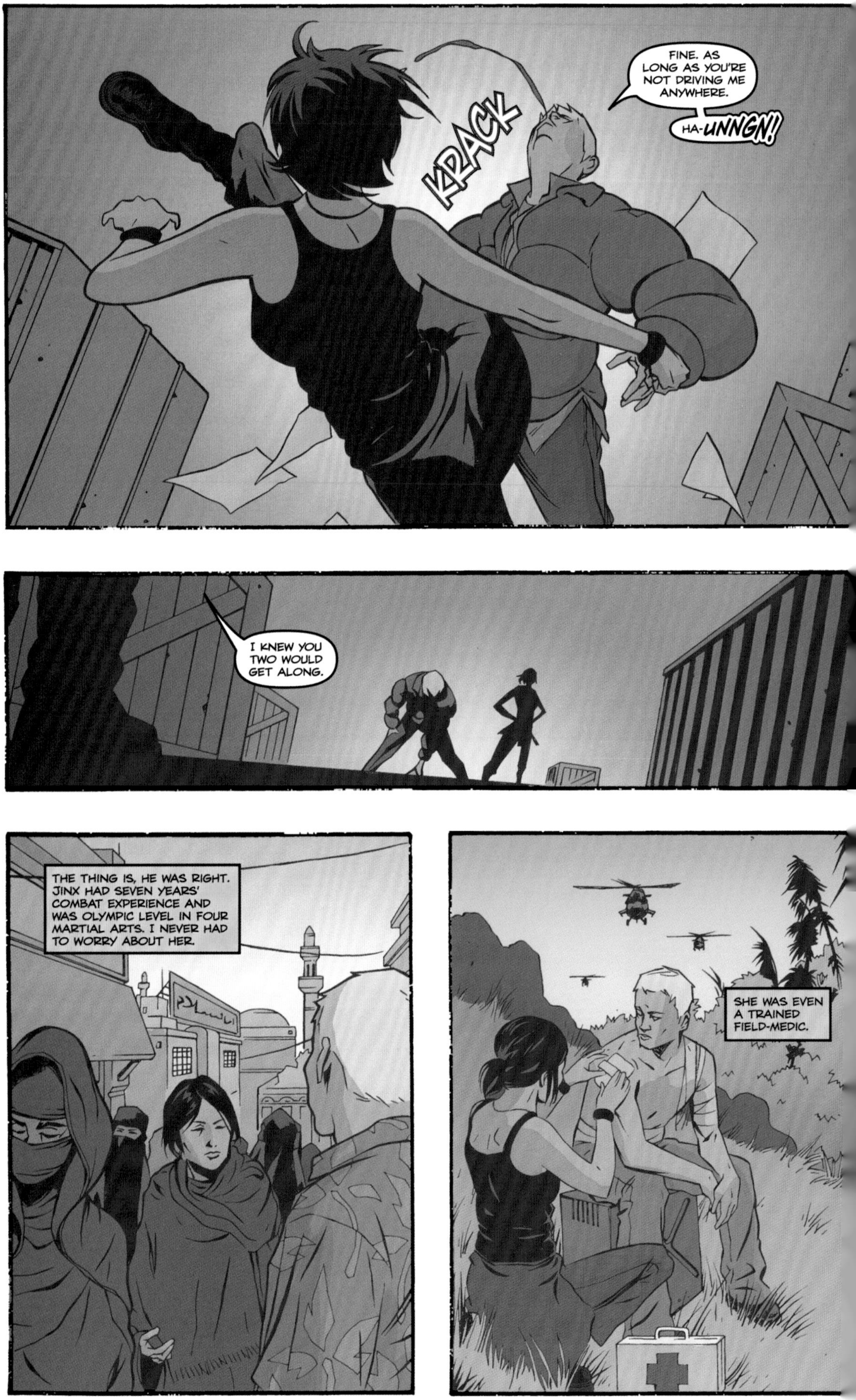
KRACK
FINE. AS LONG AS YOU'RE NOT DRIVING ME ANYWHERE.
HA-UNNGN!
I KNEW YOU TWO WOULD GET ALONG.
THE THING IS, HE WAS RIGHT. JINX HAD SEVEN YEARS' COMBAT EXPERIENCE AND WAS OLYMPIC LEVEL IN FOUR MARTIAL ARTS. I NEVER HAD TO WORRY ABOUT HER.
SHE WAS EVEN A TRAINED FIELD-MEDIC.

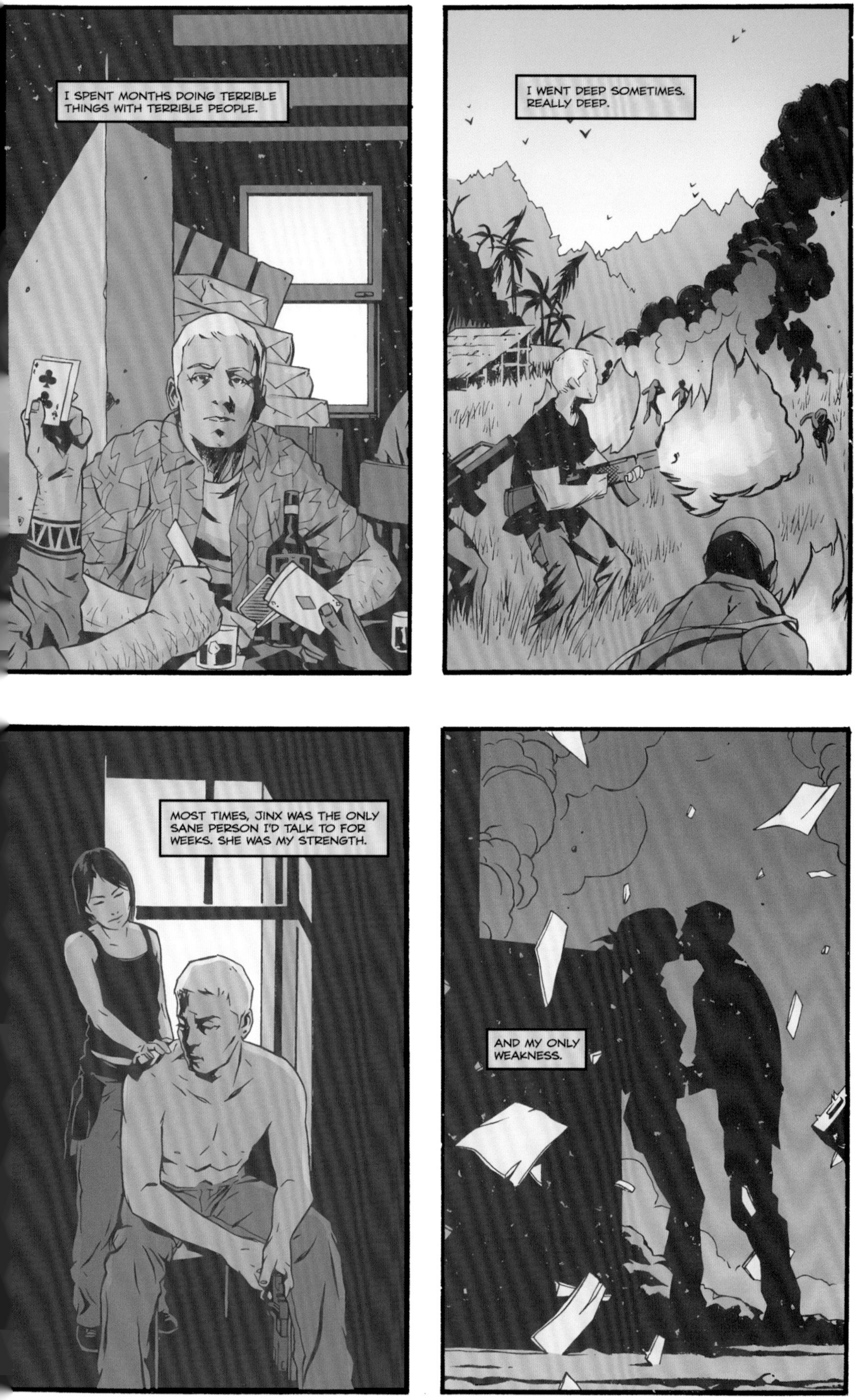
I SPENT MONTHS DOING TERRIBLE THINGS WITH TERRIBLE PEOPLE.
I WENT DEEP SOMETIMES. REALLY DEEP.
MOST TIMES, JINX WAS THE ONLY SANE PERSON I'D TALK TO FOR WEEKS. SHE WAS MY STRENGTH.
AND MY ONLY WEAKNESS.

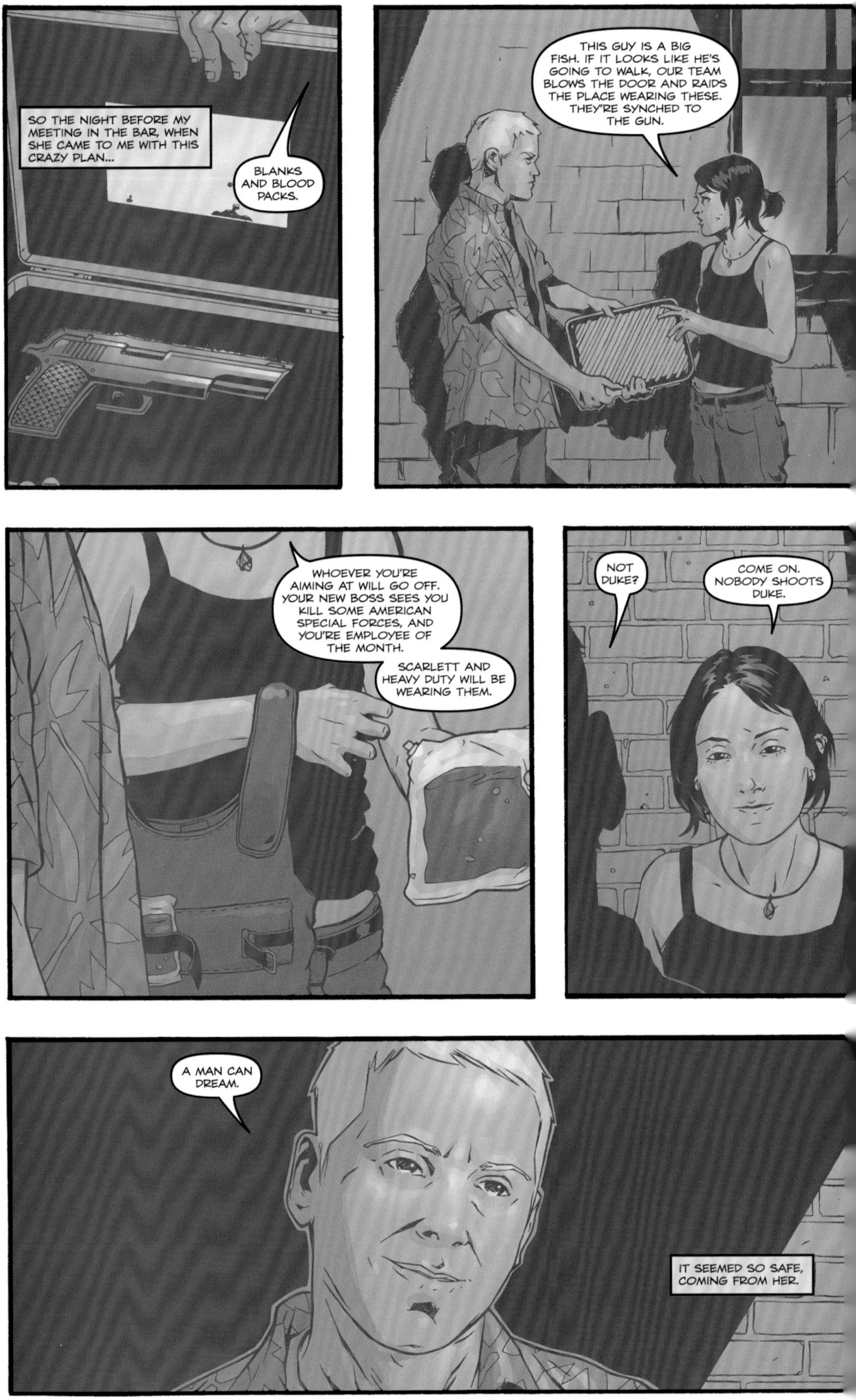
SO THE NIGHT BEFORE MY MEETING IN THE BAR, WHEN SHE CAME TO ME WITH THIS CRAZY PLAN...
BLANKS AND BLOOD PACKS.
THIS GUY IS A BIG FISH. IF IT LOOKS LIKE HE'S GOING TO WALK, OUR TEAM BLOWS THE DOOR AND RAIDS THE PLACE WEARING THESE. THEY'RE SYNCHED TO THE GUN.
WHOEVER YOU'RE AIMING AT WILL GO OFF. YOUR NEW BOSS SEES YOU KILL SOME AMERICAN SPECIAL FORCES, AND YOU'RE EMPLOYEE OF THE MONTH.
SCARLETT AND HEAVY DUTY WILL BE WEARING THEM.
NOT DUKE?
COME ON. NOBODY SHOOTS DUKE.
A MAN CAN DREAM.
IT SEEMED SO SAFE, COMING FROM HER.

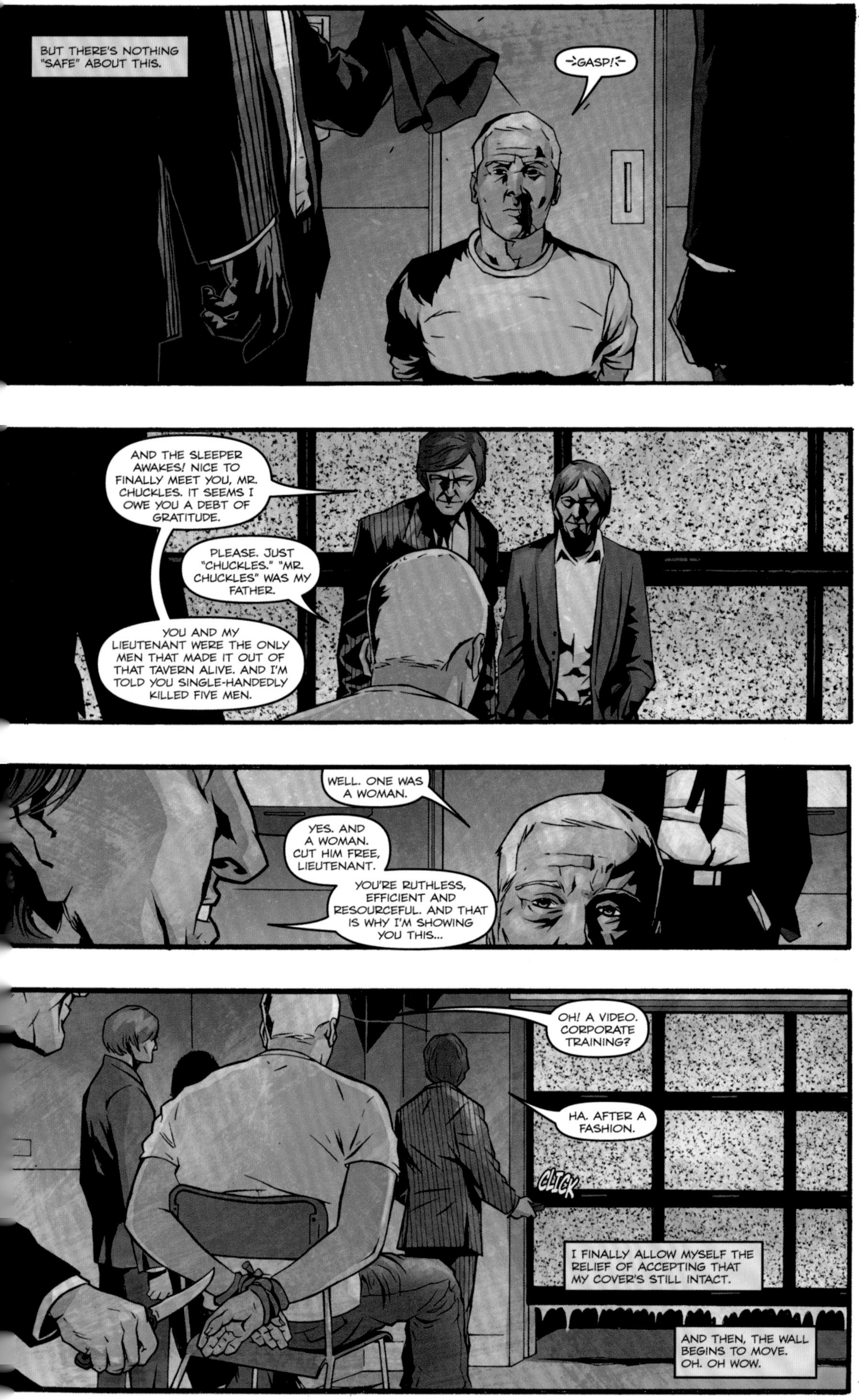

BUT THERE'S NOTHING "SAFE" ABOUT THIS.
GASP!
AND THE SLEEPER AWAKES! NICE TO FINALLY MEET YOU, MR. CHUCKLES. IT SEEMS I OWE YOU A DEBT OF GRATITUDE.
PLEASE. JUST "CHUCKLES." "MR. CHUCKLES" WAS MY FATHER.
YOU AND MY LIEUTENANT WERE THE ONLY MEN THAT MADE IT OUT OF THAT TAVERN ALIVE. AND I'M TOLD YOU SINGLE-HANDEDLY KILLED FIVE MEN.
WELL. ONE WAS A WOMAN.
YES. AND A WOMAN. CUT HIM FREE, LIEUTENANT.
YOU'RE RUTHLESS, EFFICIENT AND RESOURCEFUL. AND THAT IS WHY I'M SHOWING YOU THIS...
OH! A VIDEO. CORPORATE TRAINING?
HA. AFTER A FASHION.
CLICK
I FINALLY ALLOW MYSELF THE RELIEF OF ACCEPTING THAT MY COVER'S STILL INTACT.
AND THEN, THE WALL BEGINS TO MOVE. OH. OH WOW.

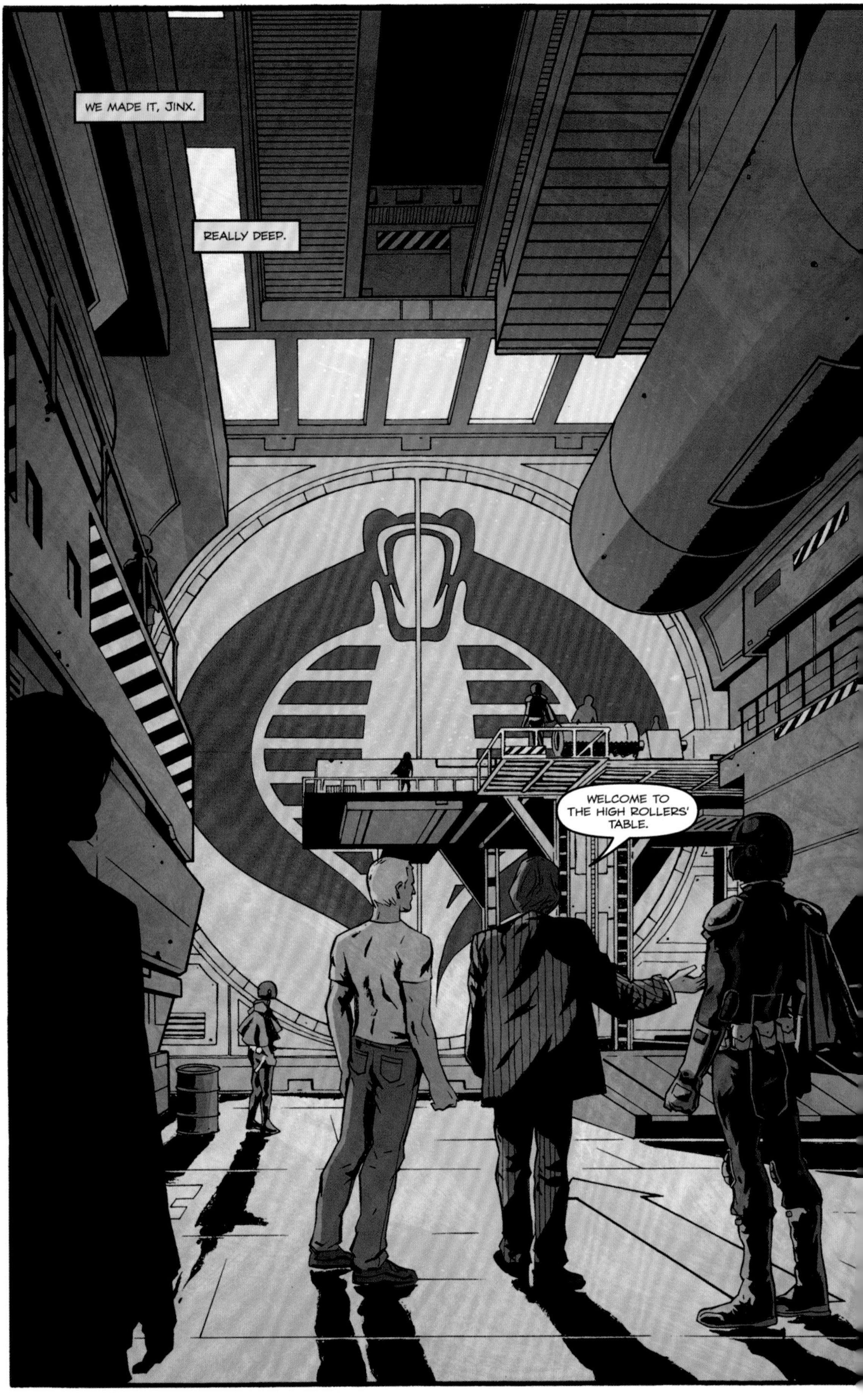
WE MADE IT, JINX.
REALLY DEEP.
WELCOME TO THE HIGH ROLLERS' TABLE.

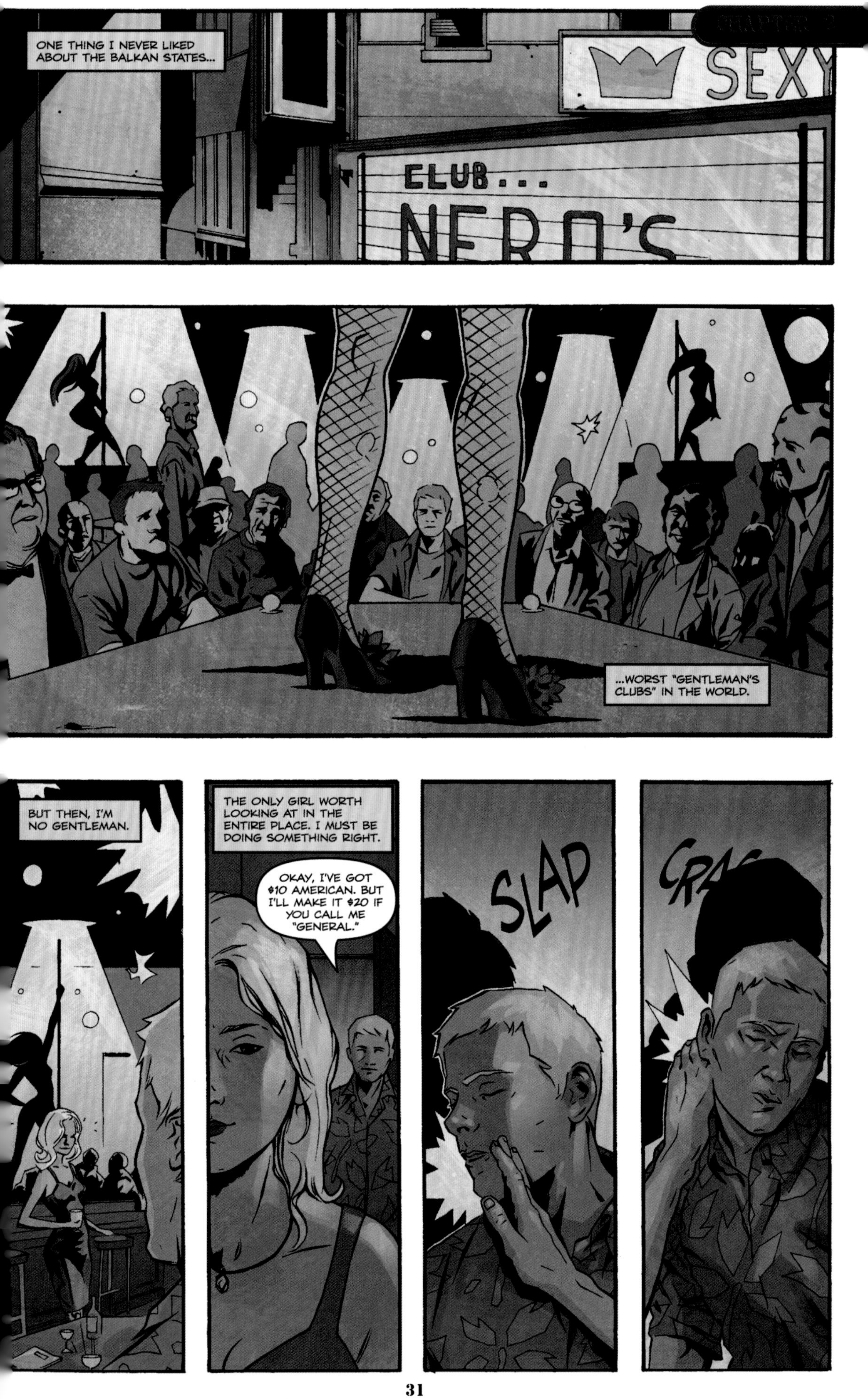
ONE THING I NEVER LIKED ABOUT THE BALKAN STATES...
SEXY
CLUB...
NERO'S
...WORST "GENTLEMAN'S CLUBS" IN THE WORLD.
BUT THEN, I'M NO GENTLEMAN.
THE ONLY GIRL WORTH LOOKING AT IN THE ENTIRE PLACE. I MUST BE DOING SOMETHING RIGHT.
OKAY, I'VE GOT $10 AMERICAN. BUT I'LL MAKE IT $20 IF YOU CALL ME "GENERAL."
SLAP

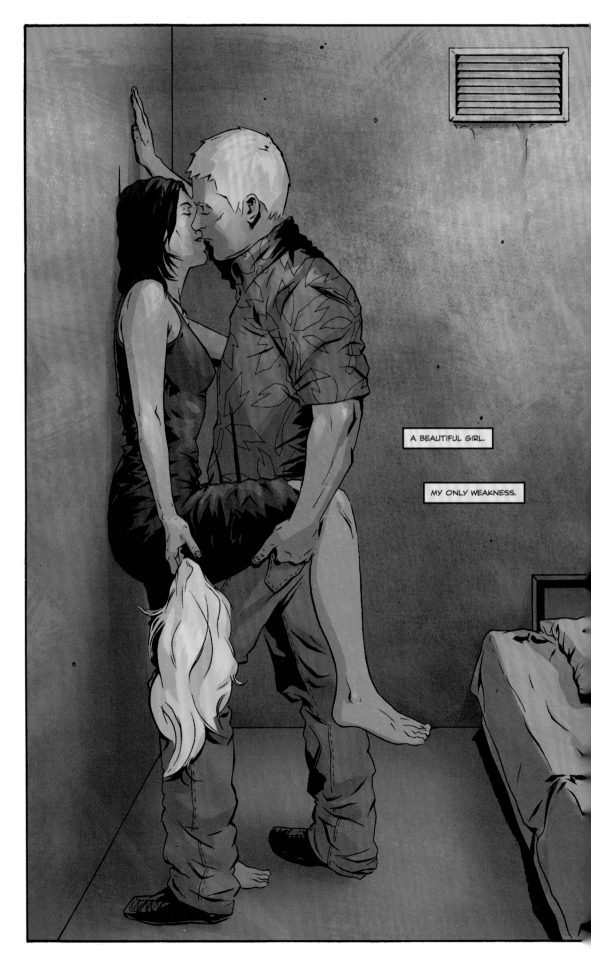

A BEAUTIFUL GIRL.

MY ONLY WEAKNESS.

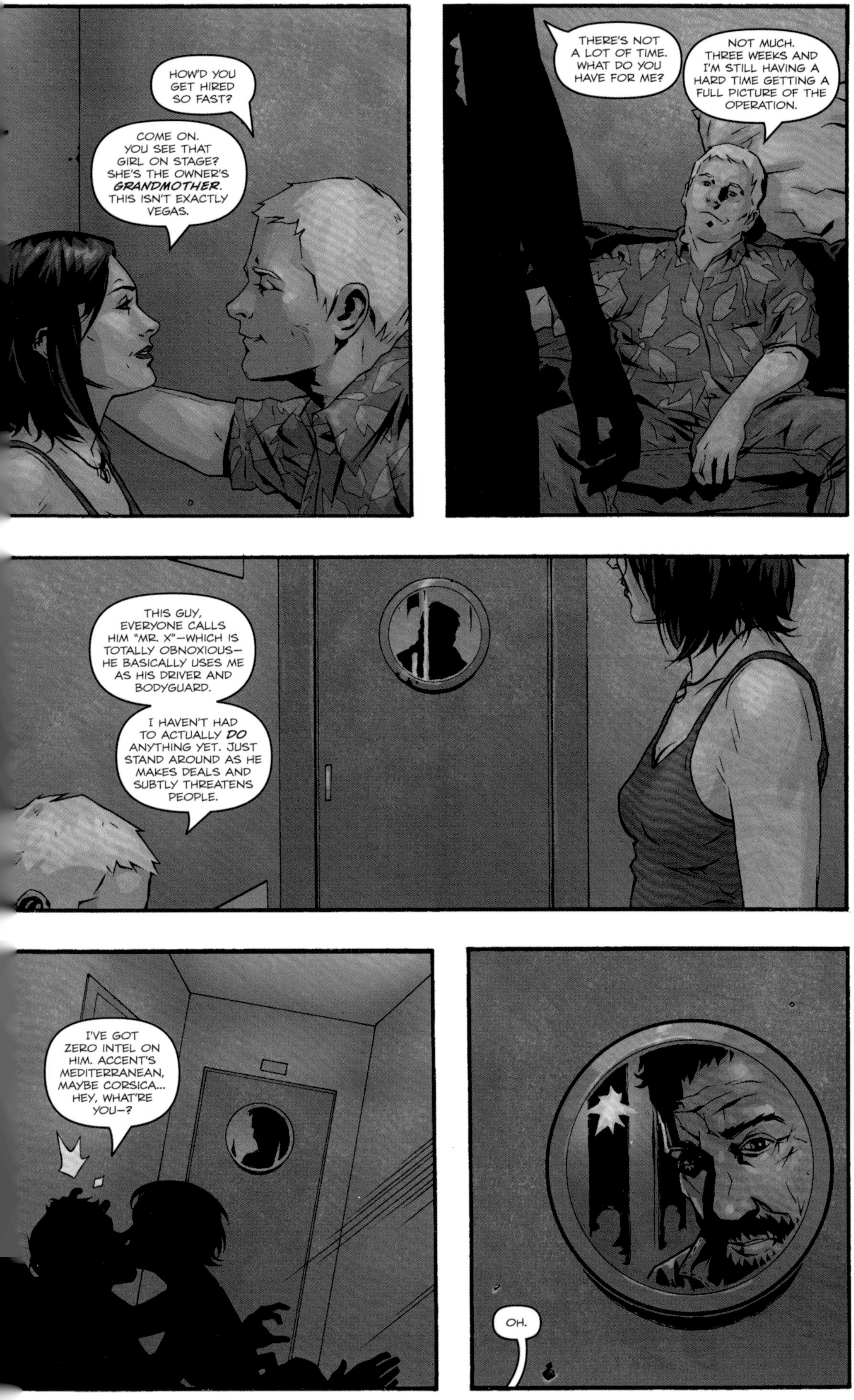
HOW'D YOU GET HIRED SO FAST?
COME ON. YOU SEE THAT GIRL ON STAGE? SHE'S THE OWNER'S GRANDMOTHER. THIS ISN'T EXACTLY VEGAS.
THERE'S NOT A LOT OF TIME. WHAT DO YOU HAVE FOR ME?
NOT MUCH. THREE WEEKS AND I'M STILL HAVING A HARD TIME GETTING A FULL PICTURE OF THE OPERATION.
THIS GUY, EVERYONE CALLS HIM "MR. X"—WHICH IS TOTALLY OBNOXIOUS—HE BASICALLY USES ME AS HIS DRIVER AND BODYGUARD.
I HAVEN'T HAD TO ACTUALLY DO ANYTHING YET. JUST STAND AROUND AS HE MAKES DEALS AND SUBTLY THREATENS PEOPLE.
I'VE GOT ZERO INTEL ON HIM. ACCENT'S MEDITERRANEAN, MAYBE CORSICA... HEY, WHAT'RE YOU—?
OH.

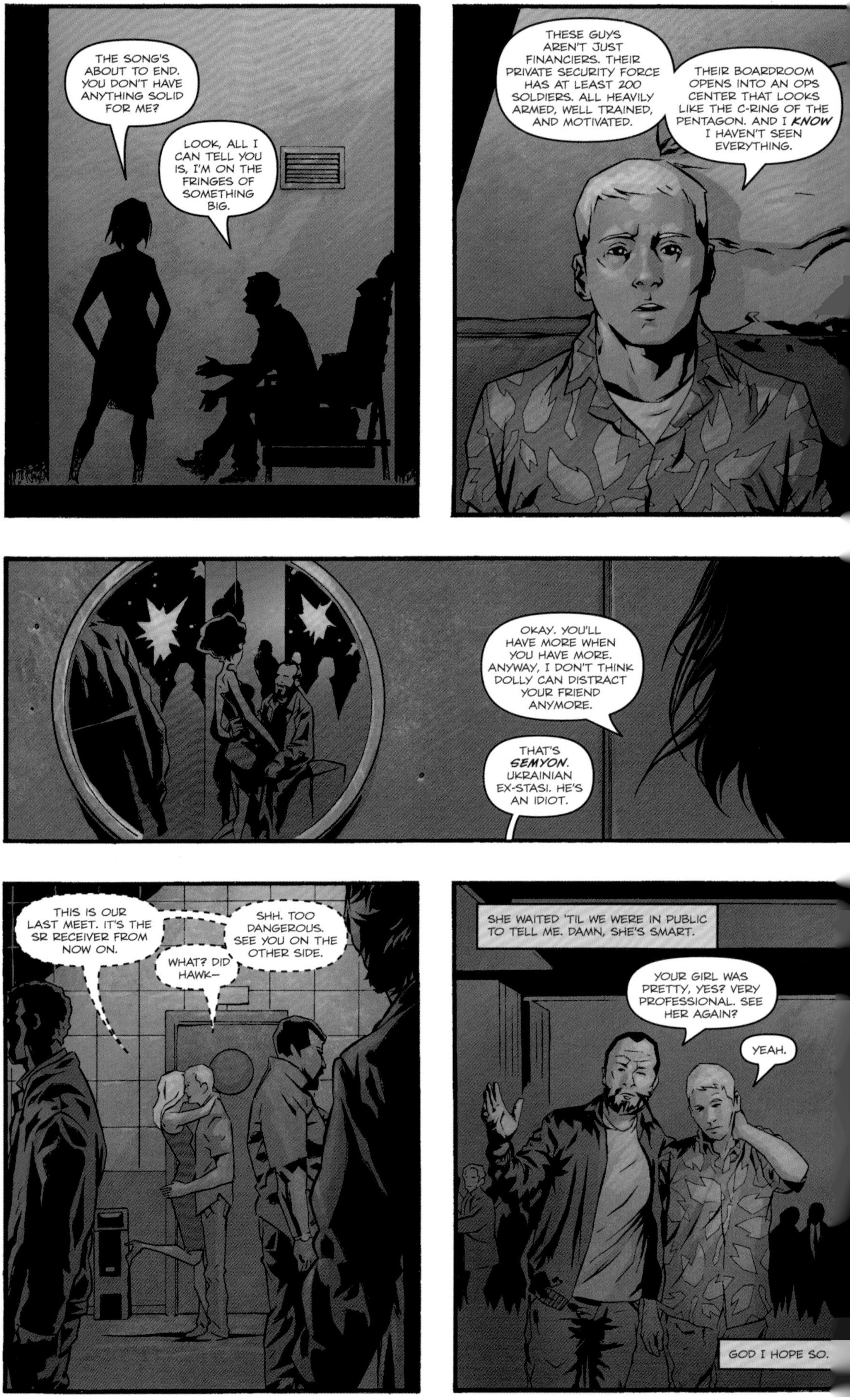
THE SONG'S ABOUT TO END. YOU DON'T HAVE ANYTHING SOLID FOR ME?
LOOK, ALL I CAN TELL YOU IS, I'M ON THE FRINGES OF SOMETHING BIG.
THESE GUYS AREN'T JUST FINANCIERS. THEIR PRIVATE SECURITY FORCE HAS AT LEAST 200 SOLDIERS. ALL HEAVILY ARMED, WELL TRAINED, AND MOTIVATED.
THEIR BOARDROOM OPENS INTO AN OPS CENTER THAT LOOKS LIKE THE C-RING OF THE PENTAGON. AND I KNOW I HAVEN'T SEEN EVERYTHING.
OKAY. YOU'LL HAVE MORE WHEN YOU HAVE MORE. ANYWAY, I DON'T THINK DOLLY CAN DISTRACT YOUR FRIEND ANYMORE.
THAT'S SEMYON. UKRAINIAN EX-STASI. HE'S AN IDIOT.
THIS IS OUR LAST MEET. IT'S THE SR RECEIVER FROM NOW ON.
WHAT? DID HAWK–
SHH. TOO DANGEROUS. SEE YOU ON THE OTHER SIDE.
SHE WAITED 'TIL WE WERE IN PUBLIC TO TELL ME. DAMN, SHE'S SMART.
YOUR GIRL WAS PRETTY, YES? VERY PROFESSIONAL. SEE HER AGAIN?
YEAH.
GOD I HOPE SO.

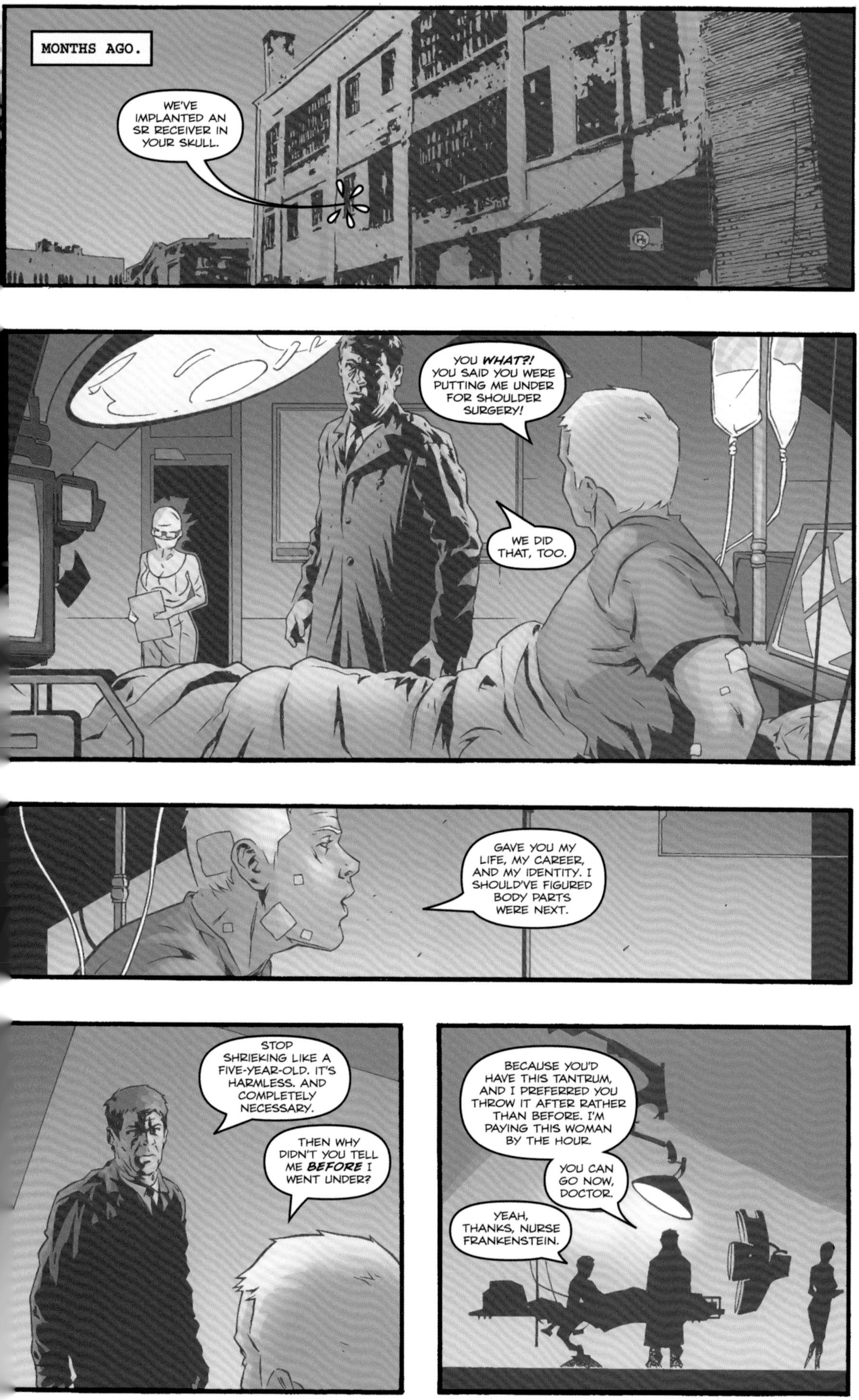
MONTHS AGO.
WE'VE IMPLANTED AN SR RECEIVER IN YOUR SKULL.
YOU WHAT?! YOU SAID YOU WERE PUTTING ME UNDER FOR SHOULDER SURGERY!
WE DID THAT, TOO.
GAVE YOU MY LIFE, MY CAREER, AND MY IDENTITY. I SHOULD'VE FIGURED BODY PARTS WERE NEXT.
STOP SHRIEKING LIKE A FIVE-YEAR-OLD. IT'S HARMLESS. AND COMPLETELY NECESSARY.
THEN WHY DIDN'T YOU TELL ME BEFORE I WENT UNDER?
BECAUSE YOU'D HAVE THIS TANTRUM, AND I PREFERRED YOU THROW IT AFTER RATHER THAN BEFORE. I'M PAYING THIS WOMAN BY THE HOUR.
YOU CAN GO NOW, DOCTOR.
YEAH, THANKS, NURSE FRANKENSTEIN.

SO WHAT IS THIS THING? DOES IT AT LEAST GET HOWARD STERN?
***SKELETAL RESONANCE RECEIVER***. IT'S NOT ALWAYS GOING TO BE SHIRTLESS REBELS IN THE CAMBODIAN JUNGLE.
EVENTUALLY YOU'LL FIND YOURSELF AMONG PEOPLE WITH COUNTERMEASURES.
NO MATTER HOW HIGH-TECH A GADGET WE GIVE YOU, THEY'LL HAVE SOMETHING HIGHER TO FIND IT. SO THE ONLY OPTION IS TO GO TO THE OTHER END OF THE SPECTRUM.
WE'VE DRILLED A SIMPLE RF RECEIVER INTO YOUR MASTOID. WE ALSO IMPLANTED SEVERAL DOZEN OTHER FRAGMENTS IN THE RIGHT SIDE OF YOUR SKULL. IT'LL SHOW UP ON ANY SCAN AS SHRAPNEL.
IT USES YOUR SKELETON AS A RECEIVER. WE CAN SEND CODED MESSAGES IN DOTS AND DASHES. 'BOUT AS CRUDE AS IT GETS.
LET'S GIVE IT A TRY.
GAH! IT'S LIKE AN ELECTRIC TOOTHBRUSH IN MY HEAD!
PERFECT. TO COMMUNICATE BACK YOU JUST BITE DOWN ON SOME FOIL TO CREATE AN INTERFERENCE CIRCUIT.
IF YOU DON'T HAVE A SWEET TOOTH... DEVELOP ONE.

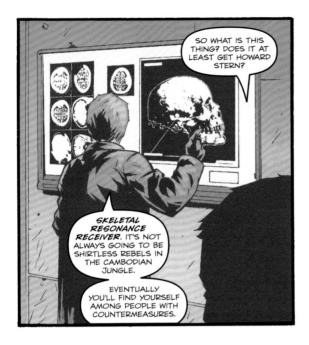

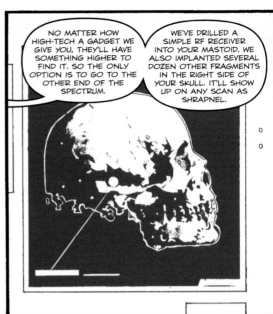

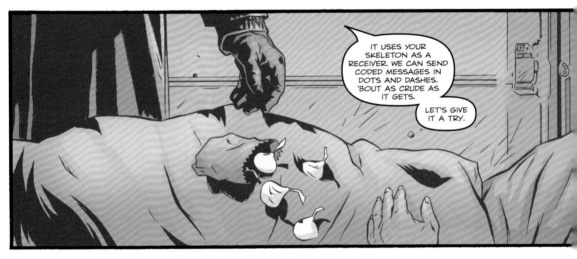

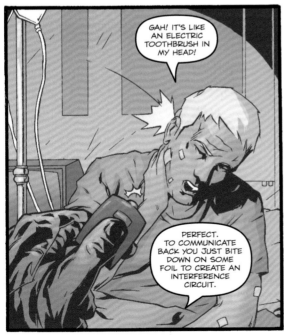

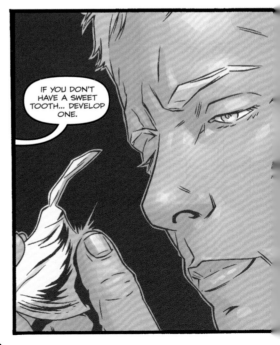

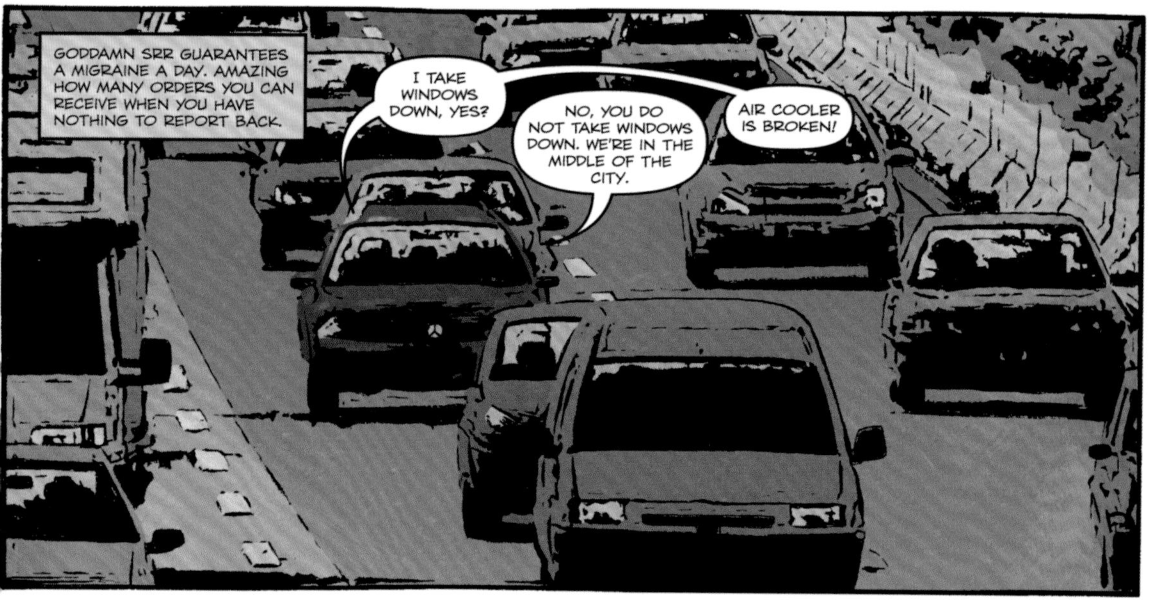
GODDAMN SRR GUARANTEES A MIGRAINE A DAY. AMAZING HOW MANY ORDERS YOU CAN RECEIVE WHEN YOU HAVE NOTHING TO REPORT BACK.
I TAKE WINDOWS DOWN, YES?
NO, YOU DO NOT TAKE WINDOWS DOWN. WE'RE IN THE MIDDLE OF THE CITY.
AIR COOLER IS BROKEN!

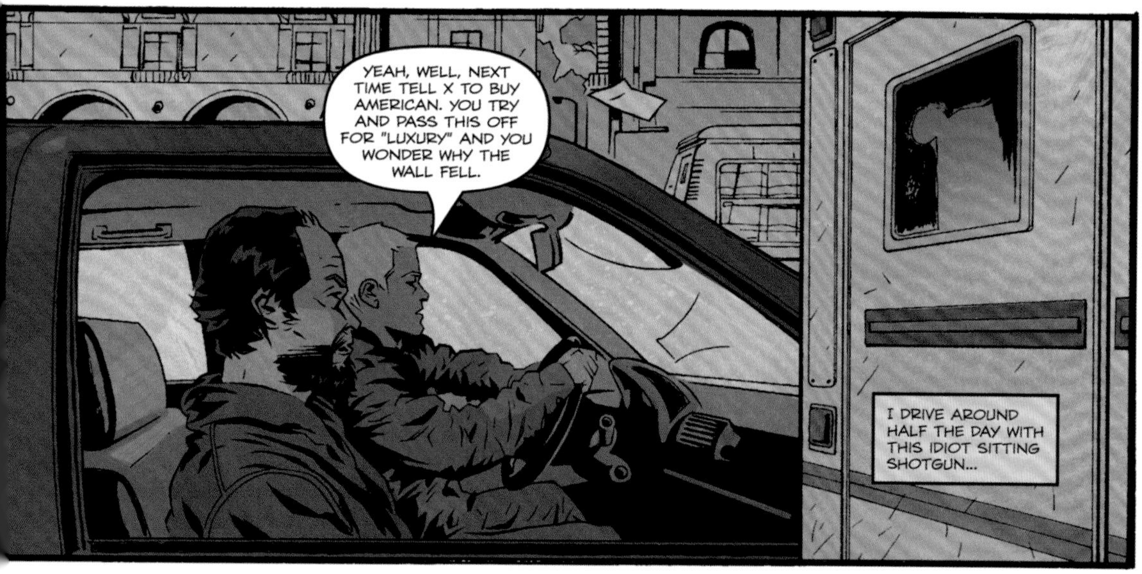
YEAH, WELL, NEXT TIME TELL X TO BUY AMERICAN. YOU TRY AND PASS THIS OFF FOR "LUXURY" AND YOU WONDER WHY THE WALL FELL.
I DRIVE AROUND HALF THE DAY WITH THIS IDIOT SITTING SHOTGUN...

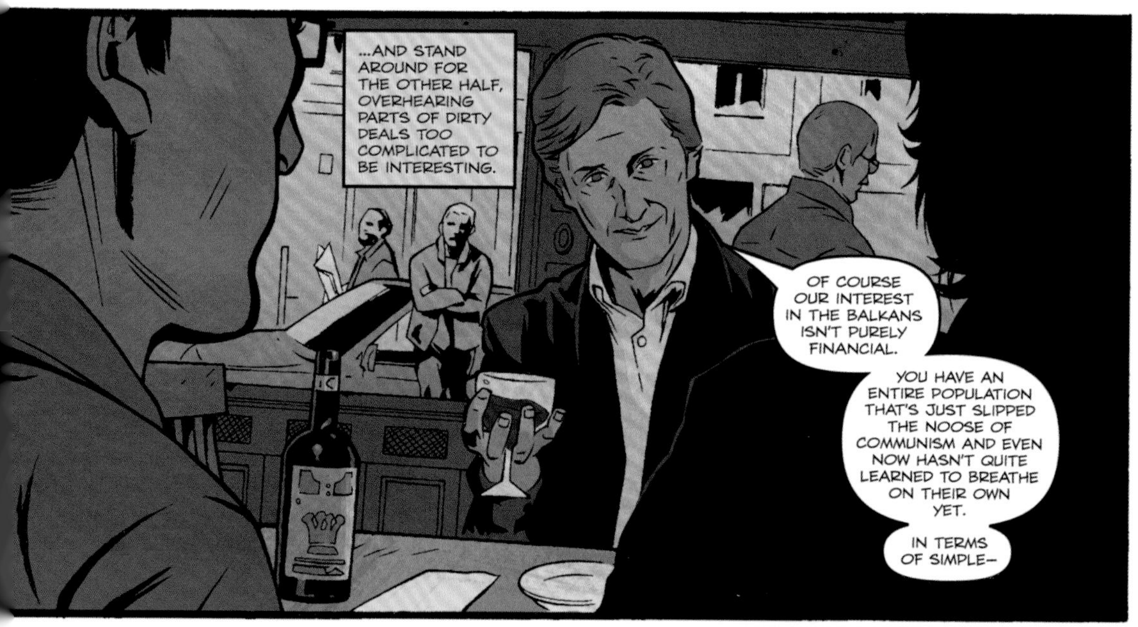
...AND STAND AROUND FOR THE OTHER HALF, OVERHEARING PARTS OF DIRTY DEALS TOO COMPLICATED TO BE INTERESTING.
OF COURSE OUR INTEREST IN THE BALKANS ISN'T PURELY FINANCIAL.
YOU HAVE AN ENTIRE POPULATION THAT'S JUST SLIPPED THE NOOSE OF COMMUNISM AND EVEN NOW HASN'T QUITE LEARNED TO BREATHE ON THEIR OWN YET.
IN TERMS OF SIMPLE–

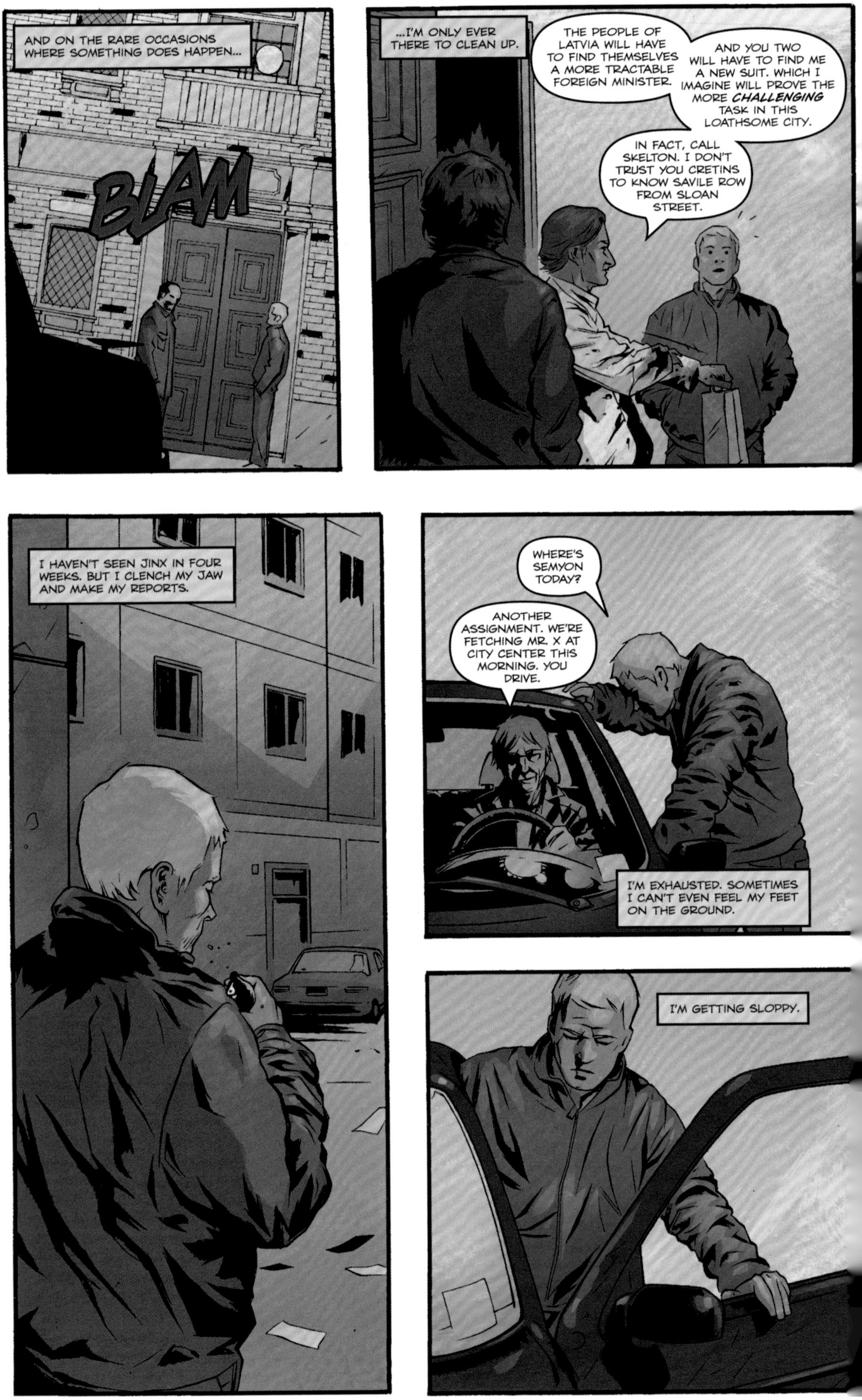
AND ON THE RARE OCCASIONS WHERE SOMETHING DOES HAPPEN...
BLAM
...I'M ONLY EVER THERE TO CLEAN UP.
THE PEOPLE OF LATVIA WILL HAVE TO FIND THEMSELVES A MORE TRACTABLE FOREIGN MINISTER.
AND YOU TWO WILL HAVE TO FIND ME A NEW SUIT. WHICH I IMAGINE WILL PROVE THE MORE CHALLENGING TASK IN THIS LOATHSOME CITY.
IN FACT, CALL SKELTON. I DON'T TRUST YOU CRETINS TO KNOW SAVILE ROW FROM SLOAN STREET.
I HAVEN'T SEEN JINX IN FOUR WEEKS. BUT I CLENCH MY JAW AND MAKE MY REPORTS.
WHERE'S SEMYON TODAY?
ANOTHER ASSIGNMENT. WE'RE FETCHING MR. X AT CITY CENTER THIS MORNING. YOU DRIVE.
I'M EXHAUSTED. SOMETIMES I CAN'T EVEN FEEL MY FEET ON THE GROUND.
I'M GETTING SLOPPY.

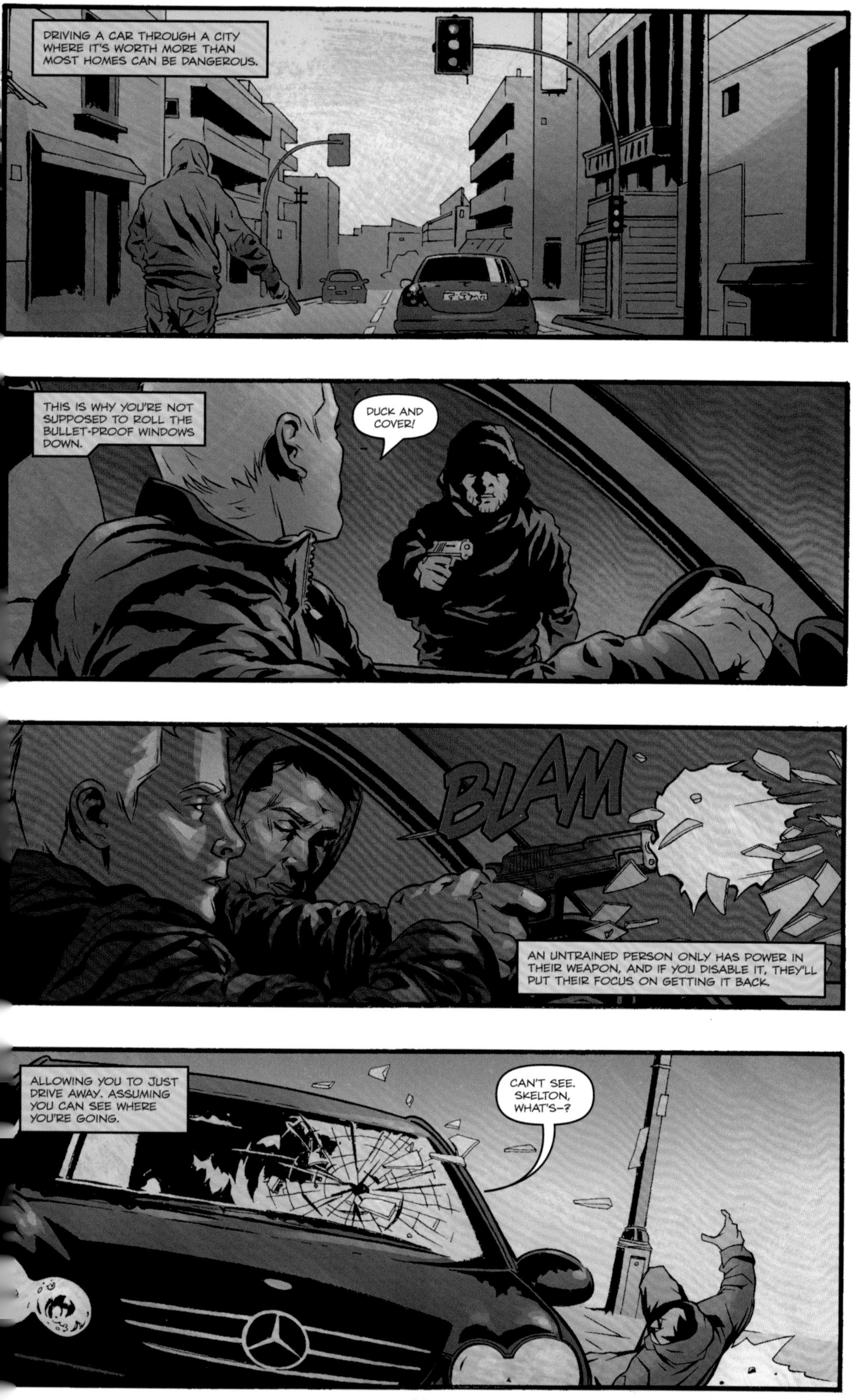
DRIVING A CAR THROUGH A CITY WHERE IT'S WORTH MORE THAN MOST HOMES CAN BE DANGEROUS.
THIS IS WHY YOU'RE NOT SUPPOSED TO ROLL THE BULLET-PROOF WINDOWS DOWN.
DUCK AND COVER!
BLAM
AN UNTRAINED PERSON ONLY HAS POWER IN THEIR WEAPON, AND IF YOU DISABLE IT, THEY'LL PUT THEIR FOCUS ON GETTING IT BACK.
ALLOWING YOU TO JUST DRIVE AWAY. ASSUMING YOU CAN SEE WHERE YOU'RE GOING.
CAN'T SEE. SKELTON, WHAT'S--?

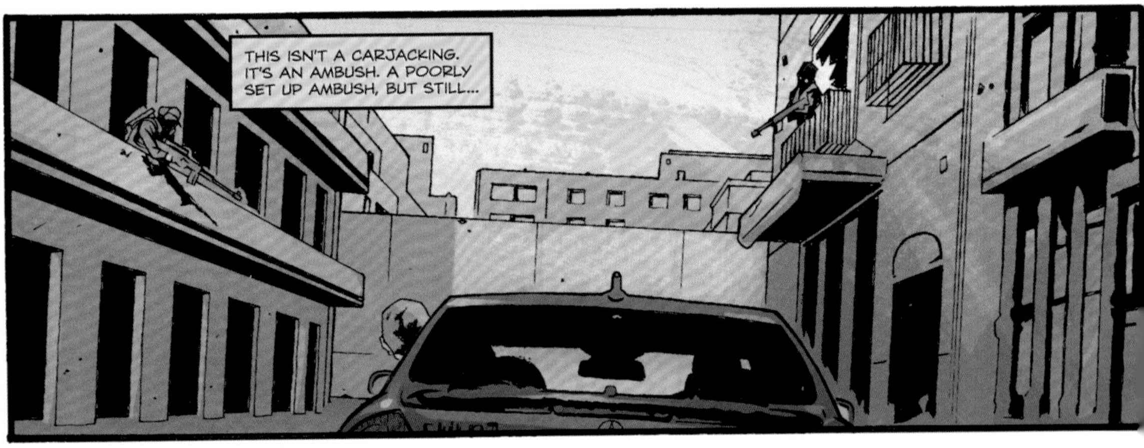
THIS ISN'T A CARJACKING. IT'S AN AMBUSH. A POORLY SET UP AMBUSH, BUT STILL...

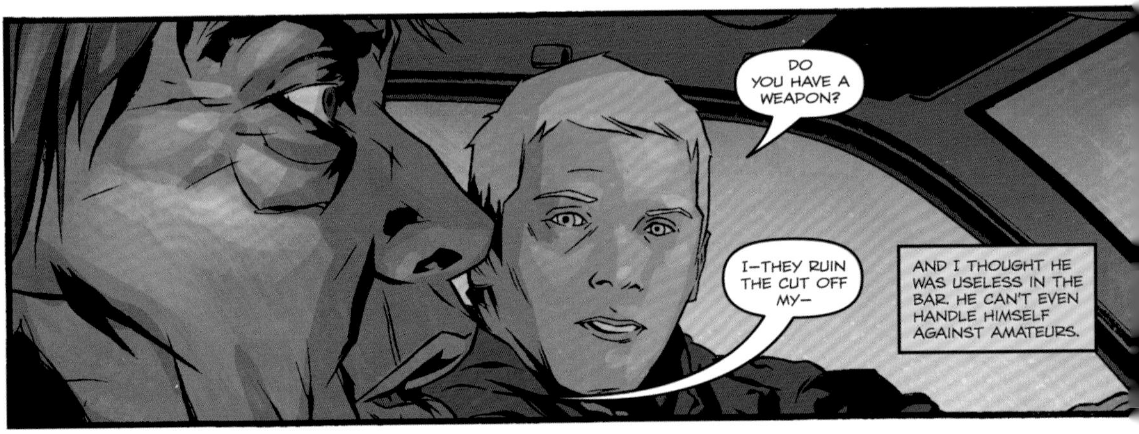
DO YOU HAVE A WEAPON?
I—THEY RUIN THE CUT OFF MY—
AND I THOUGHT HE WAS USELESS IN THE BAR. HE CAN'T EVEN HANDLE HIMSELF AGAINST AMATEURS.

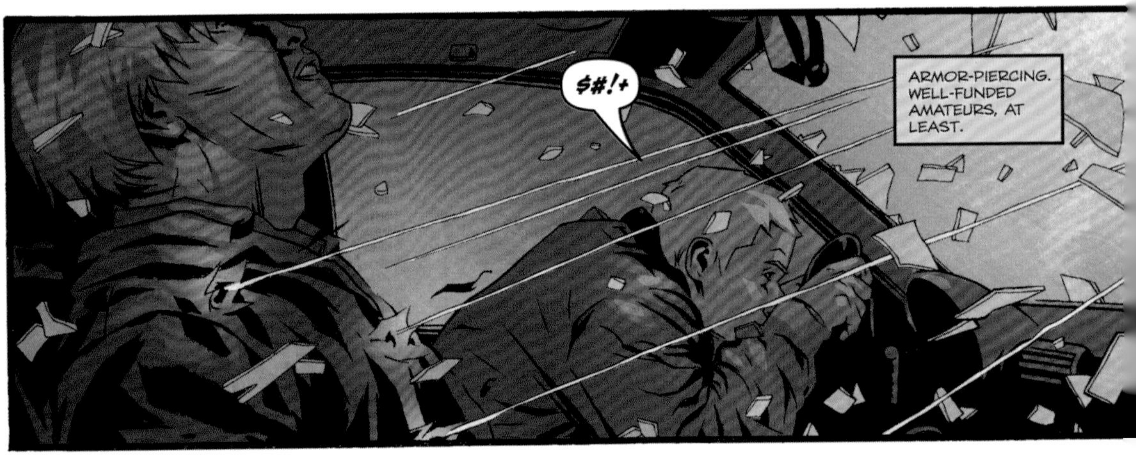
$#!+
ARMOR-PIERCING. WELL-FUNDED AMATEURS, AT LEAST.

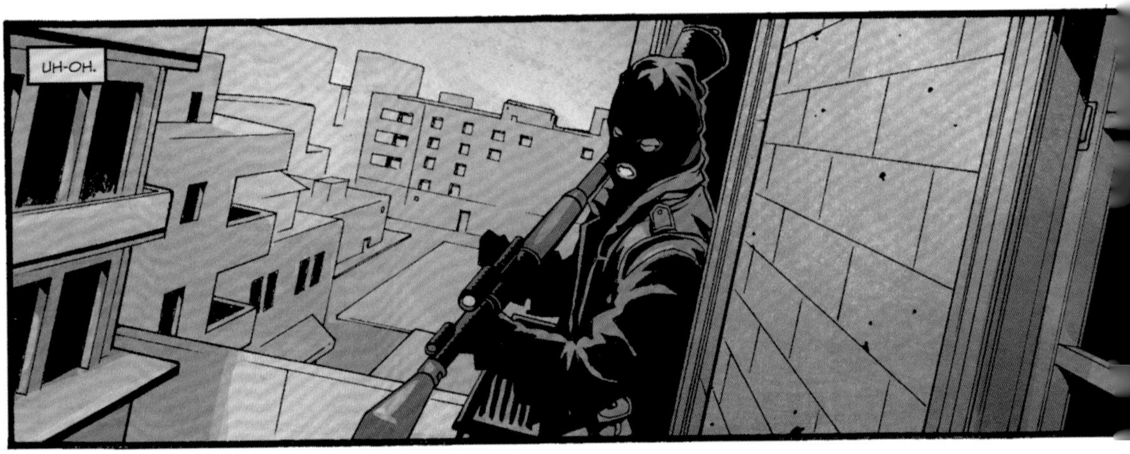
UH-OH.

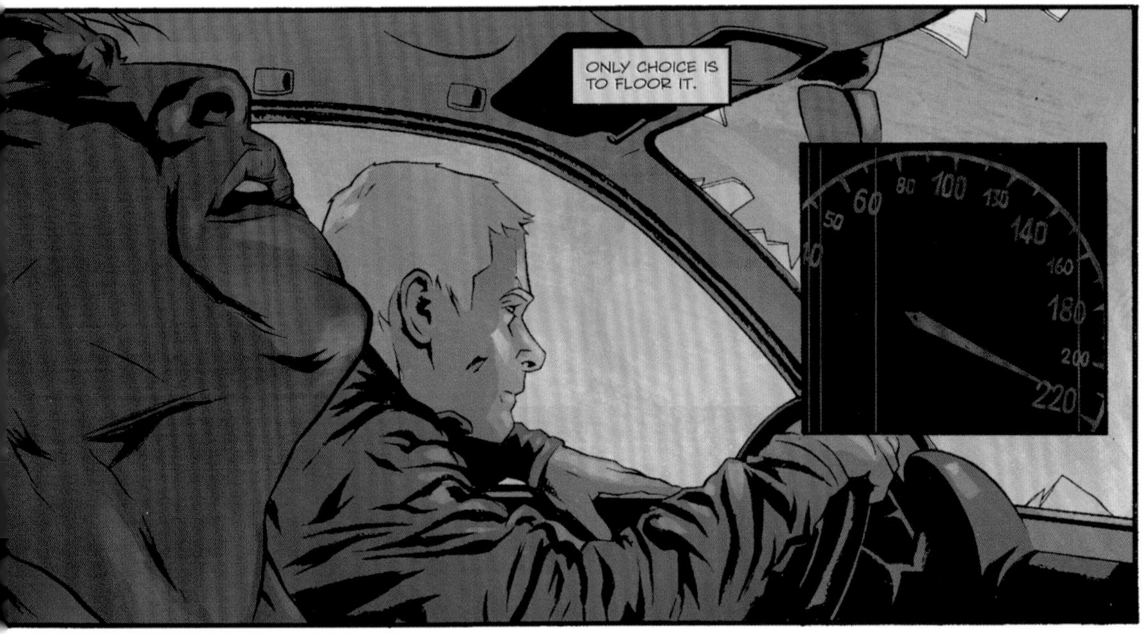
ONLY CHOICE IS TO FLOOR IT.
40 50 60 80 100 130 140 160 180 200 220

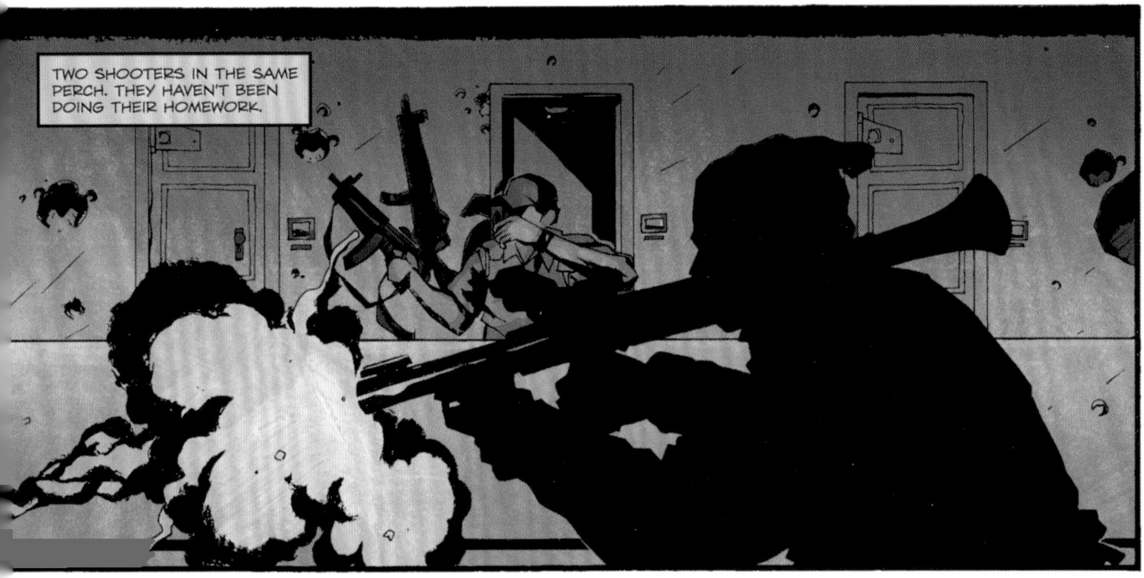
TWO SHOOTERS IN THE SAME PERCH. THEY HAVEN'T BEEN DOING THEIR HOMEWORK.

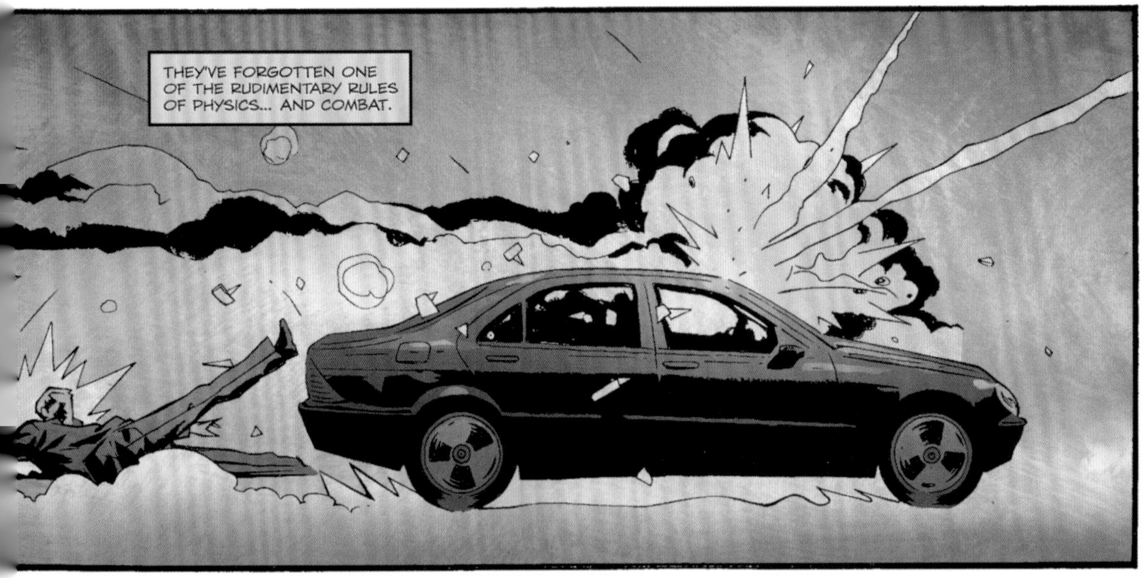
THEY'VE FORGOTTEN ONE OF THE RUDIMENTARY RULES OF PHYSICS... AND COMBAT.

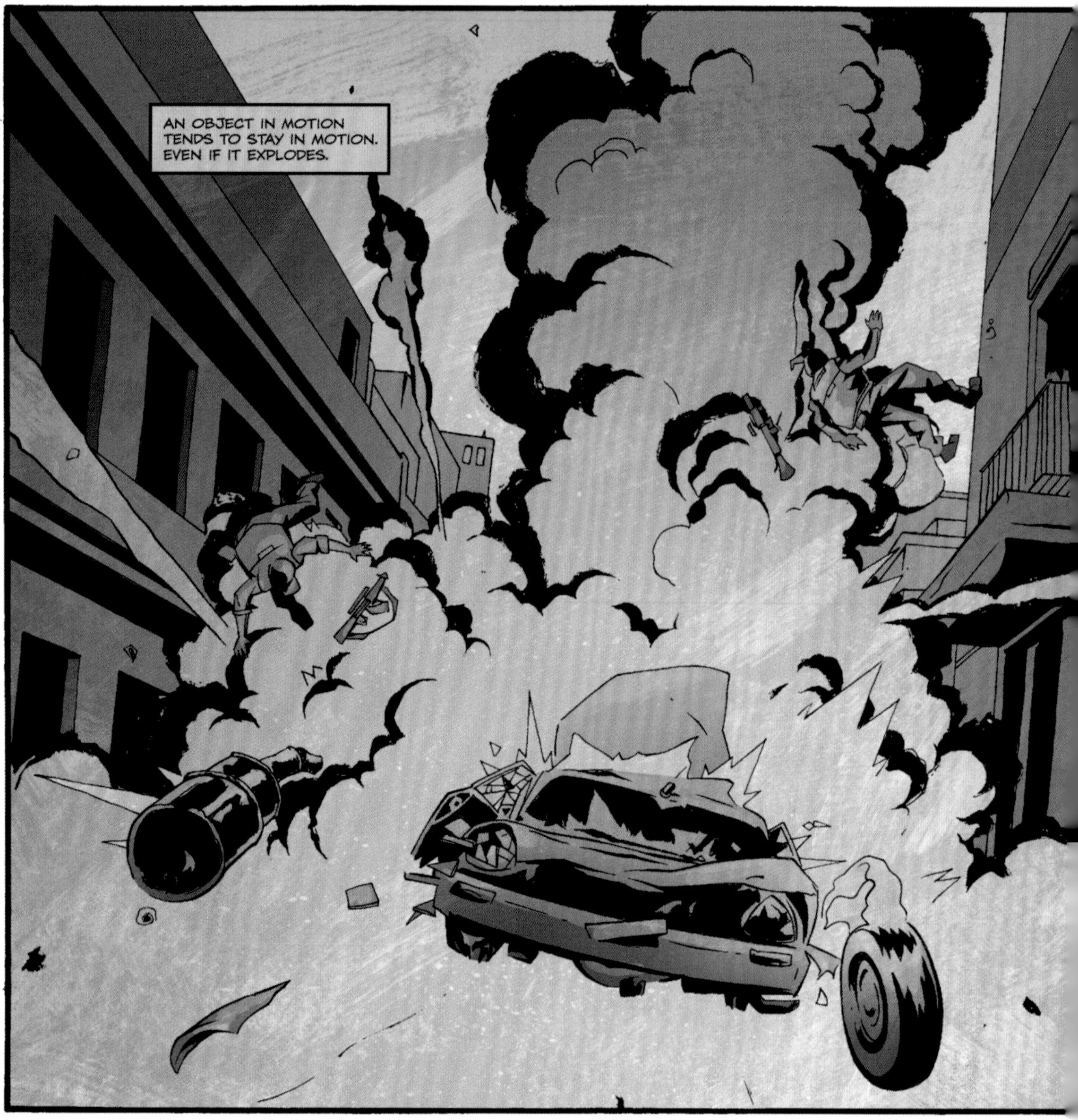
AN OBJECT IN MOTION TENDS TO STAY IN MOTION. EVEN IF IT EXPLODES.

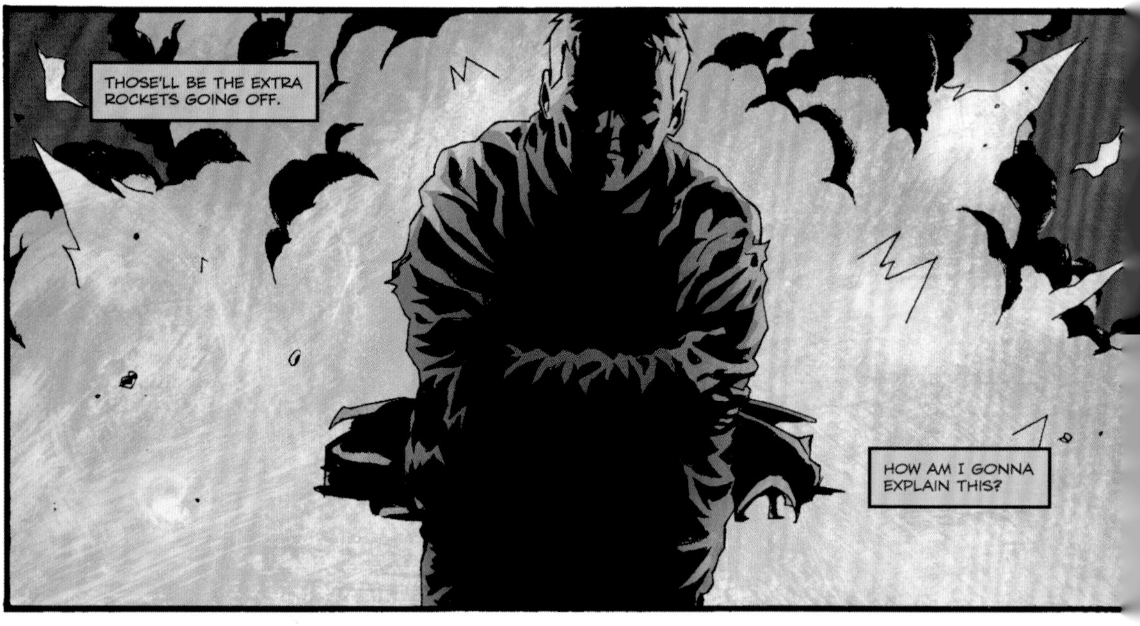
THOSE'LL BE THE EXTRA ROCKETS GOING OFF.
HOW AM I GONNA EXPLAIN THIS?

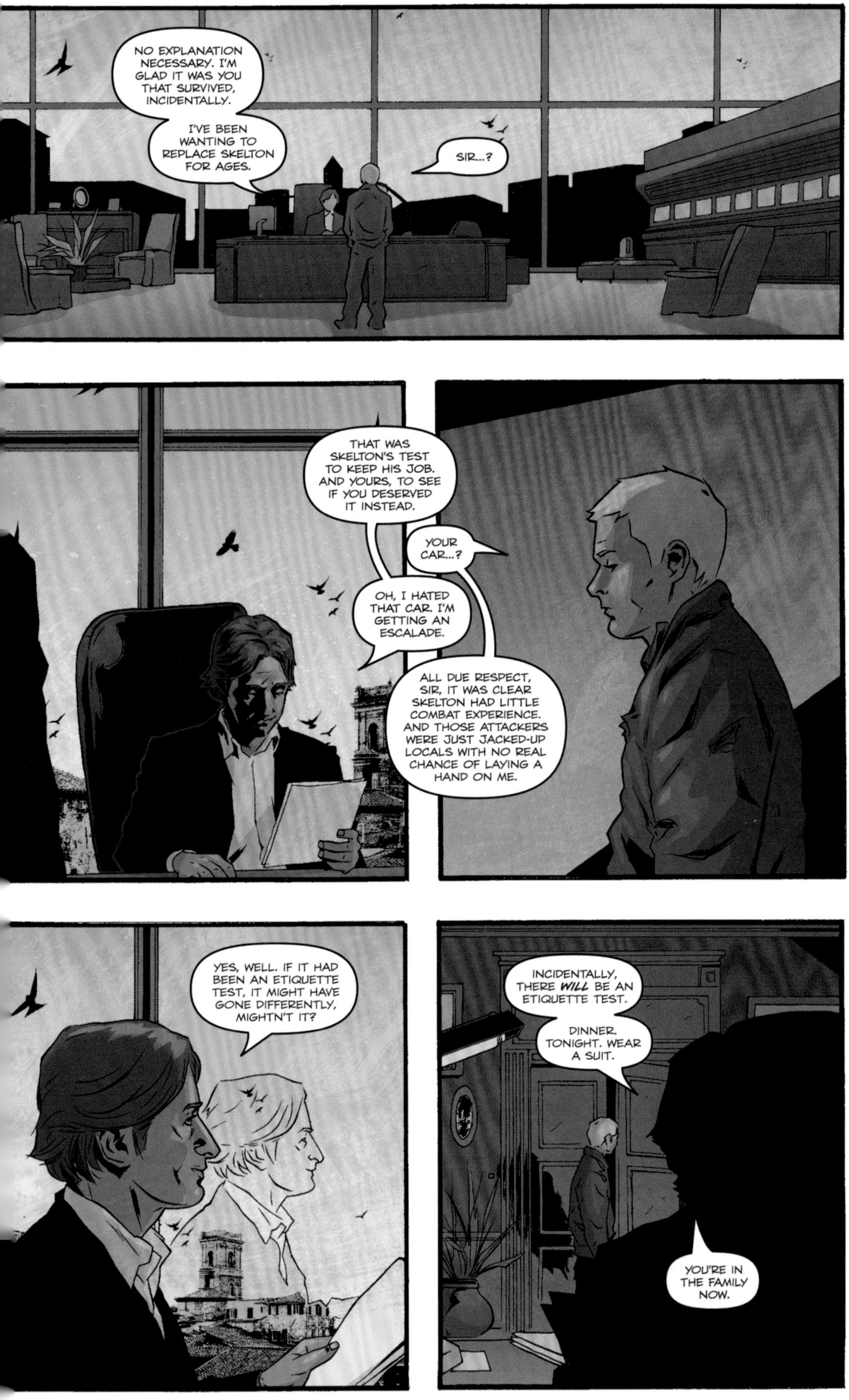
NO EXPLANATION NECESSARY. I'M GLAD IT WAS YOU THAT SURVIVED, INCIDENTALLY.
I'VE BEEN WANTING TO REPLACE SKELTON FOR AGES.
SIR...?
THAT WAS SKELTON'S TEST TO KEEP HIS JOB. AND YOURS, TO SEE IF YOU DESERVED IT INSTEAD.
YOUR CAR...?
OH, I HATED THAT CAR. I'M GETTING AN ESCALADE.
ALL DUE RESPECT, SIR, IT WAS CLEAR SKELTON HAD LITTLE COMBAT EXPERIENCE. AND THOSE ATTACKERS WERE JUST JACKED-UP LOCALS WITH NO REAL CHANCE OF LAYING A HAND ON ME.
YES, WELL. IF IT HAD BEEN AN ETIQUETTE TEST, IT MIGHT HAVE GONE DIFFERENTLY, MIGHTN'T IT?
INCIDENTALLY, THERE ***WILL*** BE AN ETIQUETTE TEST.
DINNER. TONIGHT. WEAR A SUIT.
YOU'RE IN THE FAMILY NOW.

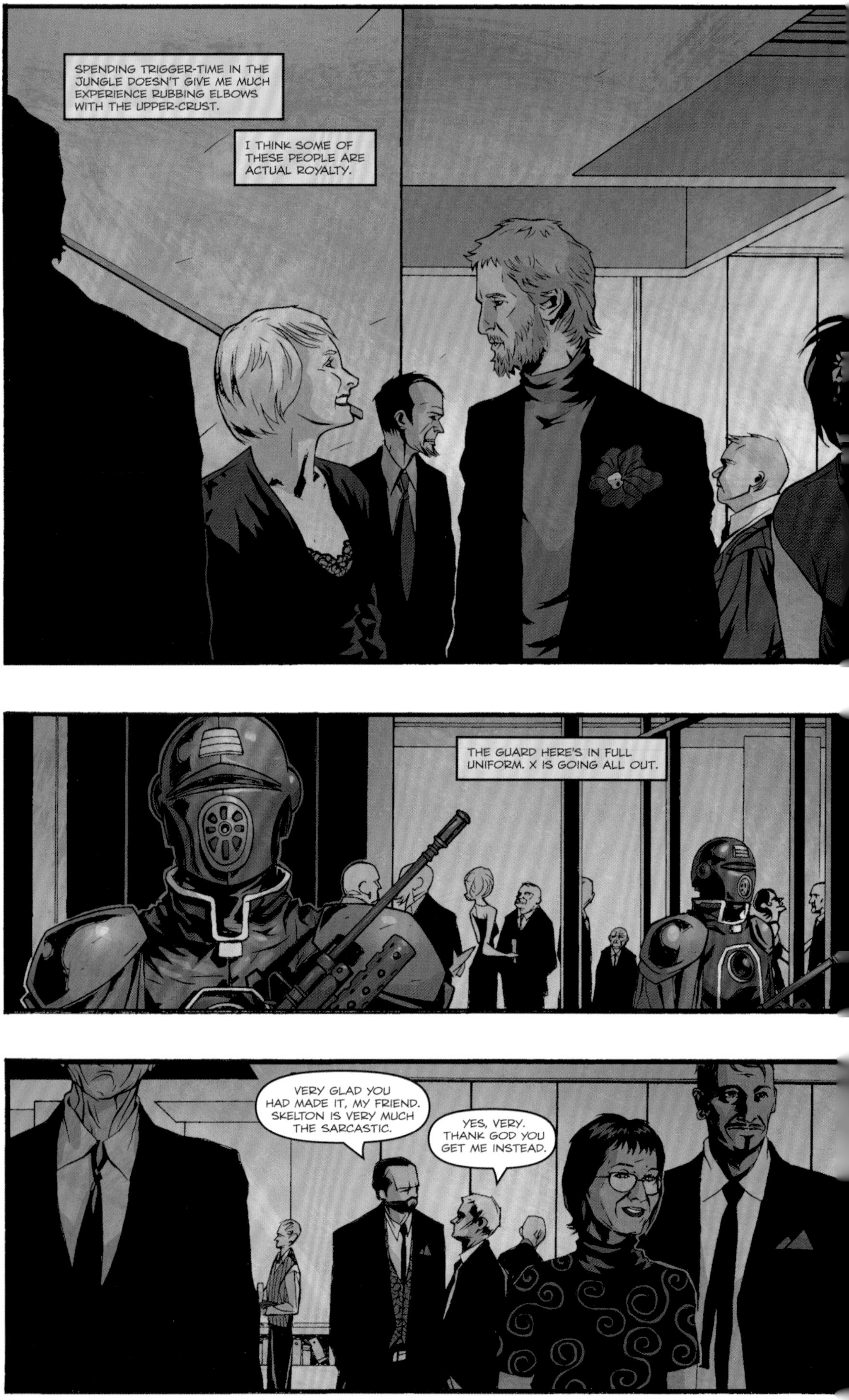
SPENDING TRIGGER-TIME IN THE JUNGLE DOESN'T GIVE ME MUCH EXPERIENCE RUBBING ELBOWS WITH THE UPPER-CRUST.
I THINK SOME OF THESE PEOPLE ARE ACTUAL ROYALTY.
THE GUARD HERE'S IN FULL UNIFORM. X IS GOING ALL OUT.
VERY GLAD YOU HAD MADE IT, MY FRIEND. SKELTON IS VERY MUCH THE SARCASTIC.
YES, VERY. THANK GOD YOU GET ME INSTEAD.

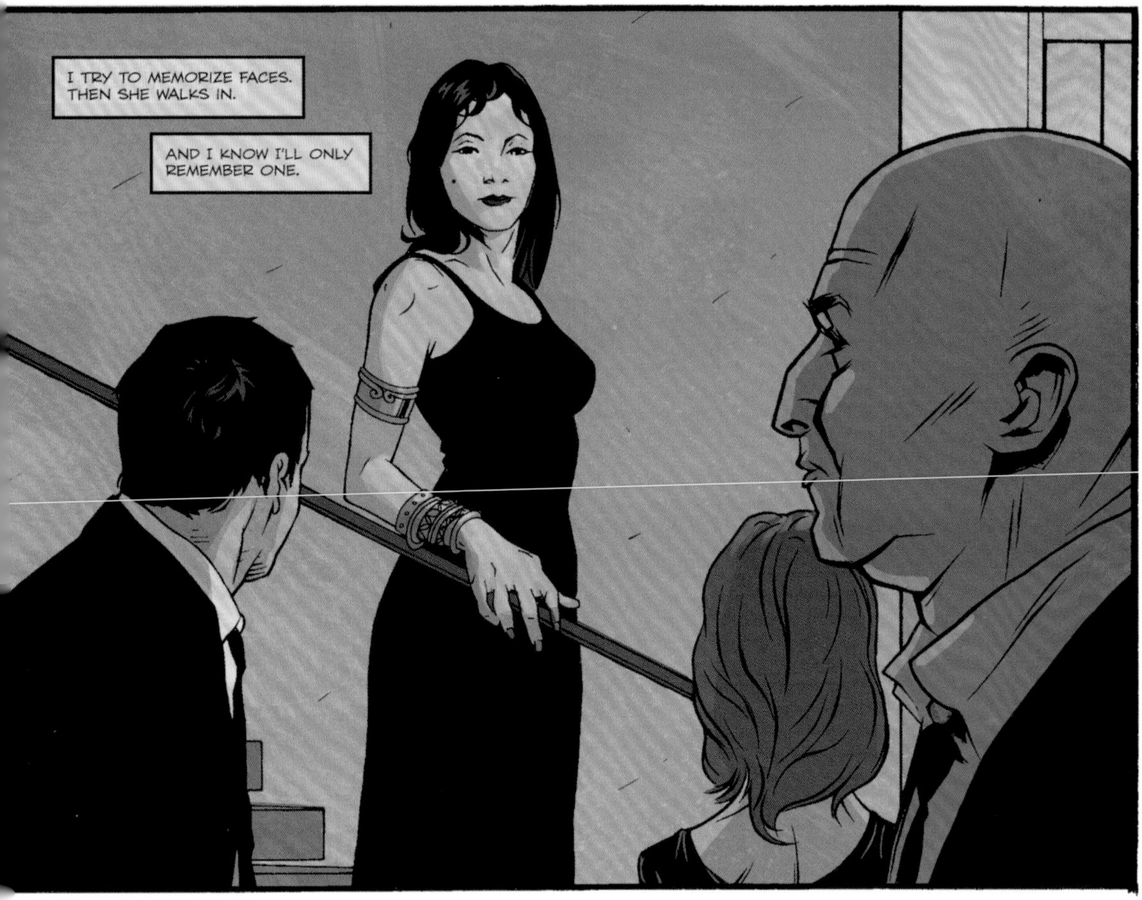
I TRY TO MEMORIZE FACES. THEN SHE WALKS IN.
AND I KNOW I'LL ONLY REMEMBER ONE.

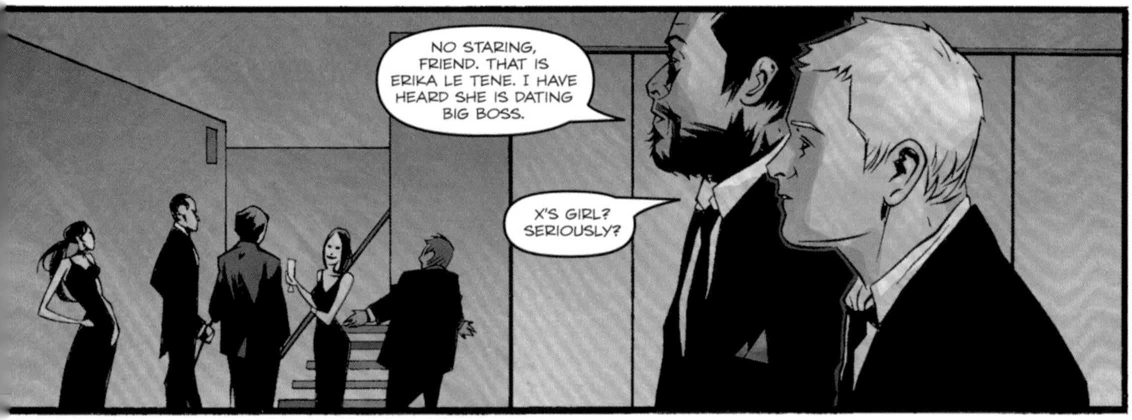
NO STARING, FRIEND. THAT IS ERIKA LE TENE. I HAVE HEARD SHE IS DATING BIG BOSS.
X'S GIRL? SERIOUSLY?

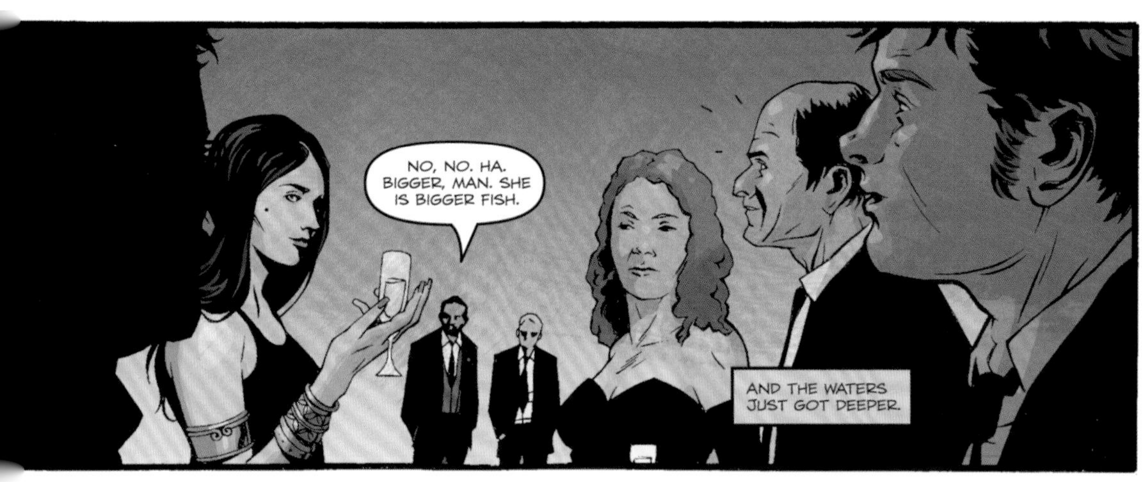
NO, NO. HA. BIGGER, MAN. SHE IS BIGGER FISH.
AND THE WATERS JUST GOT DEEPER.

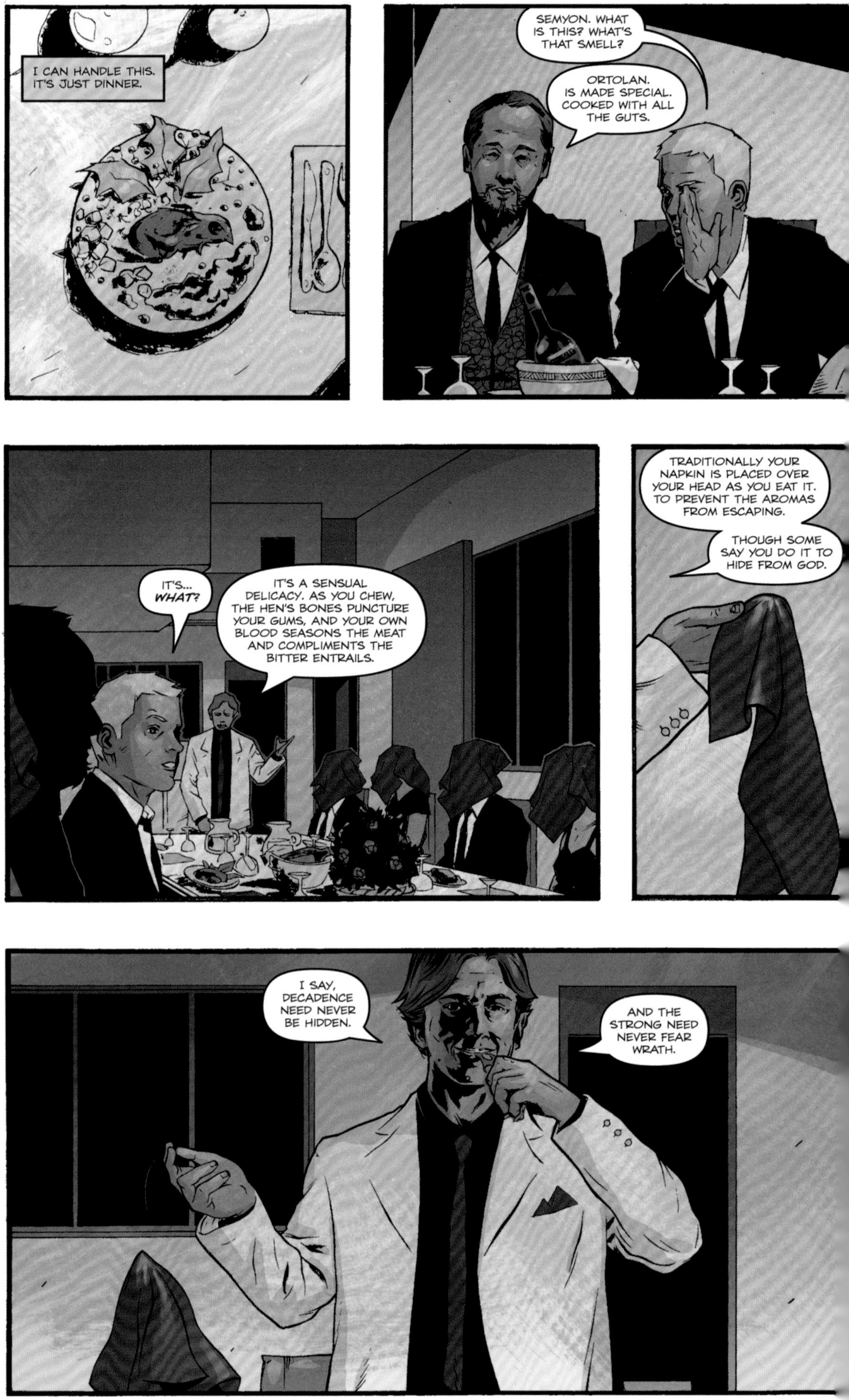
I CAN HANDLE THIS. IT'S JUST DINNER.
SEMYON. WHAT IS THIS? WHAT'S THAT SMELL?
ORTOLAN. IS MADE SPECIAL. COOKED WITH ALL THE GUTS.
IT'S... *WHAT?*
IT'S A SENSUAL DELICACY. AS YOU CHEW, THE HEN'S BONES PUNCTURE YOUR GUMS, AND YOUR OWN BLOOD SEASONS THE MEAT AND COMPLIMENTS THE BITTER ENTRAILS.
TRADITIONALLY YOUR NAPKIN IS PLACED OVER YOUR HEAD AS YOU EAT IT. TO PREVENT THE AROMAS FROM ESCAPING.
THOUGH SOME SAY YOU DO IT TO HIDE FROM GOD.
I SAY, DECADENCE NEED NEVER BE HIDDEN.
AND THE STRONG NEED NEVER FEAR WRATH.

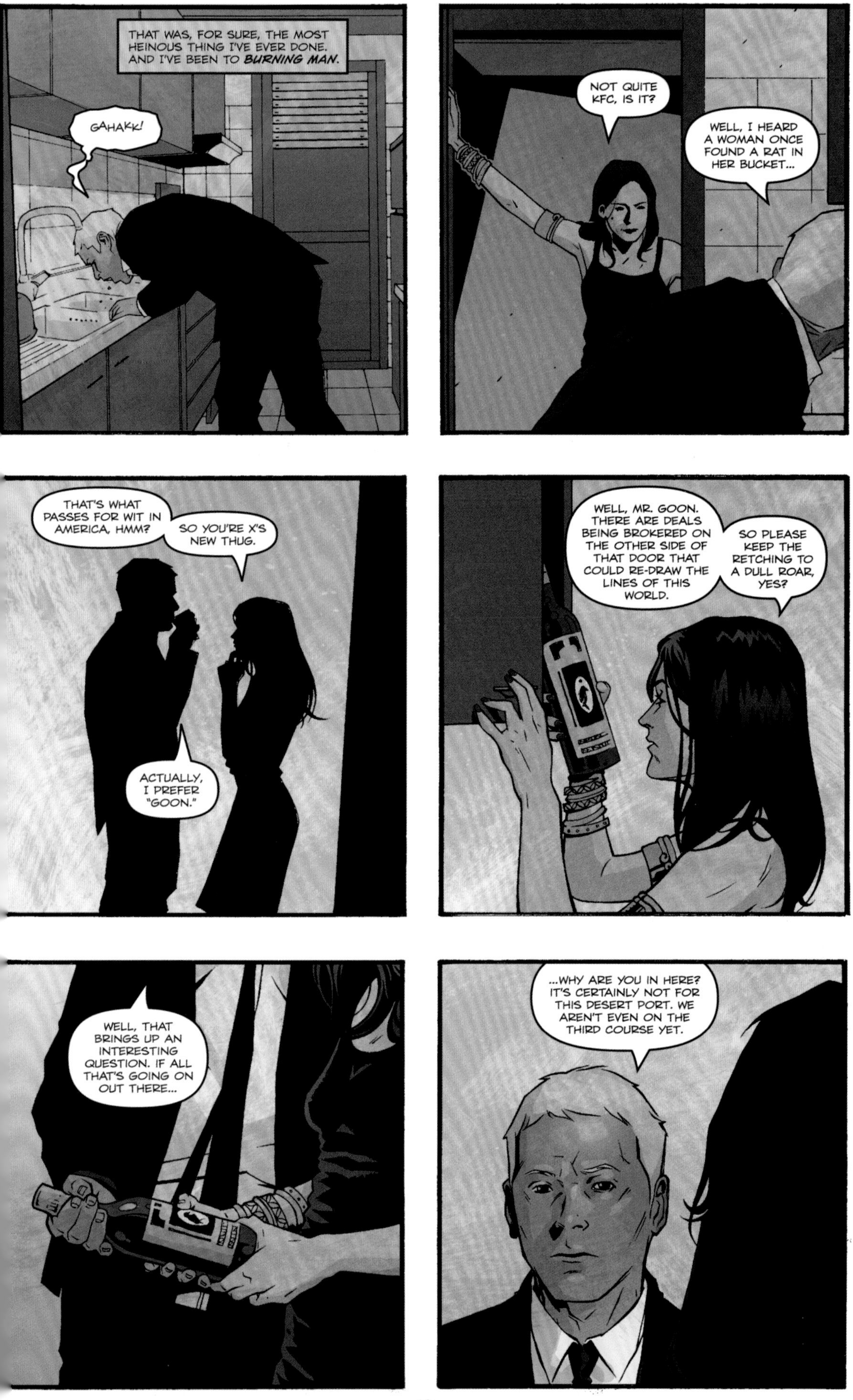
THAT WAS, FOR SURE, THE MOST HEINOUS THING I'VE EVER DONE. AND I'VE BEEN TO BURNING MAN.
GAHAKK!
NOT QUITE KFC, IS IT?
WELL, I HEARD A WOMAN ONCE FOUND A RAT IN HER BUCKET...
THAT'S WHAT PASSES FOR WIT IN AMERICA, HMM?
SO YOU'RE X'S NEW THUG.
ACTUALLY, I PREFER "GOON."
WELL, MR. GOON. THERE ARE DEALS BEING BROKERED ON THE OTHER SIDE OF THAT DOOR THAT COULD RE-DRAW THE LINES OF THIS WORLD.
SO PLEASE KEEP THE RETCHING TO A DULL ROAR, YES?
WELL, THAT BRINGS UP AN INTERESTING QUESTION. IF ALL THAT'S GOING ON OUT THERE...
...WHY ARE YOU IN HERE? IT'S CERTAINLY NOT FOR THIS DESERT PORT. WE AREN'T EVEN ON THE THIRD COURSE YET.

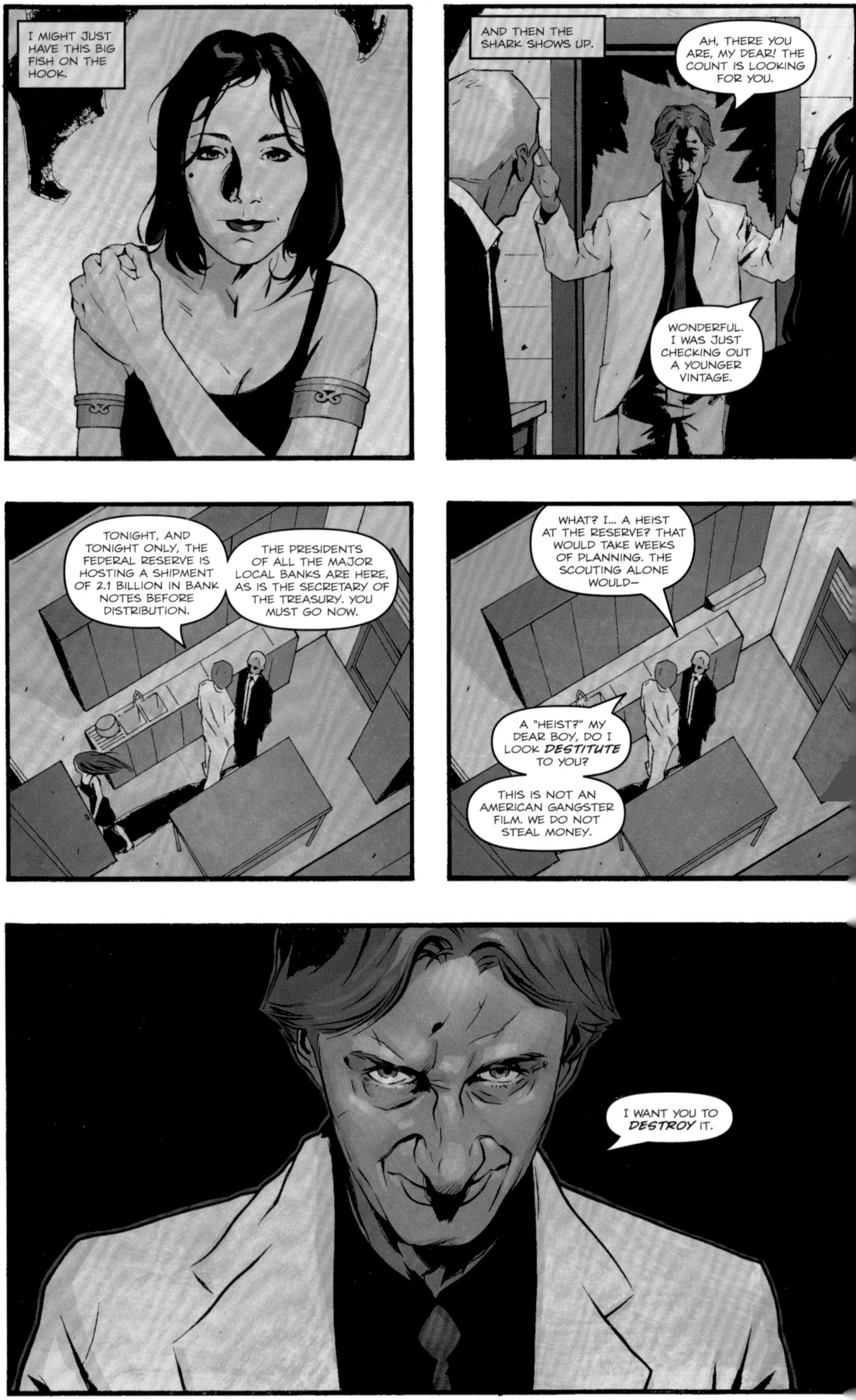
I MIGHT JUST HAVE THIS BIG FISH ON THE HOOK.
AND THEN THE SHARK SHOWS UP.
AH, THERE YOU ARE, MY DEAR! THE COUNT IS LOOKING FOR YOU.
WONDERFUL. I WAS JUST CHECKING OUT A YOUNGER VINTAGE.
TONIGHT, AND TONIGHT ONLY, THE FEDERAL RESERVE IS HOSTING A SHIPMENT OF 2.1 BILLION IN BANK NOTES BEFORE DISTRIBUTION.
THE PRESIDENTS OF ALL THE MAJOR LOCAL BANKS ARE HERE, AS IS THE SECRETARY OF THE TREASURY. YOU MUST GO NOW.
WHAT? I... A HEIST AT THE RESERVE? THAT WOULD TAKE WEEKS OF PLANNING. THE SCOUTING ALONE WOULD–
A "HEIST?" MY DEAR BOY, DO I LOOK *DESTITUTE* TO YOU?
THIS IS NOT AN AMERICAN GANGSTER FILM. WE DO NOT STEAL MONEY.
I WANT YOU TO *DESTROY* IT.

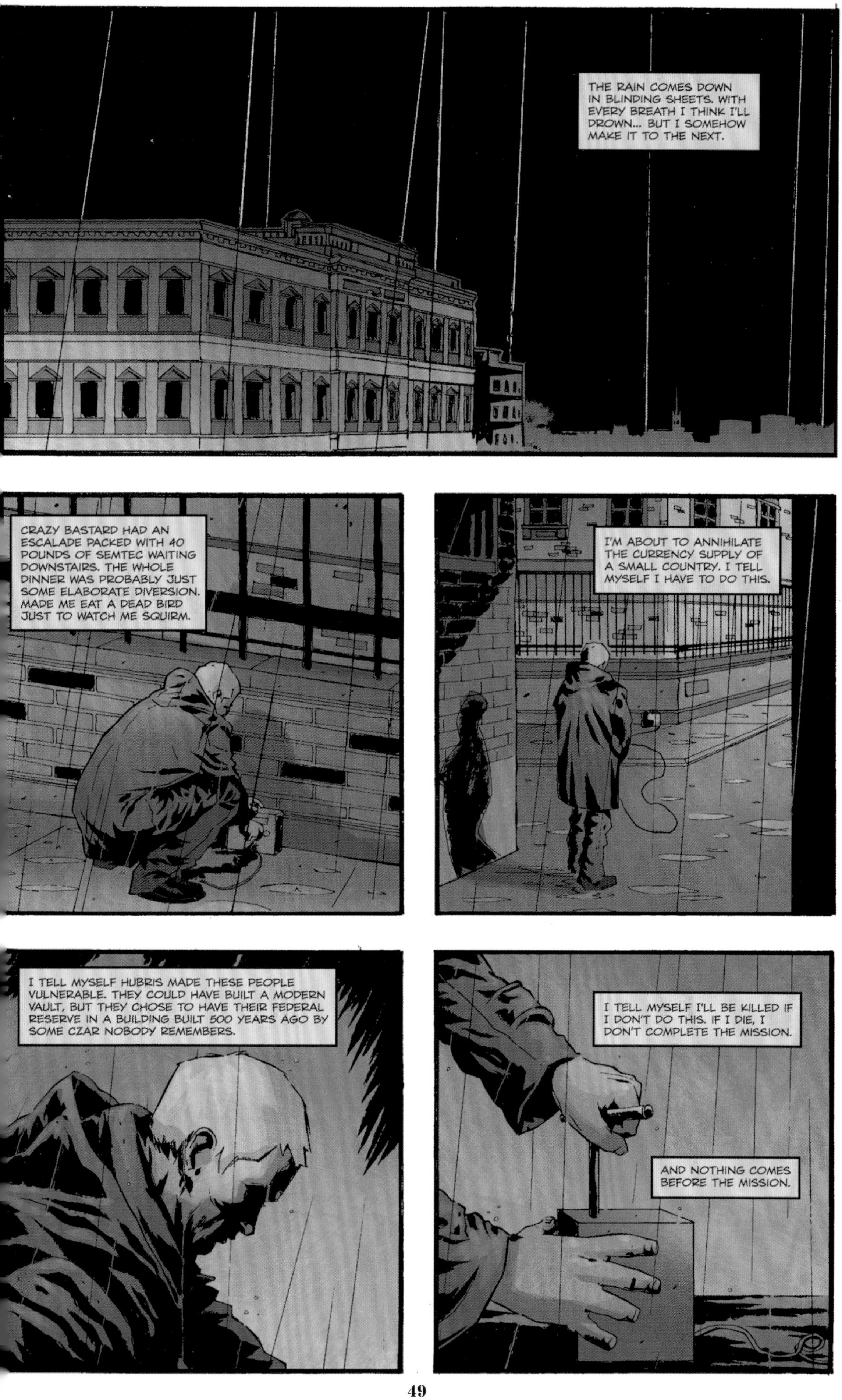
THE RAIN COMES DOWN IN BLINDING SHEETS. WITH EVERY BREATH I THINK I'LL DROWN... BUT I SOMEHOW MAKE IT TO THE NEXT.
CRAZY BASTARD HAD AN ESCALADE PACKED WITH 40 POUNDS OF SEMTEC WAITING DOWNSTAIRS. THE WHOLE DINNER WAS PROBABLY JUST SOME ELABORATE DIVERSION. MADE ME EAT A DEAD BIRD JUST TO WATCH ME SQUIRM.
I'M ABOUT TO ANNIHILATE THE CURRENCY SUPPLY OF A SMALL COUNTRY. I TELL MYSELF I HAVE TO DO THIS.
I TELL MYSELF HUBRIS MADE THESE PEOPLE VULNERABLE. THEY COULD HAVE BUILT A MODERN VAULT, BUT THEY CHOSE TO HAVE THEIR FEDERAL RESERVE IN A BUILDING BUILT 500 YEARS AGO BY SOME CZAR NOBODY REMEMBERS.
I TELL MYSELF I'LL BE KILLED IF I DON'T DO THIS. IF I DIE, I DON'T COMPLETE THE MISSION.
AND NOTHING COMES BEFORE THE MISSION.

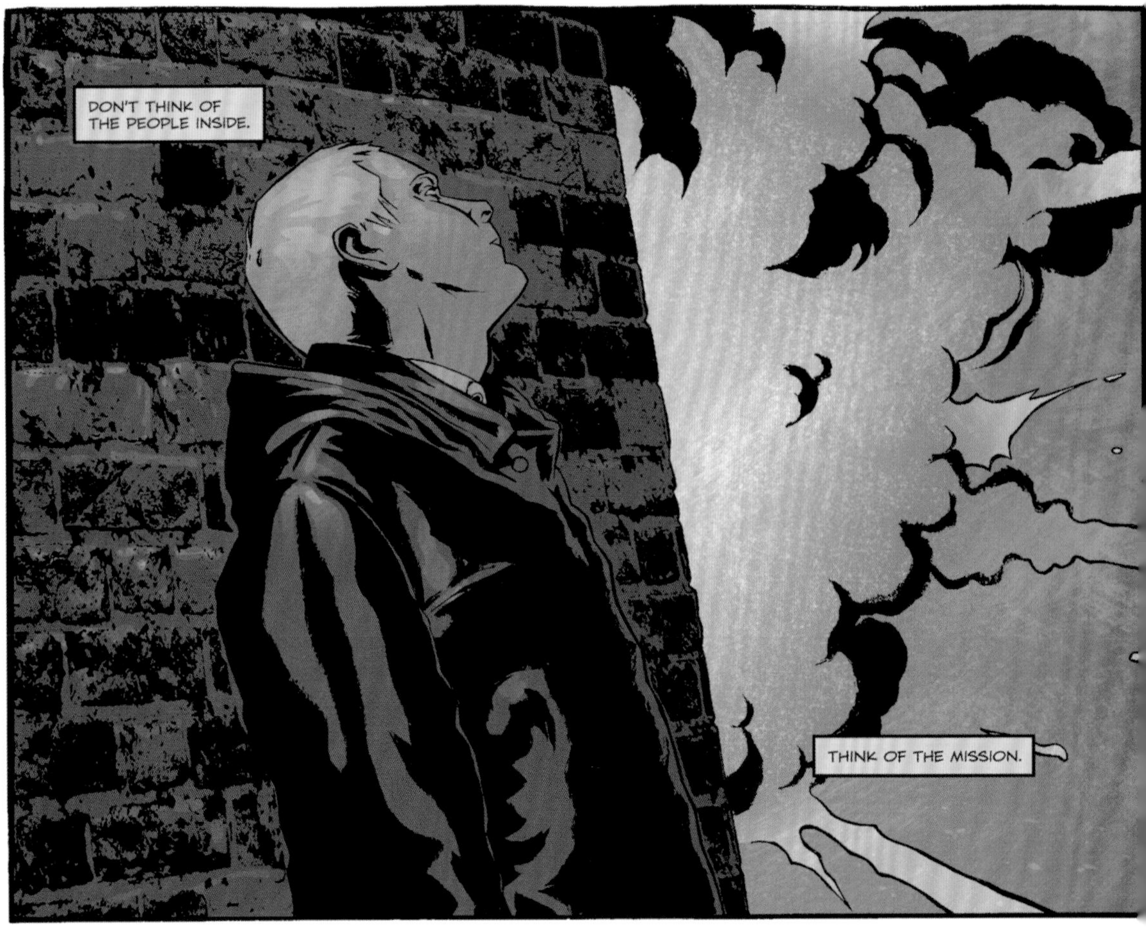
DON'T THINK OF
THE PEOPLE INSIDE.
THINK OF THE MISSION.

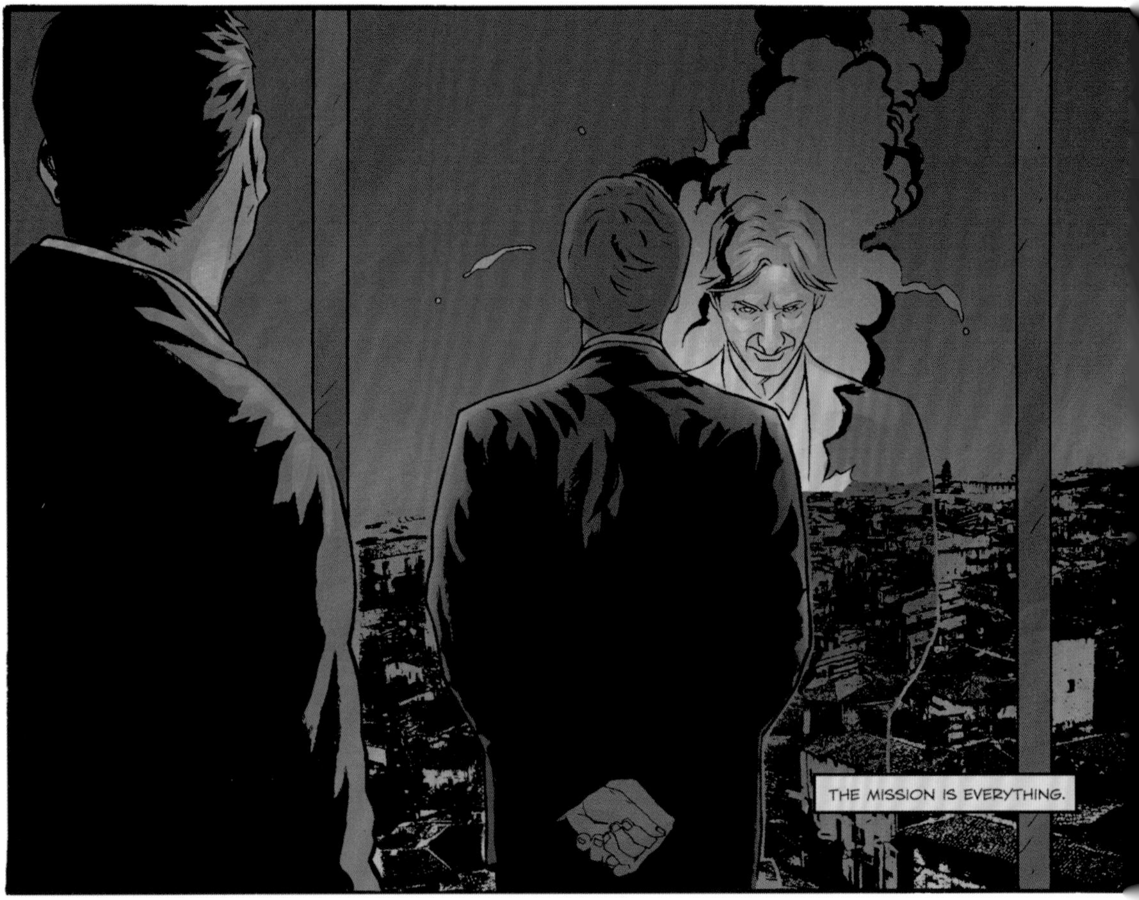
THE MISSION IS EVERYTHING.

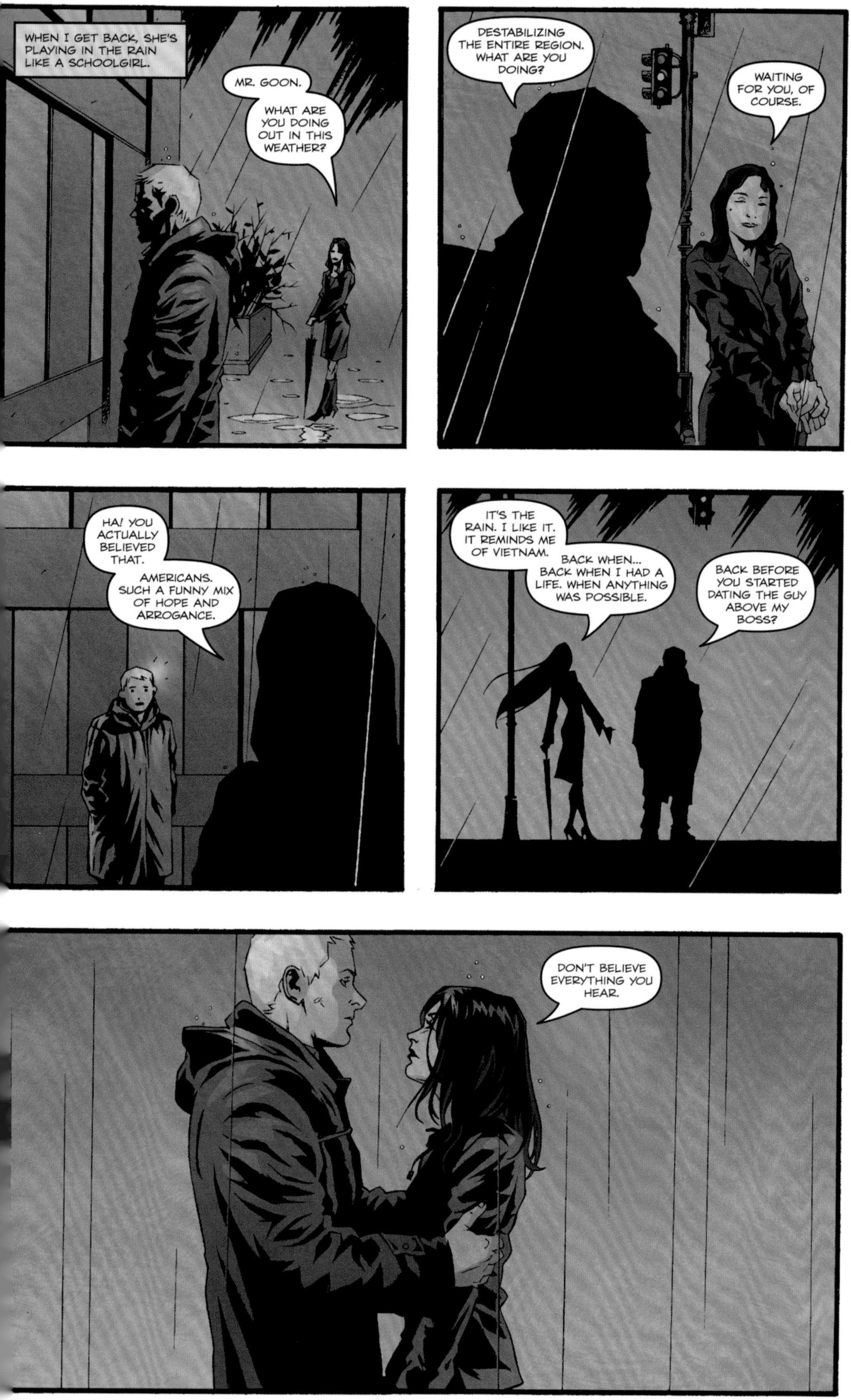

WHEN I GET BACK, SHE'S PLAYING IN THE RAIN LIKE A SCHOOLGIRL.
MR. GOON.
WHAT ARE YOU DOING OUT IN THIS WEATHER?
DESTABILIZING THE ENTIRE REGION. WHAT ARE YOU DOING?
WAITING FOR YOU, OF COURSE.
HA! YOU ACTUALLY BELIEVED THAT.
AMERICANS. SUCH A FUNNY MIX OF HOPE AND ARROGANCE.
IT'S THE RAIN. I LIKE IT. IT REMINDS ME OF VIETNAM.
BACK WHEN... BACK WHEN I HAD A LIFE. WHEN ANYTHING WAS POSSIBLE.
BACK BEFORE YOU STARTED DATING THE GUY ABOVE MY BOSS?
DON'T BELIEVE EVERYTHING YOU HEAR.

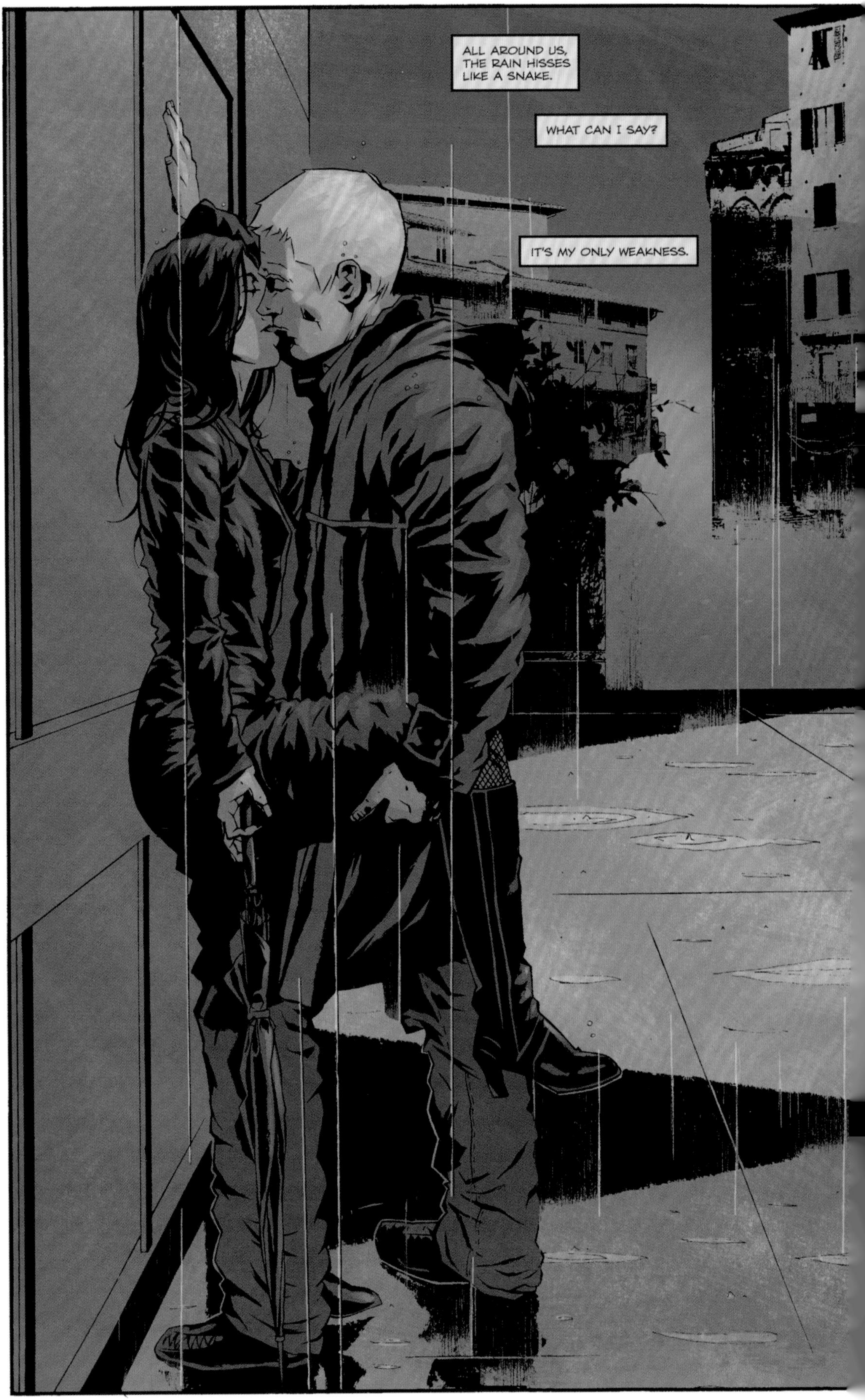
ALL AROUND US, THE RAIN HISSES LIKE A SNAKE.
WHAT CAN I SAY?
IT'S MY ONLY WEAKNESS.

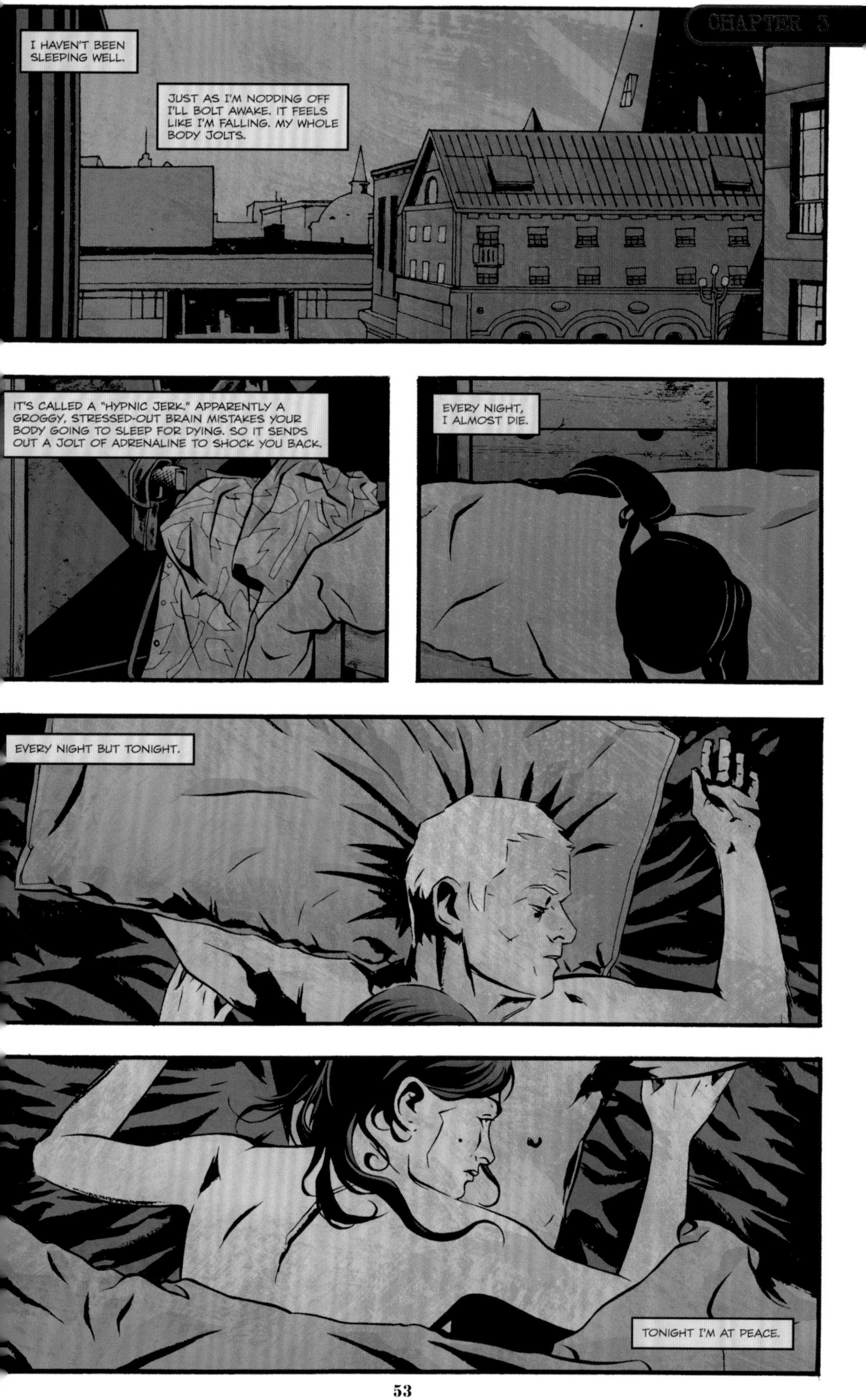
CHAPTER 3
I HAVEN'T BEEN SLEEPING WELL.
JUST AS I'M NODDING OFF I'LL BOLT AWAKE. IT FEELS LIKE I'M FALLING. MY WHOLE BODY JOLTS.
IT'S CALLED A "HYPNIC JERK." APPARENTLY A GROGGY, STRESSED-OUT BRAIN MISTAKES YOUR BODY GOING TO SLEEP FOR DYING. SO IT SENDS OUT A JOLT OF ADRENALINE TO SHOCK YOU BACK.
EVERY NIGHT, I ALMOST DIE.
EVERY NIGHT BUT TONIGHT.
TONIGHT I'M AT PEACE.

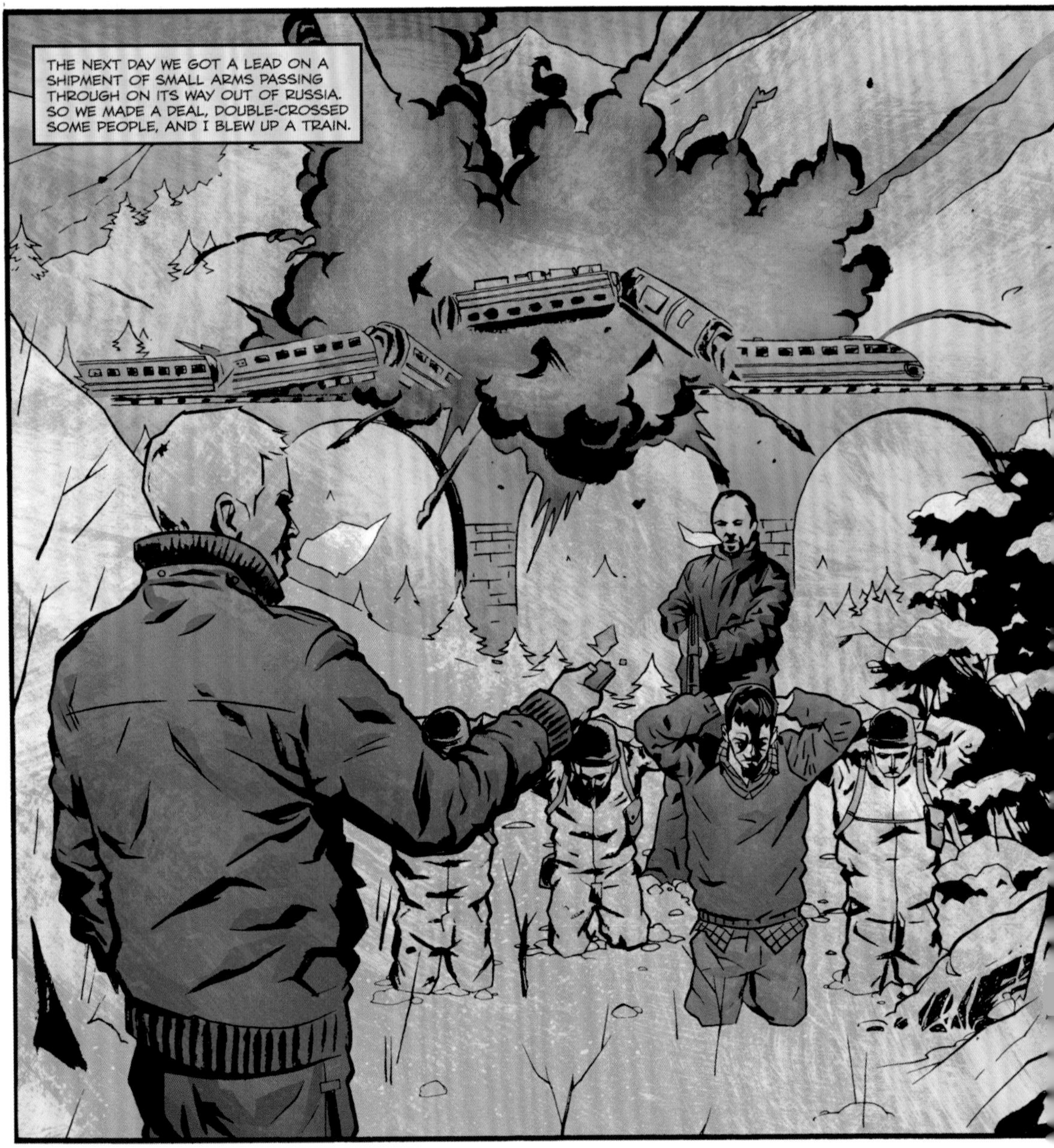
THE NEXT DAY WE GOT A LEAD ON A SHIPMENT OF SMALL ARMS PASSING THROUGH ON ITS WAY OUT OF RUSSIA. SO WE MADE A DEAL, DOUBLE-CROSSED SOME PEOPLE, AND I BLEW UP A TRAIN.

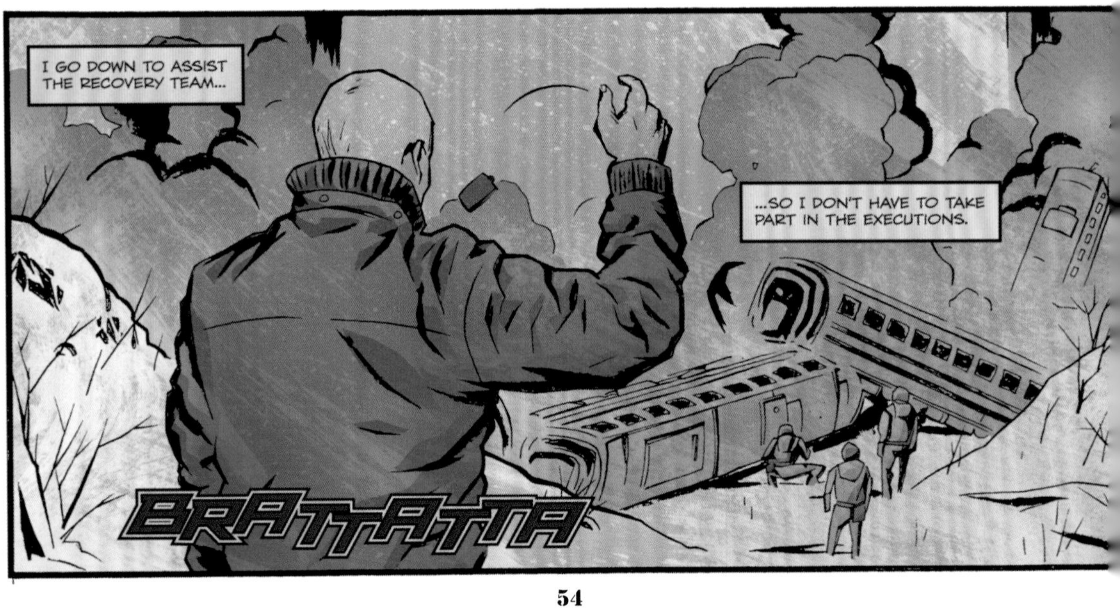
I GO DOWN TO ASSIST THE RECOVERY TEAM...
...SO I DON'T HAVE TO TAKE PART IN THE EXECUTIONS.
BRATTATTA

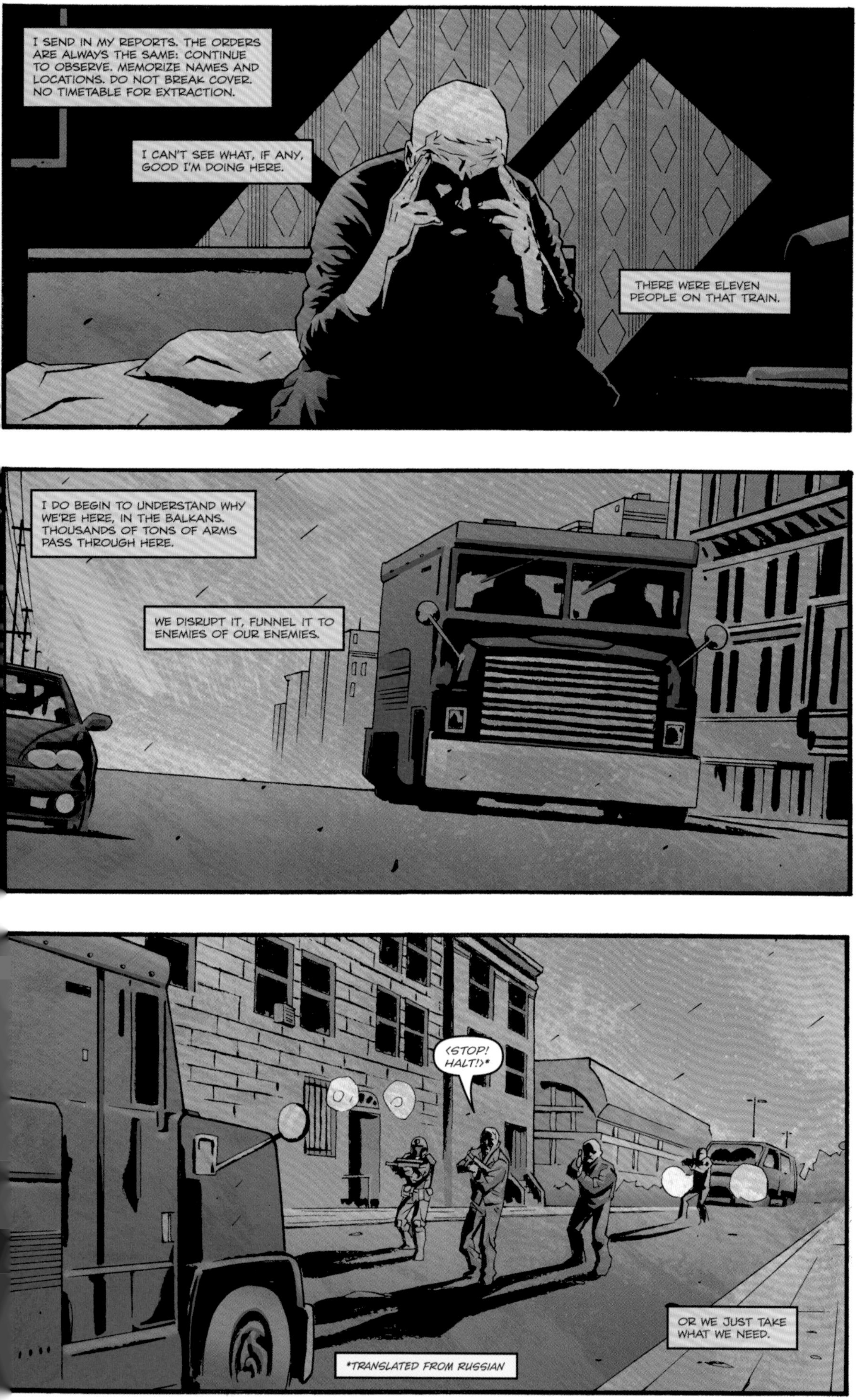
I SEND IN MY REPORTS. THE ORDERS ARE ALWAYS THE SAME: CONTINUE TO OBSERVE. MEMORIZE NAMES AND LOCATIONS. DO NOT BREAK COVER. NO TIMETABLE FOR EXTRACTION.
I CAN'T SEE WHAT, IF ANY, GOOD I'M DOING HERE.
THERE WERE ELEVEN PEOPLE ON THAT TRAIN.
I DO BEGIN TO UNDERSTAND WHY WE'RE HERE, IN THE BALKANS. THOUSANDS OF TONS OF ARMS PASS THROUGH HERE.
WE DISRUPT IT, FUNNEL IT TO ENEMIES OF OUR ENEMIES.
<STOP! HALT!>*
OR WE JUST TAKE WHAT WE NEED.
*TRANSLATED FROM RUSSIAN

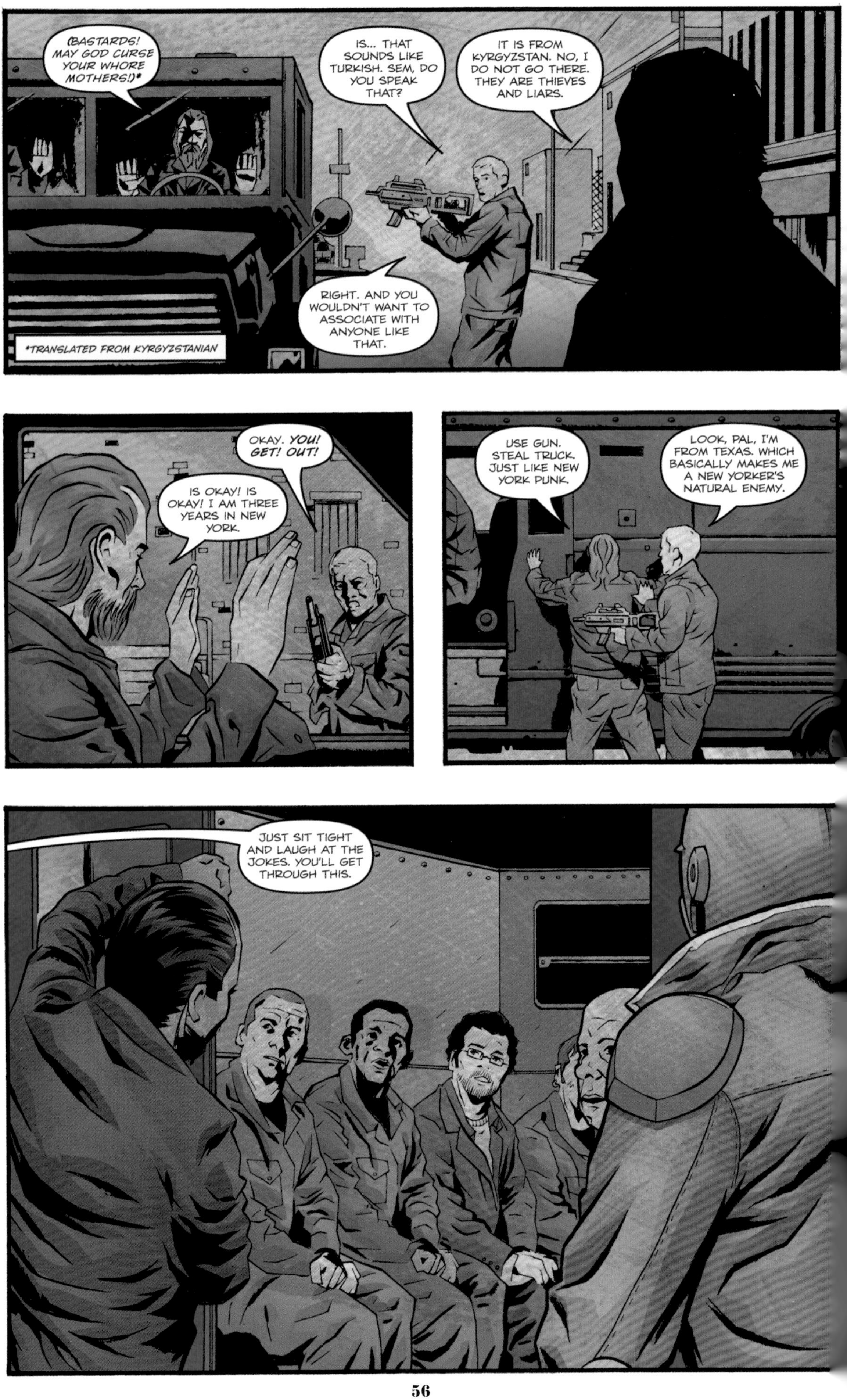
(BASTARDS! MAY GOD CURSE YOUR WHORE MOTHERS!)*
IS... THAT SOUNDS LIKE TURKISH. SEM, DO YOU SPEAK THAT?
IT IS FROM KYRGYZSTAN. NO, I DO NOT GO THERE. THEY ARE THIEVES AND LIARS.
RIGHT. AND YOU WOULDN'T WANT TO ASSOCIATE WITH ANYONE LIKE THAT.
*TRANSLATED FROM KYRGYZSTANIAN
OKAY. YOU! GET! OUT!
IS OKAY! IS OKAY! I AM THREE YEARS IN NEW YORK.
USE GUN. STEAL TRUCK. JUST LIKE NEW YORK PUNK.
LOOK, PAL, I'M FROM TEXAS. WHICH BASICALLY MAKES ME A NEW YORKER'S NATURAL ENEMY.
JUST SIT TIGHT AND LAUGH AT THE JOKES. YOU'LL GET THROUGH THIS.

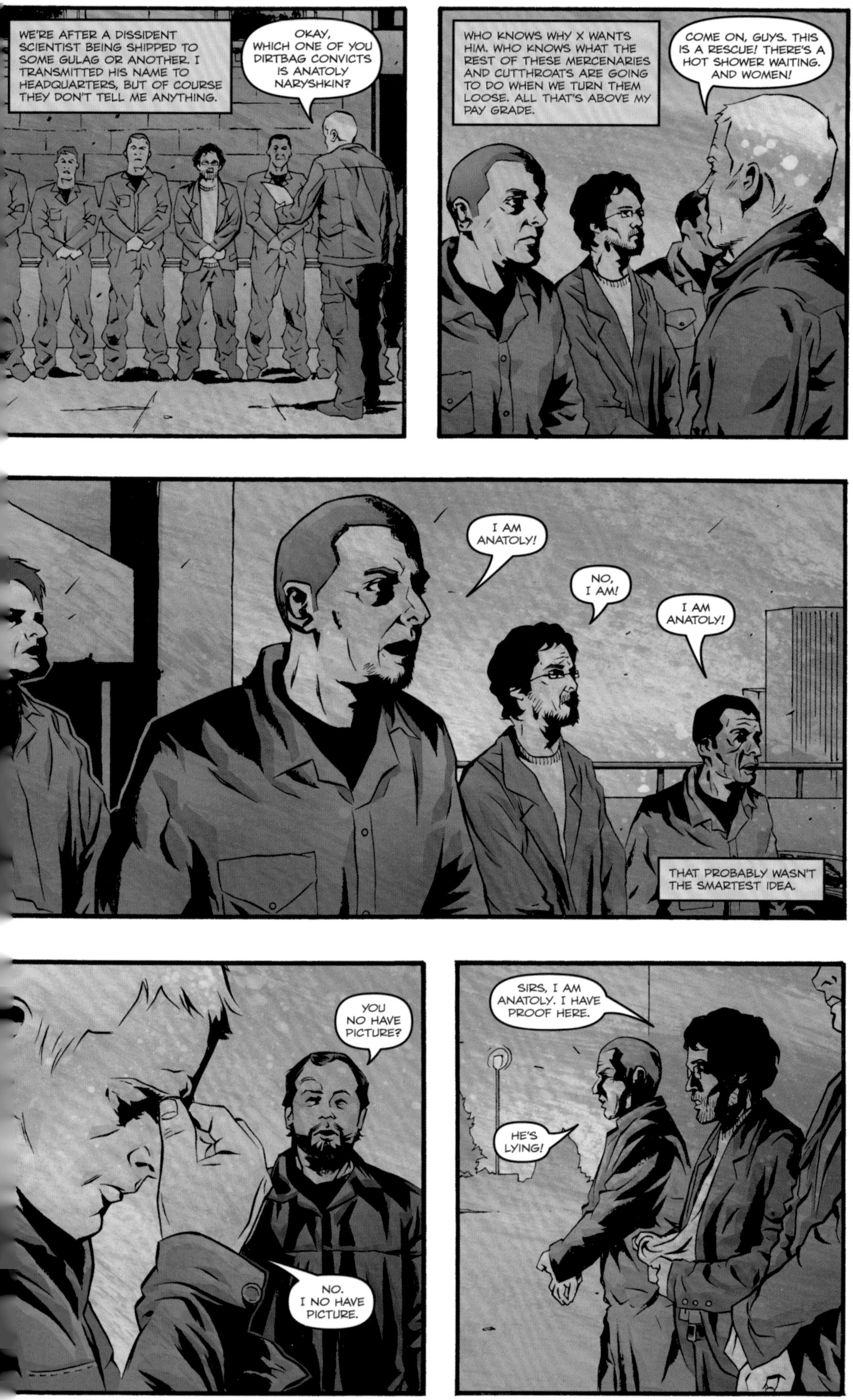
WE'RE AFTER A DISSIDENT SCIENTIST BEING SHIPPED TO SOME GULAG OR ANOTHER. I TRANSMITTED HIS NAME TO HEADQUARTERS, BUT OF COURSE THEY DON'T TELL ME ANYTHING.
OKAY, WHICH ONE OF YOU DIRTBAG CONVICTS IS ANATOLY NARYSHKIN?
WHO KNOWS WHY X WANTS HIM. WHO KNOWS WHAT THE REST OF THESE MERCENARIES AND CUTTHROATS ARE GOING TO DO WHEN WE TURN THEM LOOSE. ALL THAT'S ABOVE MY PAY GRADE.
COME ON, GUYS. THIS IS A RESCUE! THERE'S A HOT SHOWER WAITING. AND WOMEN!
I AM ANATOLY!
NO, I AM!
I AM ANATOLY!
THAT PROBABLY WASN'T THE SMARTEST IDEA.
YOU NO HAVE PICTURE?
NO. I NO HAVE PICTURE.
SIRS, I AM ANATOLY. I HAVE PROOF HERE.
HE'S LYING!

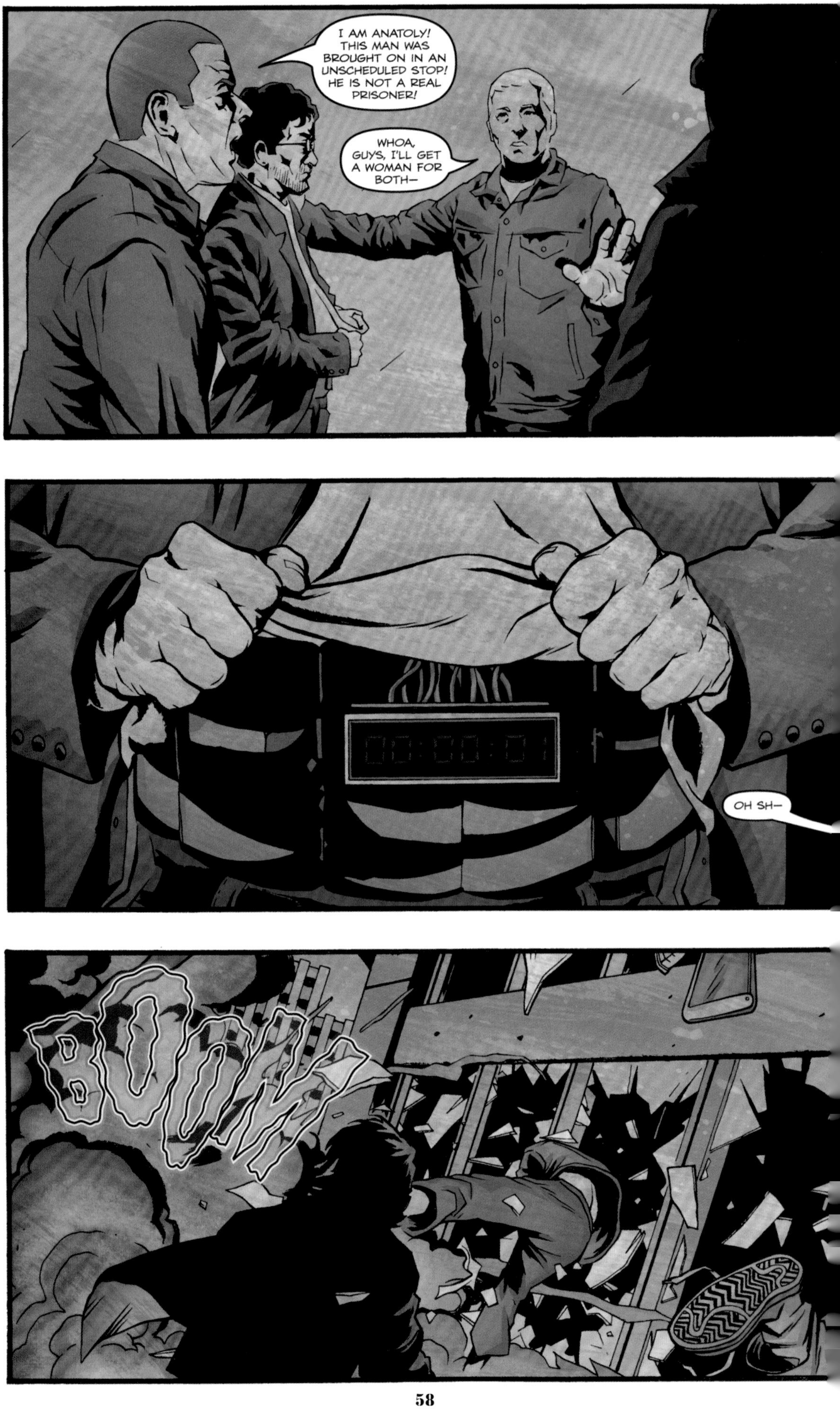
I AM ANATOLY! THIS MAN WAS BROUGHT ON IN AN UNSCHEDULED STOP! HE IS NOT A REAL PRISONER!
WHOA, GUYS, I'LL GET A WOMAN FOR BOTH—
OH SH—
BOOM

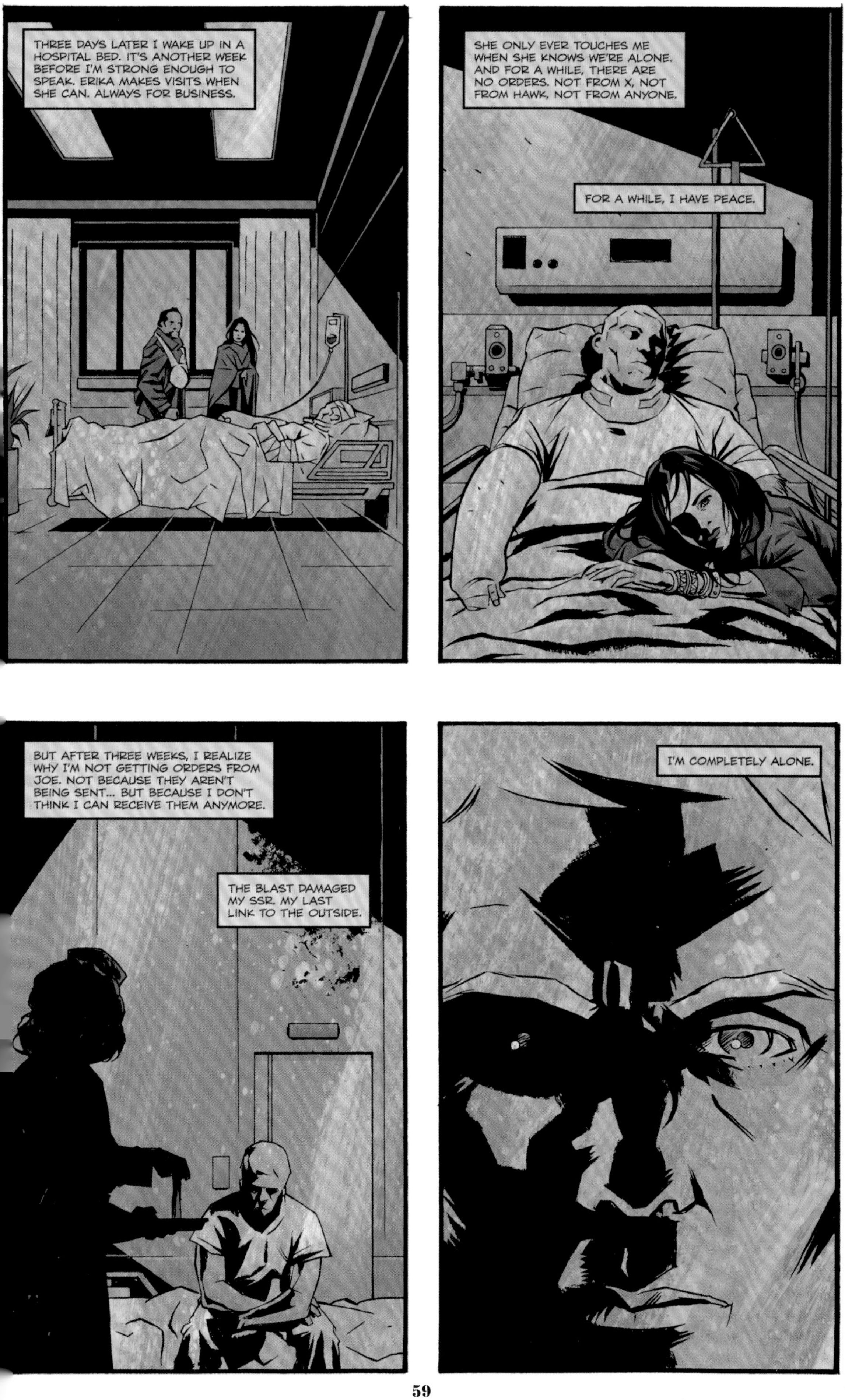
THREE DAYS LATER I WAKE UP IN A HOSPITAL BED. IT'S ANOTHER WEEK BEFORE I'M STRONG ENOUGH TO SPEAK. ERIKA MAKES VISITS WHEN SHE CAN. ALWAYS FOR BUSINESS.
SHE ONLY EVER TOUCHES ME WHEN SHE KNOWS WE'RE ALONE. AND FOR A WHILE, THERE ARE NO ORDERS. NOT FROM X, NOT FROM HAWK, NOT FROM ANYONE.
FOR A WHILE, I HAVE PEACE.
BUT AFTER THREE WEEKS, I REALIZE WHY I'M NOT GETTING ORDERS FROM JOE. NOT BECAUSE THEY AREN'T BEING SENT... BUT BECAUSE I DON'T THINK I CAN RECEIVE THEM ANYMORE.
THE BLAST DAMAGED MY SSR. MY LAST LINK TO THE OUTSIDE.
I'M COMPLETELY ALONE.

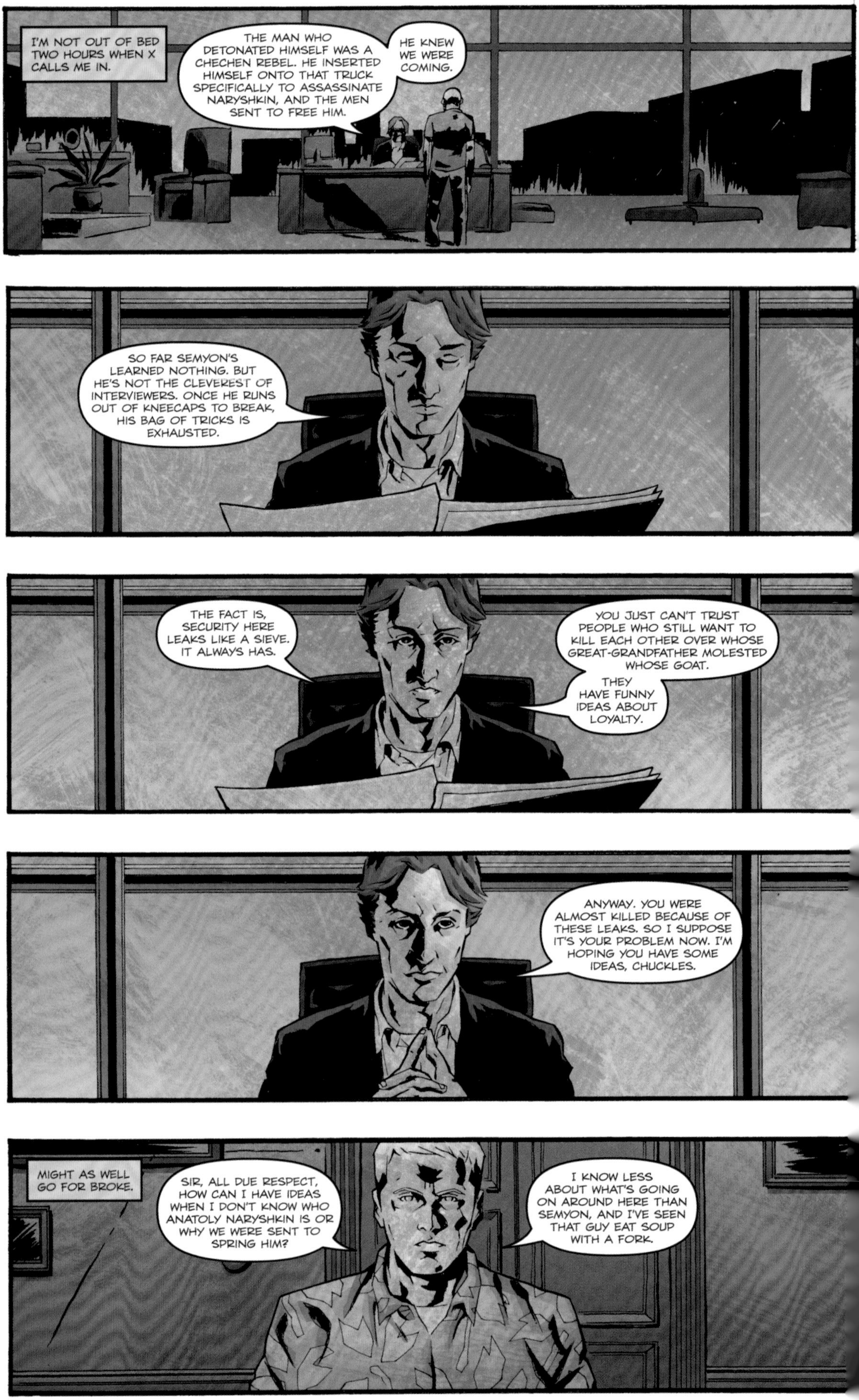

I'M NOT OUT OF BED TWO HOURS WHEN X CALLS ME IN.
THE MAN WHO DETONATED HIMSELF WAS A CHECHEN REBEL. HE INSERTED HIMSELF ONTO THAT TRUCK SPECIFICALLY TO ASSASSINATE NARYSHKIN, AND THE MEN SENT TO FREE HIM.
HE KNEW WE WERE COMING.
SO FAR SEMYON'S LEARNED NOTHING. BUT HE'S NOT THE CLEVEREST OF INTERVIEWERS. ONCE HE RUNS OUT OF KNEECAPS TO BREAK, HIS BAG OF TRICKS IS EXHAUSTED.
THE FACT IS, SECURITY HERE LEAKS LIKE A SIEVE. IT ALWAYS HAS.
YOU JUST CAN'T TRUST PEOPLE WHO STILL WANT TO KILL EACH OTHER OVER WHOSE GREAT-GRANDFATHER MOLESTED WHOSE GOAT.
THEY HAVE FUNNY IDEAS ABOUT LOYALTY.
ANYWAY. YOU WERE ALMOST KILLED BECAUSE OF THESE LEAKS. SO I SUPPOSE IT'S YOUR PROBLEM NOW. I'M HOPING YOU HAVE SOME IDEAS, CHUCKLES.
MIGHT AS WELL GO FOR BROKE.
SIR, ALL DUE RESPECT, HOW CAN I HAVE IDEAS WHEN I DON'T KNOW WHO ANATOLY NARYSHKIN IS OR WHY WE WERE SENT TO SPRING HIM?
I KNOW LESS ABOUT WHAT'S GOING ON AROUND HERE THAN SEMYON, AND I'VE SEEN THAT GUY EAT SOUP WITH A FORK.

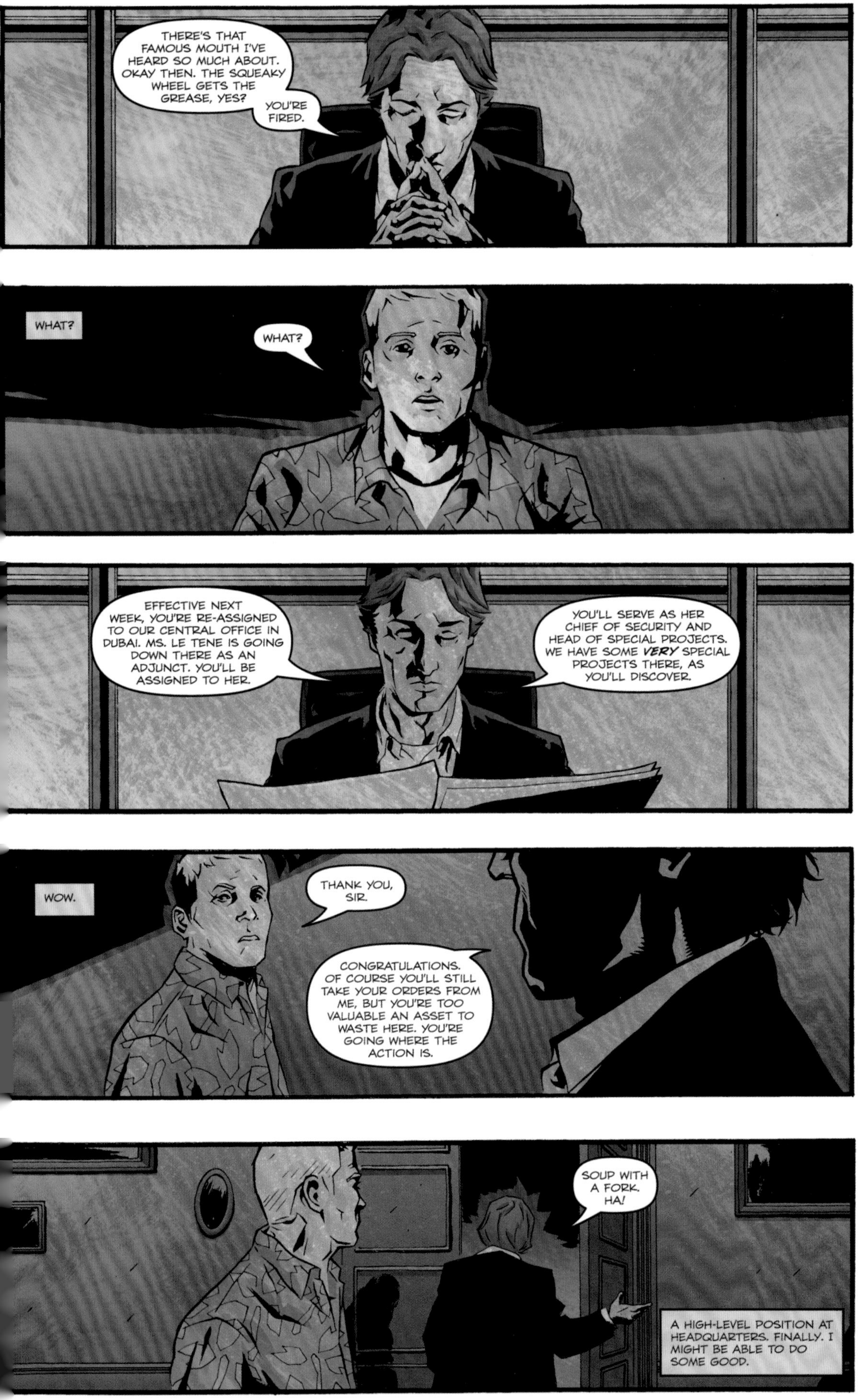
THERE'S THAT FAMOUS MOUTH I'VE HEARD SO MUCH ABOUT. OKAY THEN. THE SQUEAKY WHEEL GETS THE GREASE, YES?
YOU'RE FIRED.
WHAT?
WHAT?
EFFECTIVE NEXT WEEK, YOU'RE RE-ASSIGNED TO OUR CENTRAL OFFICE IN DUBAI. MS. LE TENE IS GOING DOWN THERE AS AN ADJUNCT. YOU'LL BE ASSIGNED TO HER.
YOU'LL SERVE AS HER CHIEF OF SECURITY AND HEAD OF SPECIAL PROJECTS. WE HAVE SOME VERY SPECIAL PROJECTS THERE, AS YOU'LL DISCOVER.
WOW.
THANK YOU, SIR.
CONGRATULATIONS. OF COURSE YOU'LL STILL TAKE YOUR ORDERS FROM ME, BUT YOU'RE TOO VALUABLE AN ASSET TO WASTE HERE. YOU'RE GOING WHERE THE ACTION IS.
SOUP WITH A FORK. HA!
A HIGH-LEVEL POSITION AT HEADQUARTERS. FINALLY. I MIGHT BE ABLE TO DO SOME GOOD.

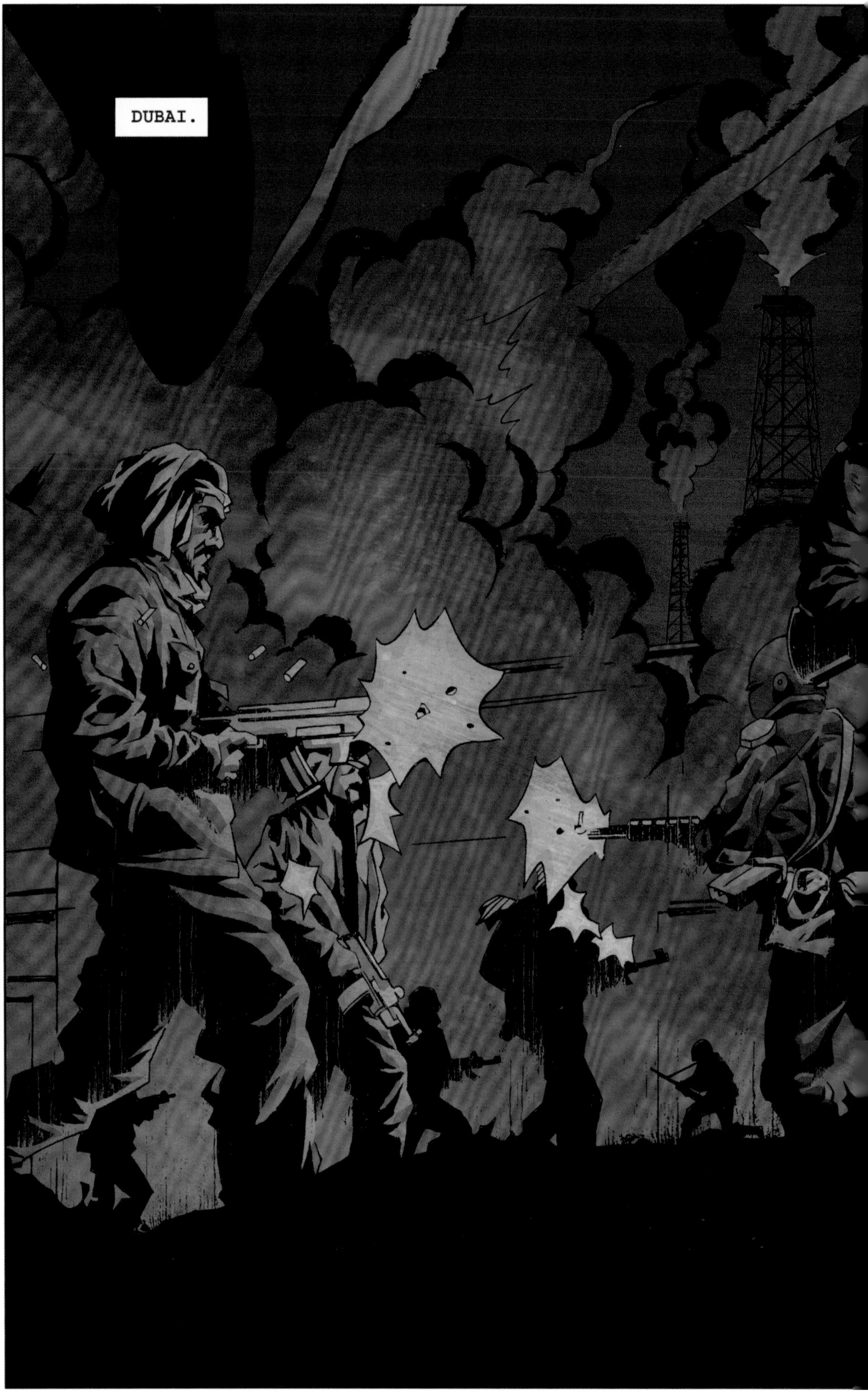
DUBAI.

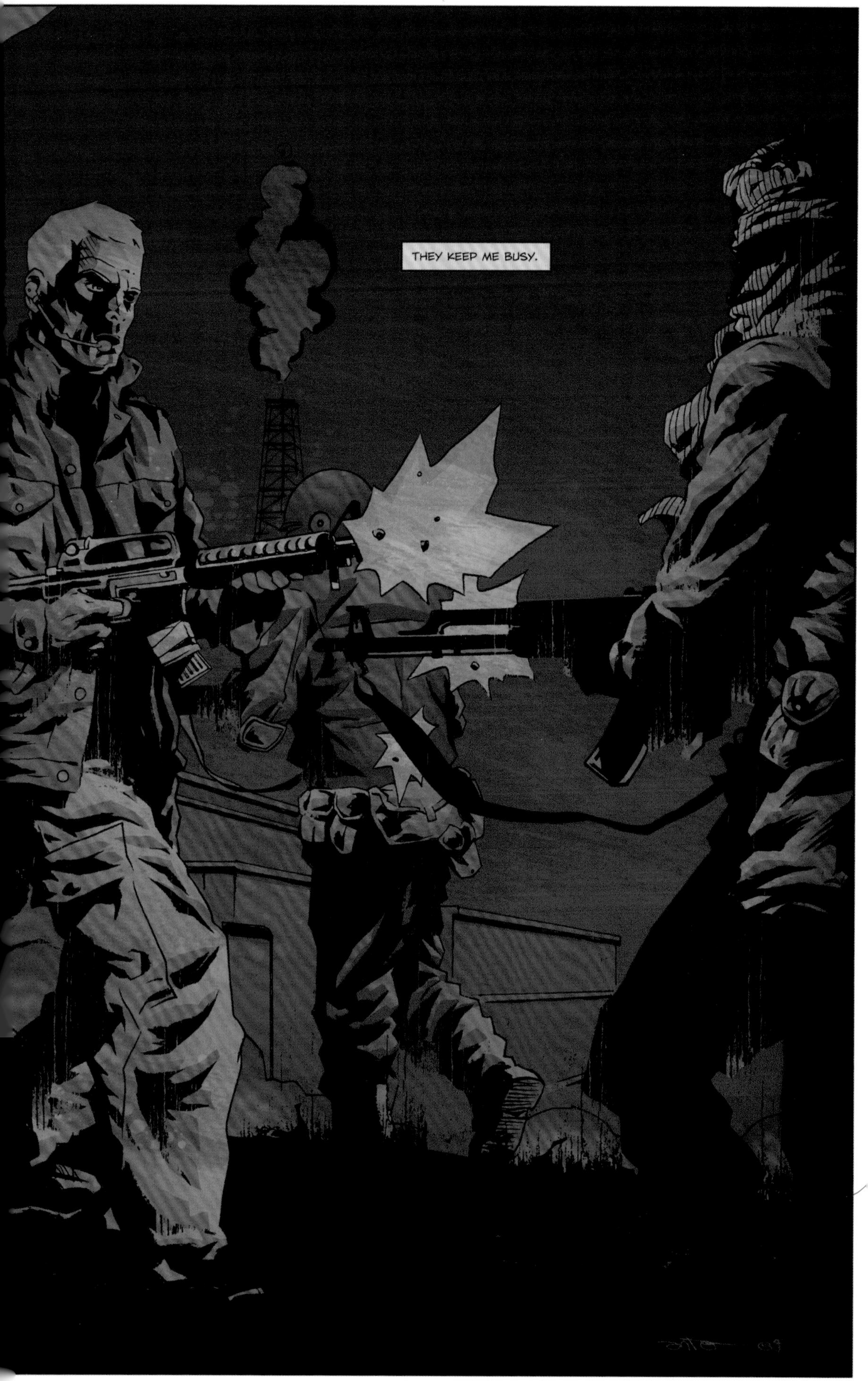
THEY KEEP ME BUSY.

TURNS OUT "CHIEF OF SECURITY" MEANS "EVERY DIRTY JOB WE CAN'T TRUST TO SOMEONE WITH ENGLISH AS HIS SECOND LANGUAGE."

EXHALE *THEN* FIRE. AND SQUEEZE, DON'T PULL. YOU GUYS GOTTA LOOSEN UP OUT HERE.

I TRAIN THE TERRORISTS OF TOMORROW. I TRAIN THEM TO KILL MY FRIENDS MORE EFFECTIVELY.

THE NERVE GAS IS IN A GARBAGE TRUCK THAT WILL BE DRIVEN ONTO THE CONSULATE TOMORROW. THE DRIVER'S A FANATIC. GUY CAN'T WAIT TO GO TO HEAVEN.

NO SHORTAGE OF THOSE TYPES IN THIS PART OF THE WORLD.

I TELL MYSELF I HAVE TO DO THIS. THE CLOSER I GET TO THE TOP, THE EASIER IT'LL BE TO BRING DOWN THE WHOLE THING.

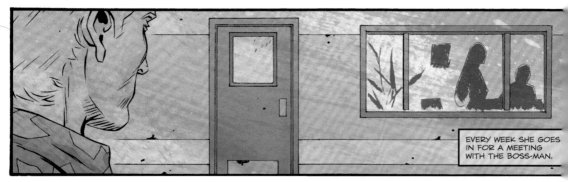

EVERY WEEK SHE GOES IN FOR A MEETING WITH THE BOSS-MAN.

I'VE NEVER SEEN HIM. NEITHER HAS SEMYON.

SEM CALLS HIM THE "COMMANDER." CAN'T TELL IF THAT'S AN ACTUAL TITLE OR JUST SEM BEING SEM.

SEM WAS RIGHT THOUGH. ERIKA DEFINITELY HAS A HISTORY WITH THIS GUY. IT'S ALL OVER HER FACE WHENEVER SHE LEAVES THE MEETINGS.

THAT'LL BE ALL. COME BY MY PLACE AT 11:45 TONIGHT.

I HAVE TO USE THAT SOMEHOW.

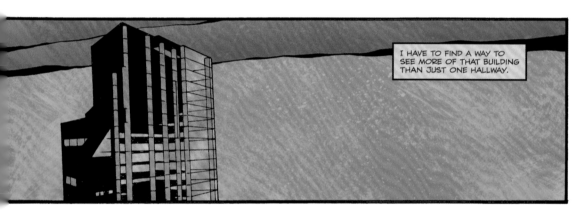

I HAVE TO FIND A WAY TO SEE MORE OF THAT BUILDING THAN JUST ONE HALLWAY.

OR WHAT I CAN SEE FROM ERIKA'S WINDOW.

IS THE VIEW IN HERE DISAPPOINTING YOU?

I WAS TOLD I'D BE IN CHARGE OF SPECIAL PROJECTS. SO FAR THIS HAS ALL BEEN RUN AND GUN.

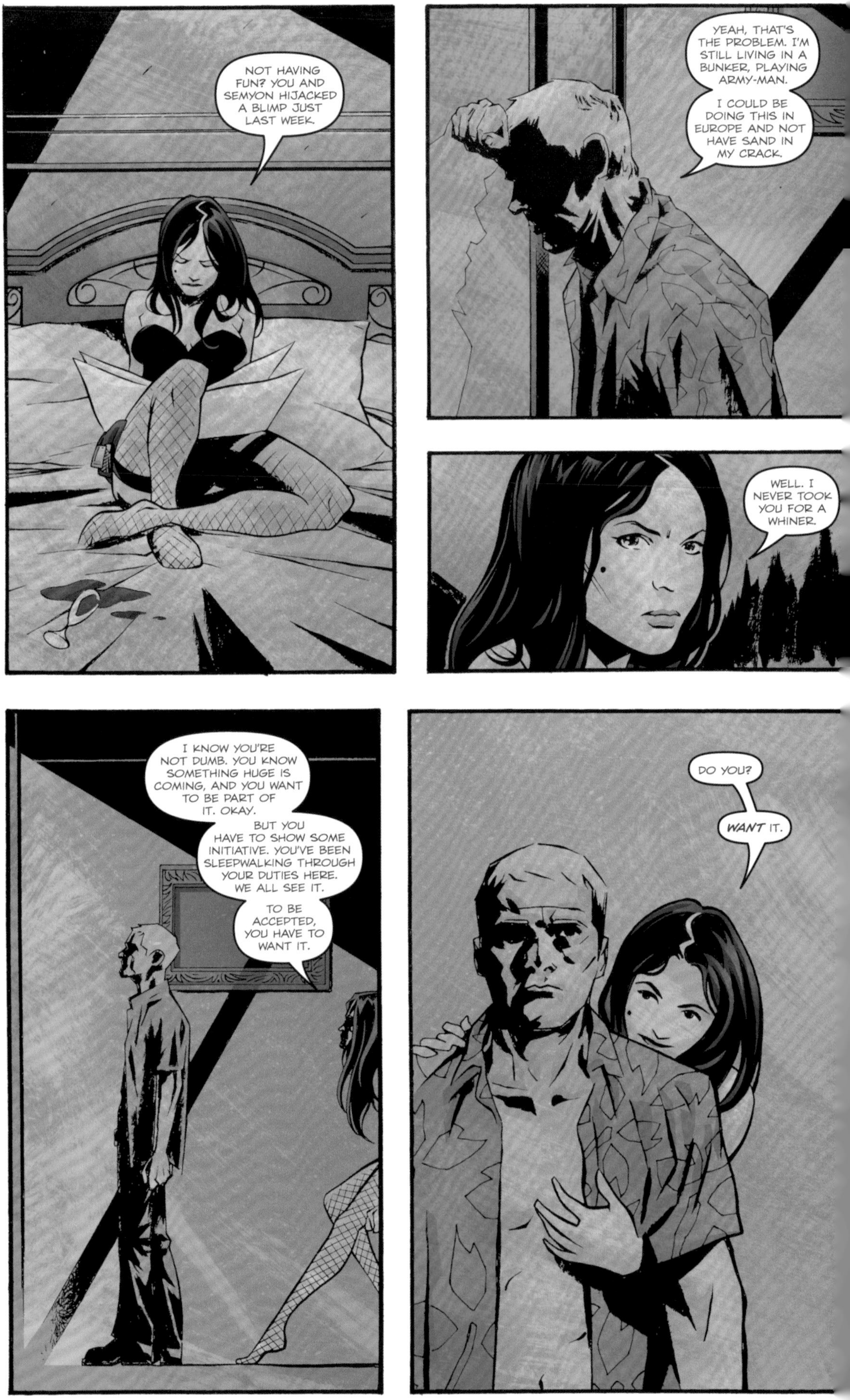
NOT HAVING FUN? YOU AND SEMYON HIJACKED A BLIMP JUST LAST WEEK.
YEAH, THAT'S THE PROBLEM. I'M STILL LIVING IN A BUNKER, PLAYING ARMY-MAN.
I COULD BE DOING THIS IN EUROPE AND NOT HAVE SAND IN MY CRACK.
WELL. I NEVER TOOK YOU FOR A WHINER.
I KNOW YOU'RE NOT DUMB. YOU KNOW SOMETHING HUGE IS COMING, AND YOU WANT TO BE PART OF IT. OKAY.
BUT YOU HAVE TO SHOW SOME INITIATIVE. YOU'VE BEEN SLEEPWALKING THROUGH YOUR DUTIES HERE. WE ALL SEE IT.
TO BE ACCEPTED, YOU HAVE TO WANT IT.
DO YOU?
*WANT* IT.

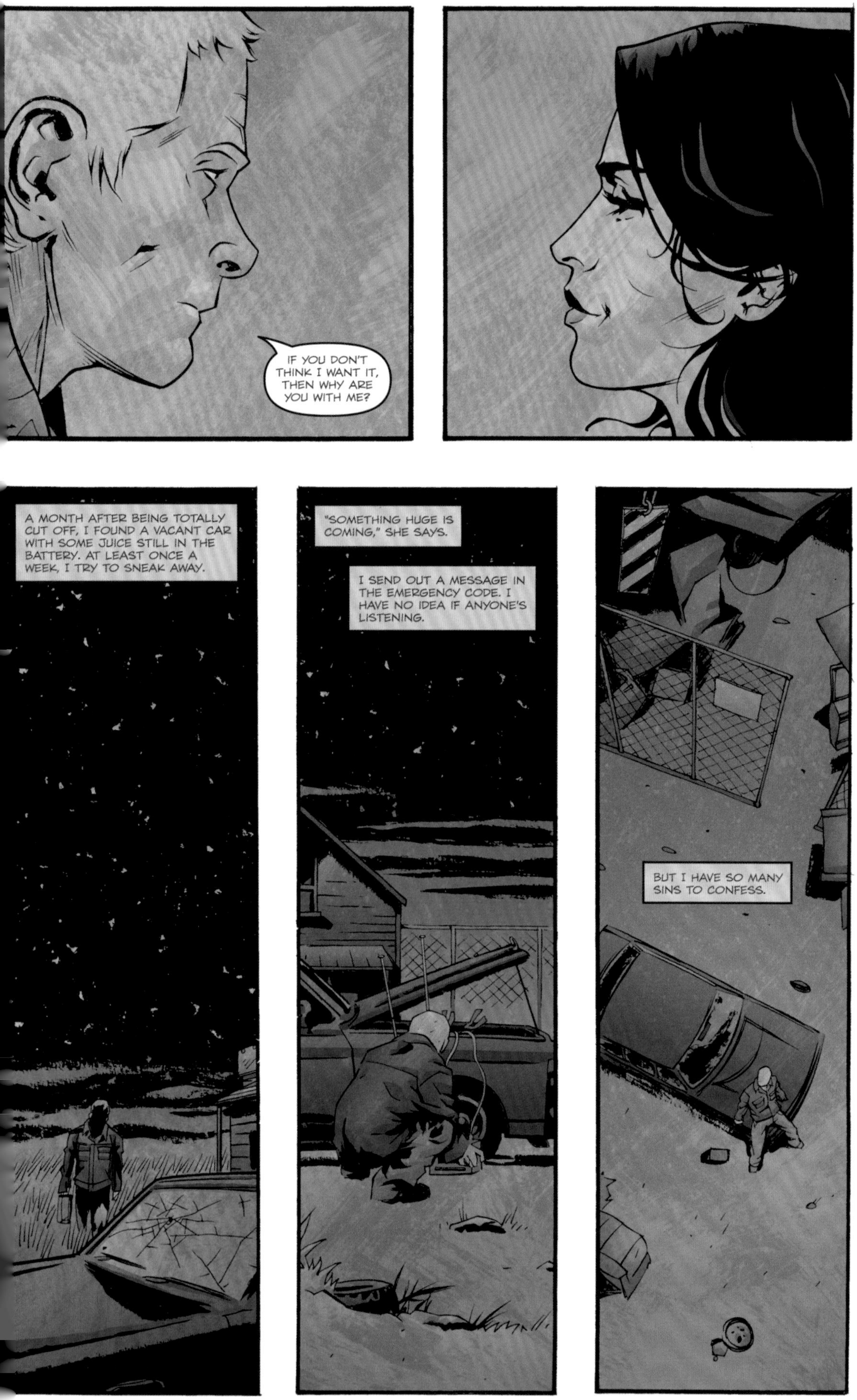
IF YOU DON'T THINK I WANT IT, THEN WHY ARE YOU WITH ME?
A MONTH AFTER BEING TOTALLY CUT OFF, I FOUND A VACANT CAR WITH SOME JUICE STILL IN THE BATTERY. AT LEAST ONCE A WEEK, I TRY TO SNEAK AWAY.
"SOMETHING HUGE IS COMING," SHE SAYS.
I SEND OUT A MESSAGE IN THE EMERGENCY CODE. I HAVE NO IDEA IF ANYONE'S LISTENING.
BUT I HAVE SO MANY SINS TO CONFESS.

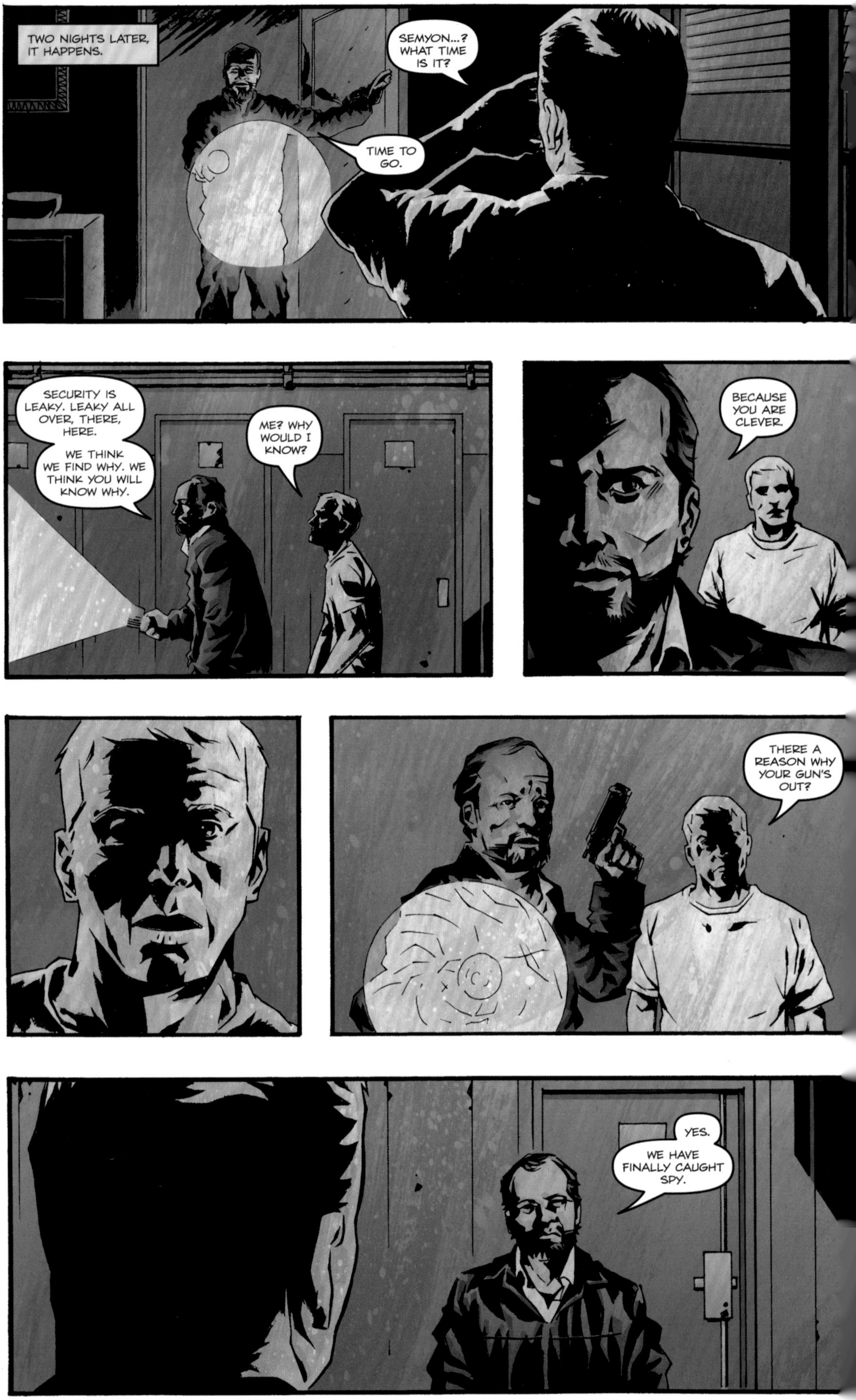
TWO NIGHTS LATER, IT HAPPENS.
SEMYON...? WHAT TIME IS IT?
TIME TO GO.
SECURITY IS LEAKY. LEAKY ALL OVER, THERE, HERE.
WE THINK WE FIND WHY. WE THINK YOU WILL KNOW WHY.
ME? WHY WOULD I KNOW?
BECAUSE YOU ARE CLEVER.
THERE A REASON WHY YOUR GUN'S OUT?
YES.
WE HAVE FINALLY CAUGHT SPY.

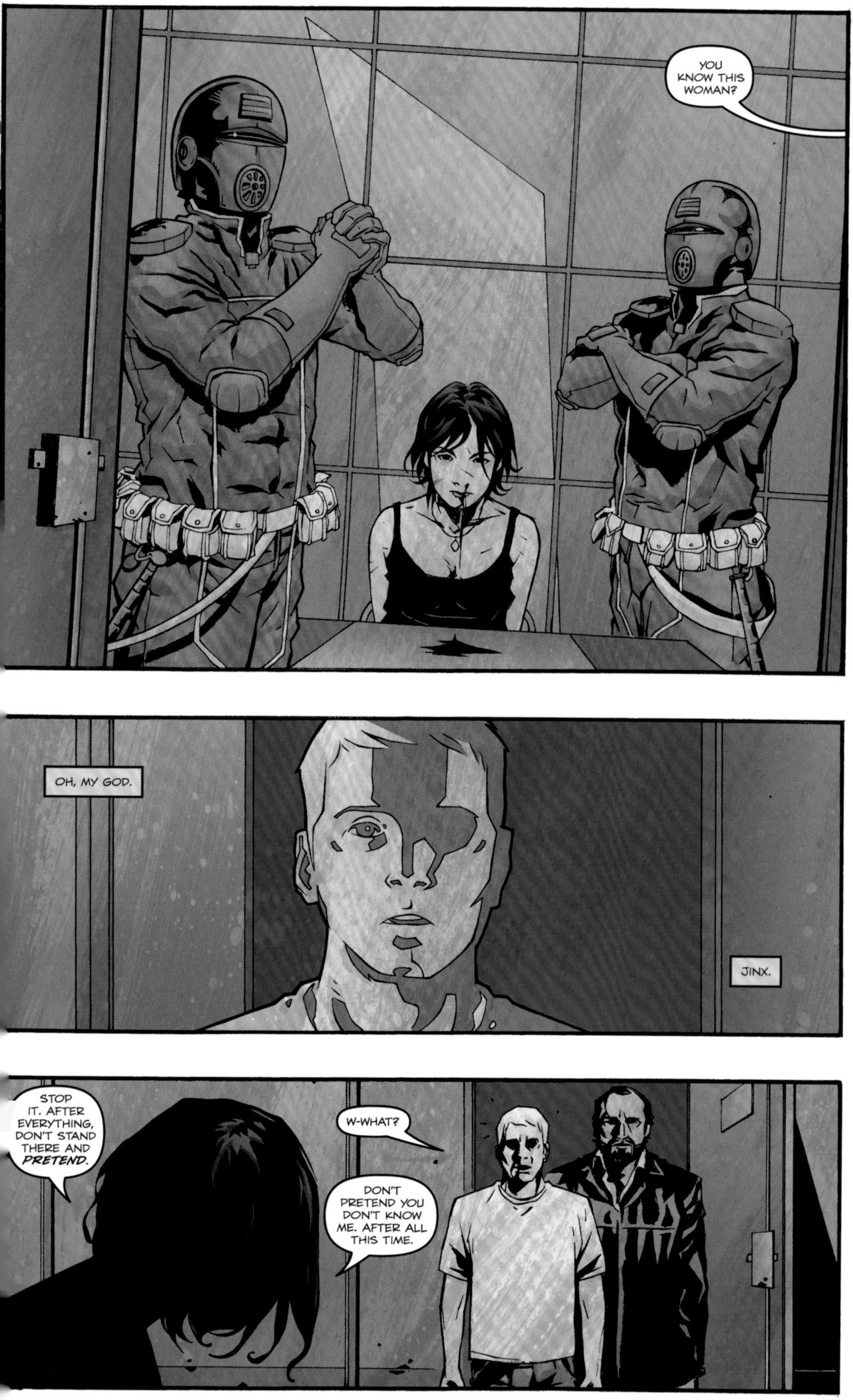
YOU KNOW THIS WOMAN?
OH, MY GOD.
JINX.
STOP IT. AFTER EVERYTHING, DON'T STAND THERE AND *PRETEND*.
W-WHAT?
DON'T PRETEND YOU DON'T KNOW ME. AFTER ALL THIS TIME.

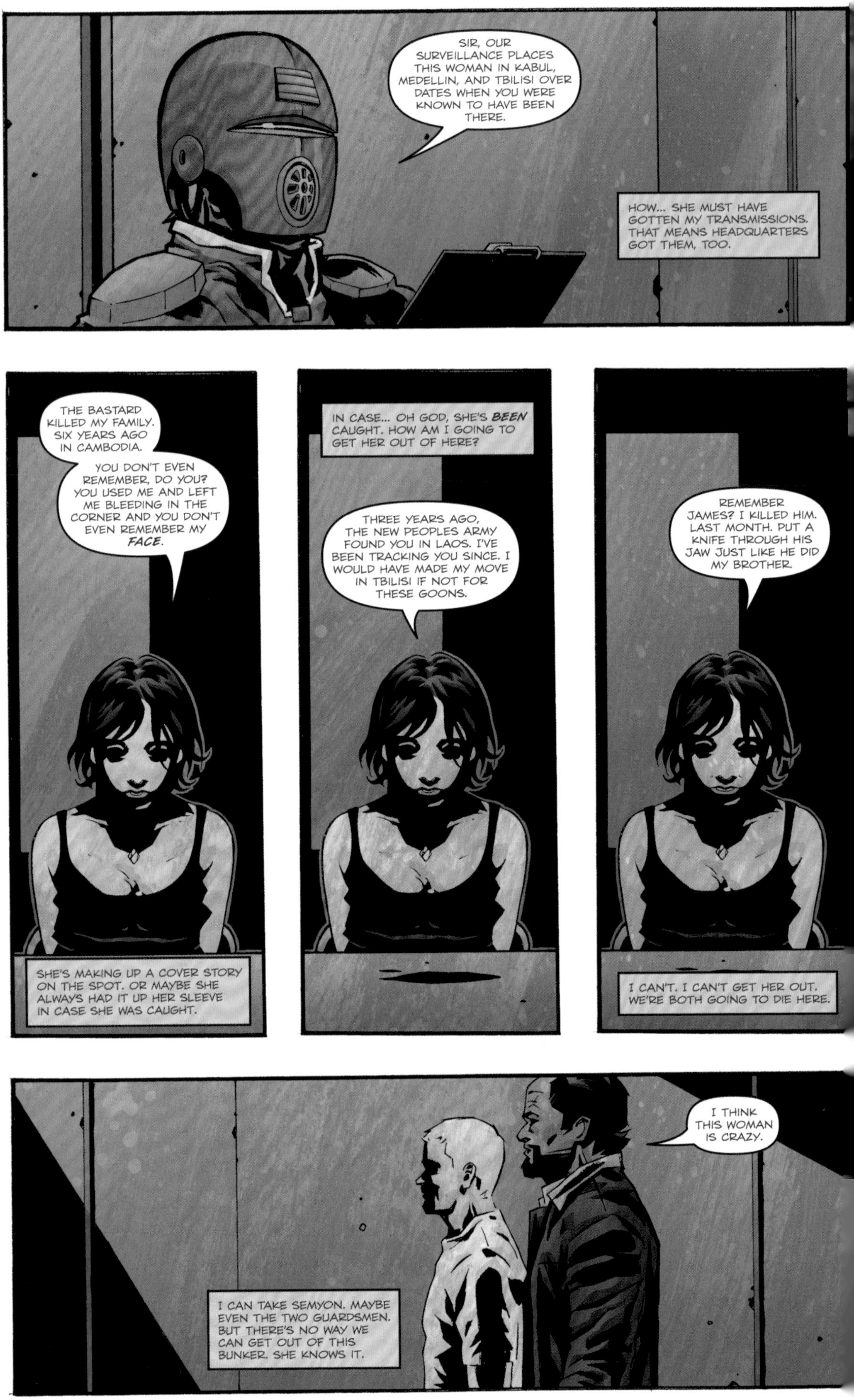
SIR, OUR SURVEILLANCE PLACES THIS WOMAN IN KABUL, MEDELLIN, AND TBILISI OVER DATES WHEN YOU WERE KNOWN TO HAVE BEEN THERE.
HOW... SHE MUST HAVE GOTTEN MY TRANSMISSIONS. THAT MEANS HEADQUARTERS GOT THEM, TOO.
THE BASTARD KILLED MY FAMILY. SIX YEARS AGO IN CAMBODIA.
YOU DON'T EVEN REMEMBER, DO YOU? YOU USED ME AND LEFT ME BLEEDING IN THE CORNER AND YOU DON'T EVEN REMEMBER MY FACE.
SHE'S MAKING UP A COVER STORY ON THE SPOT. OR MAYBE SHE ALWAYS HAD IT UP HER SLEEVE IN CASE SHE WAS CAUGHT.
IN CASE... OH GOD, SHE'S BEEN CAUGHT. HOW AM I GOING TO GET HER OUT OF HERE?
THREE YEARS AGO, THE NEW PEOPLES ARMY FOUND YOU IN LAOS. I'VE BEEN TRACKING YOU SINCE. I WOULD HAVE MADE MY MOVE IN TBILISI IF NOT FOR THESE GOONS.
REMEMBER JAMES? I KILLED HIM. LAST MONTH. PUT A KNIFE THROUGH HIS JAW JUST LIKE HE DID MY BROTHER.
I CAN'T. I CAN'T GET HER OUT. WE'RE BOTH GOING TO DIE HERE.
I THINK THIS WOMAN IS CRAZY.
I CAN TAKE SEMYON. MAYBE EVEN THE TWO GUARDSMEN. BUT THERE'S NO WAY WE CAN GET OUT OF THIS BUNKER. SHE KNOWS IT.

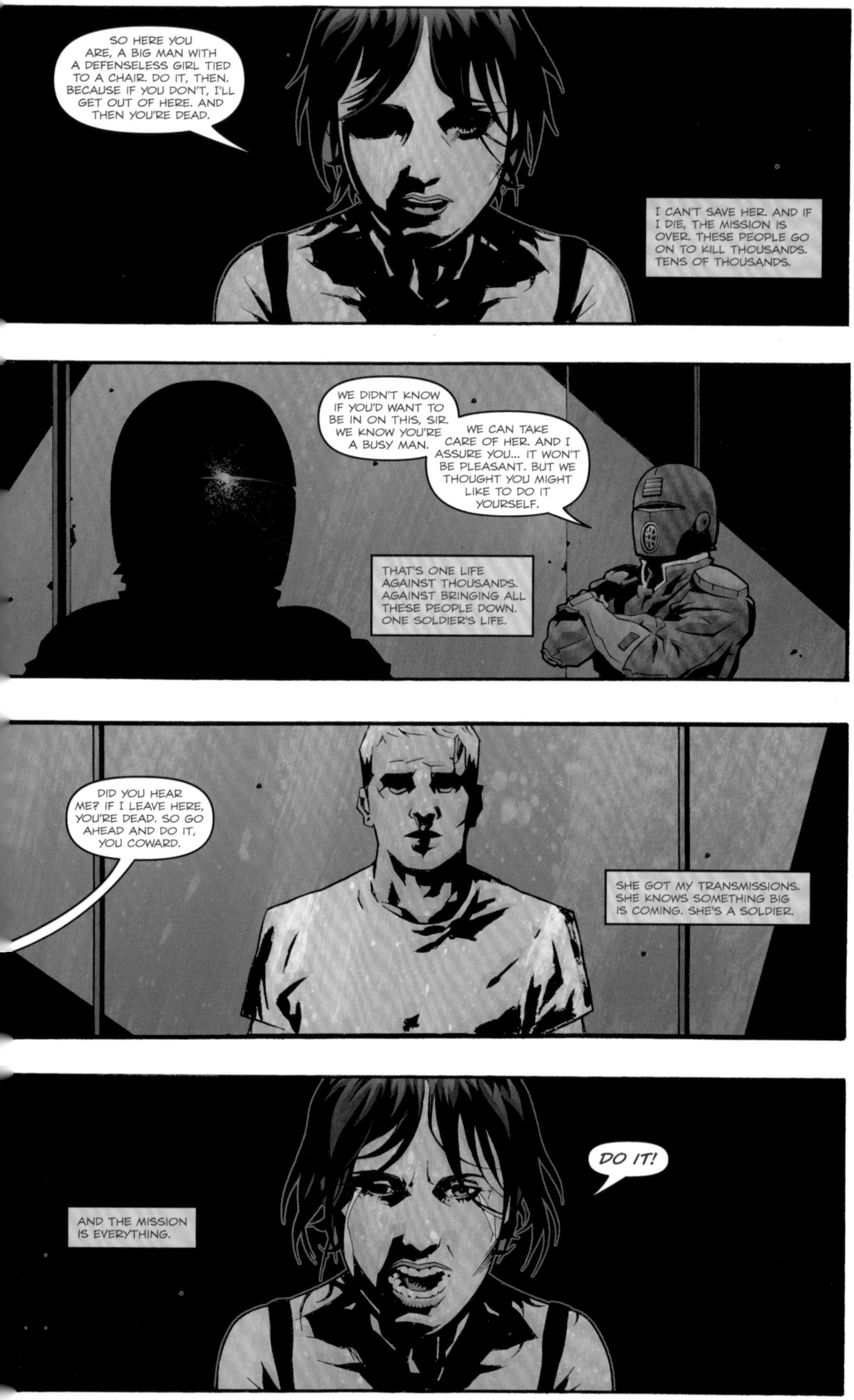
SO HERE YOU ARE, A BIG MAN WITH A DEFENSELESS GIRL TIED TO A CHAIR. DO IT, THEN. BECAUSE IF YOU DON'T, I'LL GET OUT OF HERE. AND THEN YOU'RE DEAD.
I CAN'T SAVE HER. AND IF I DIE, THE MISSION IS OVER. THESE PEOPLE GO ON TO KILL THOUSANDS. TENS OF THOUSANDS.
WE DIDN'T KNOW IF YOU'D WANT TO BE IN ON THIS, SIR. WE KNOW YOU'RE A BUSY MAN.
WE CAN TAKE CARE OF HER. AND I ASSURE YOU... IT WON'T BE PLEASANT. BUT WE THOUGHT YOU MIGHT LIKE TO DO IT YOURSELF.
THAT'S ONE LIFE AGAINST THOUSANDS. AGAINST BRINGING ALL THESE PEOPLE DOWN. ONE SOLDIER'S LIFE.
DID YOU HEAR ME? IF I LEAVE HERE, YOU'RE DEAD. SO GO AHEAD AND DO IT, YOU COWARD.
SHE GOT MY TRANSMISSIONS. SHE KNOWS SOMETHING BIG IS COMING. SHE'S A SOLDIER.
DO IT!
AND THE MISSION IS EVERYTHING.

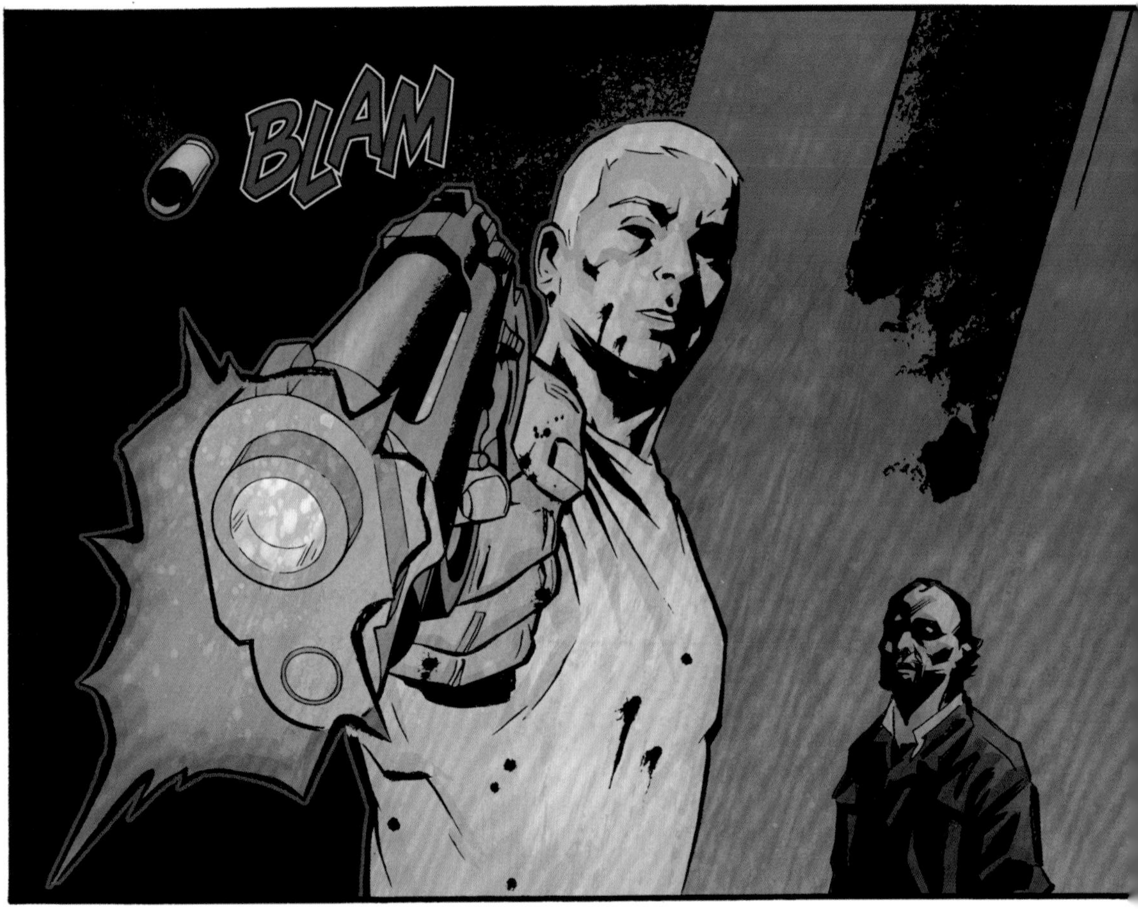
BLAM

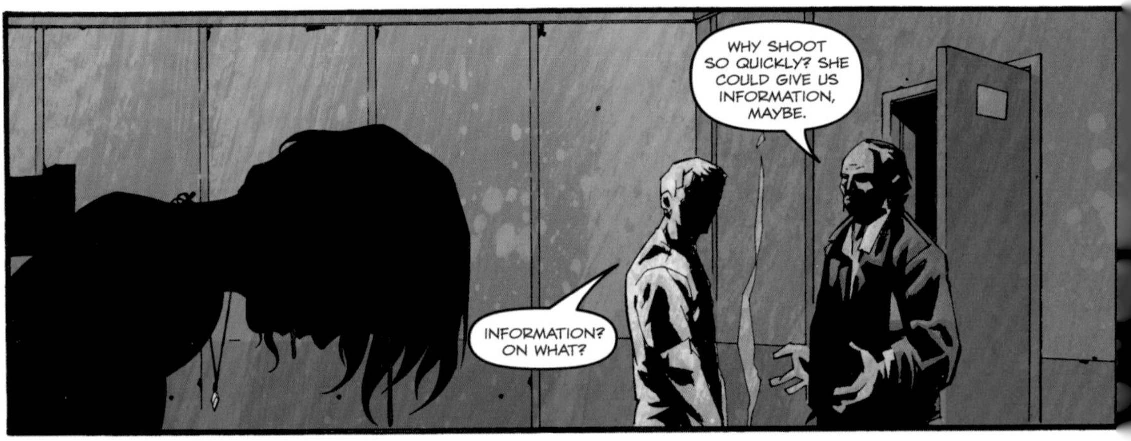
WHY SHOOT SO QUICKLY? SHE COULD GIVE US INFORMATION, MAYBE.
INFORMATION? ON WHAT?

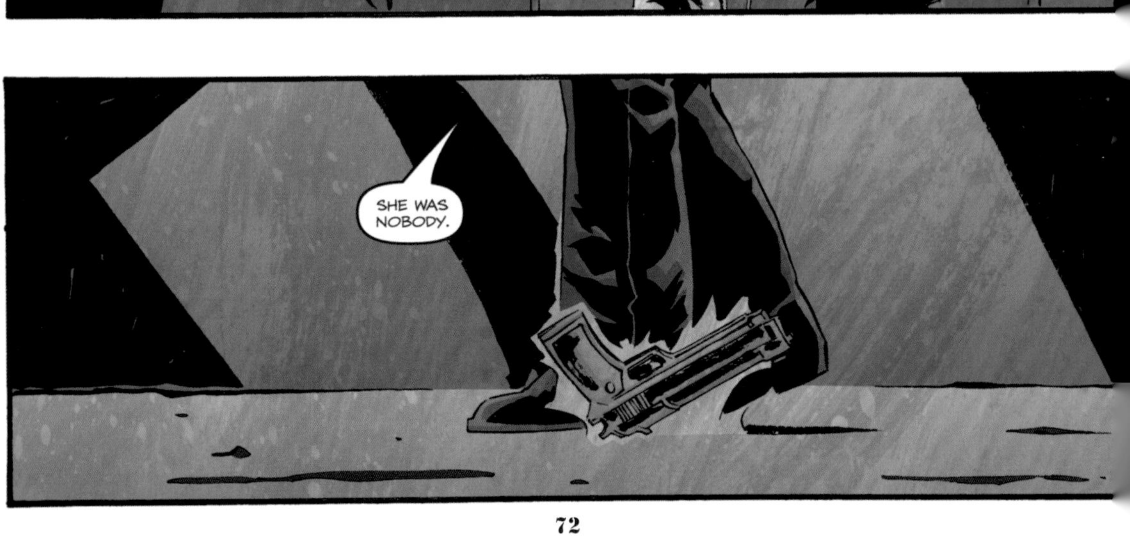
SHE WAS NOBODY.

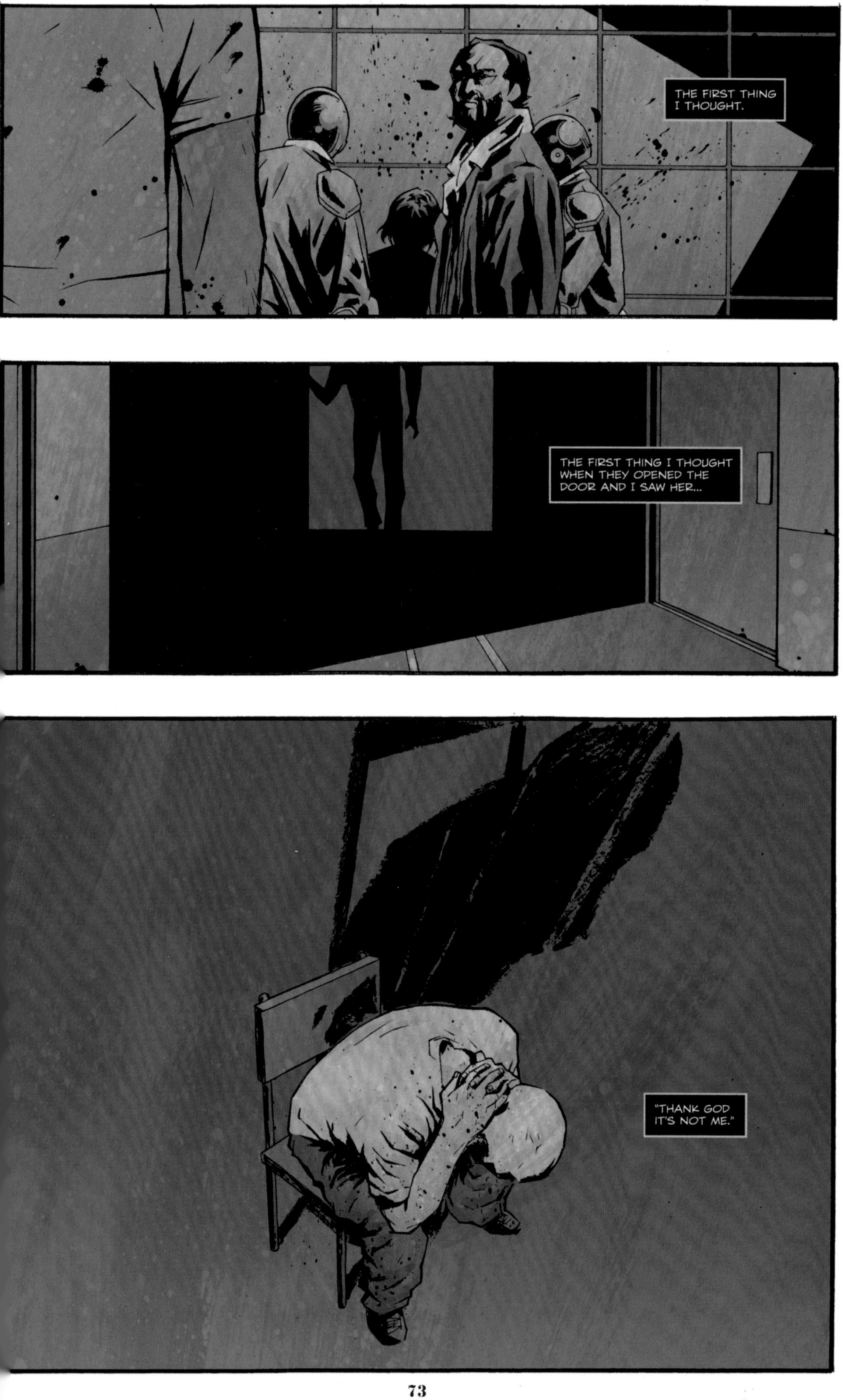
THE FIRST THING I THOUGHT.
THE FIRST THING I THOUGHT WHEN THEY OPENED THE DOOR AND I SAW HER...
"THANK GOD IT'S NOT ME."

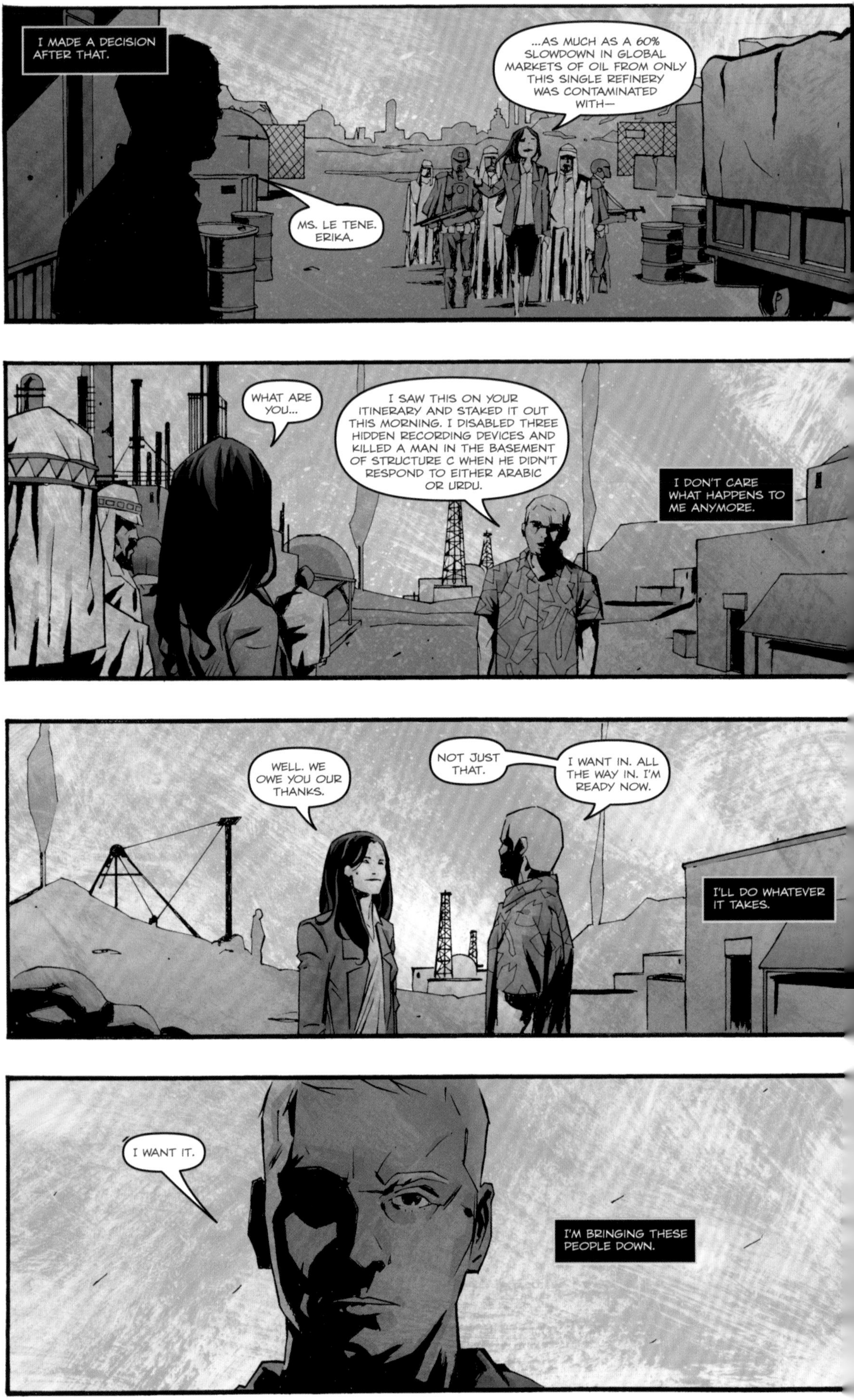
I MADE A DECISION AFTER THAT.
...AS MUCH AS A 60% SLOWDOWN IN GLOBAL MARKETS OF OIL FROM ONLY THIS SINGLE REFINERY WAS CONTAMINATED WITH—
MS. LE TENE. ERIKA.
WHAT ARE YOU...
I SAW THIS ON YOUR ITINERARY AND STAKED IT OUT THIS MORNING. I DISABLED THREE HIDDEN RECORDING DEVICES AND KILLED A MAN IN THE BASEMENT OF STRUCTURE C WHEN HE DIDN'T RESPOND TO EITHER ARABIC OR URDU.
I DON'T CARE WHAT HAPPENS TO ME ANYMORE.
WELL. WE OWE YOU OUR THANKS.
NOT JUST THAT.
I WANT IN. ALL THE WAY IN. I'M READY NOW.
I'LL DO WHATEVER IT TAKES.
I WANT IT.
I'M BRINGING THESE PEOPLE DOWN.

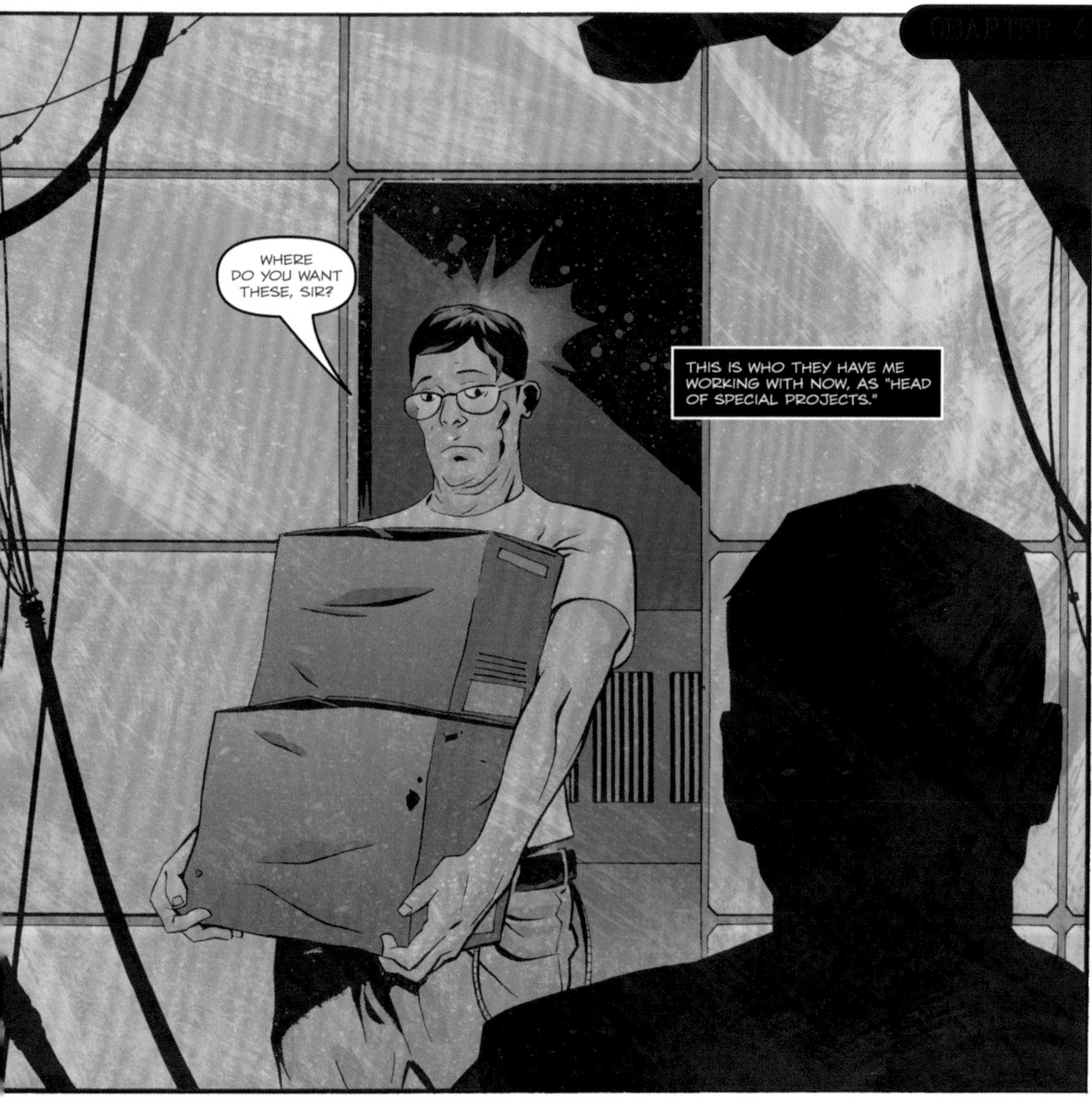
WHERE DO YOU WANT THESE, SIR?
THIS IS WHO THEY HAVE ME WORKING WITH NOW, AS "HEAD OF SPECIAL PROJECTS."

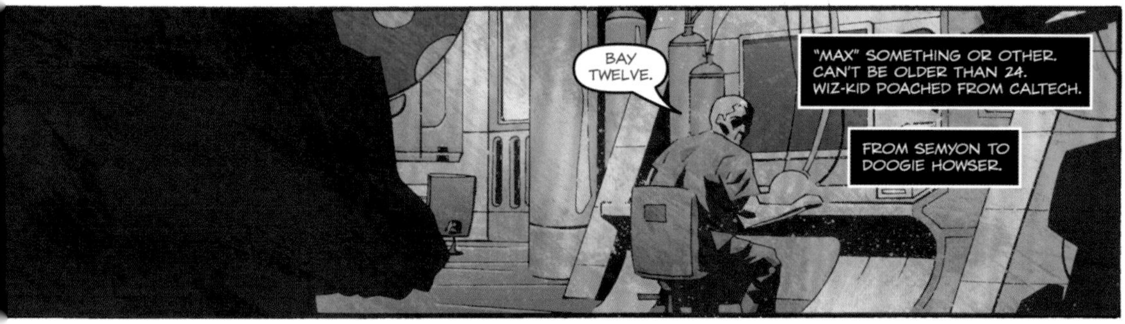
BAY TWELVE.
"MAX" SOMETHING OR OTHER. CAN'T BE OLDER THAN 24. WIZ-KID POACHED FROM CALTECH.
FROM SEMYON TO DOOGIE HOWSER.

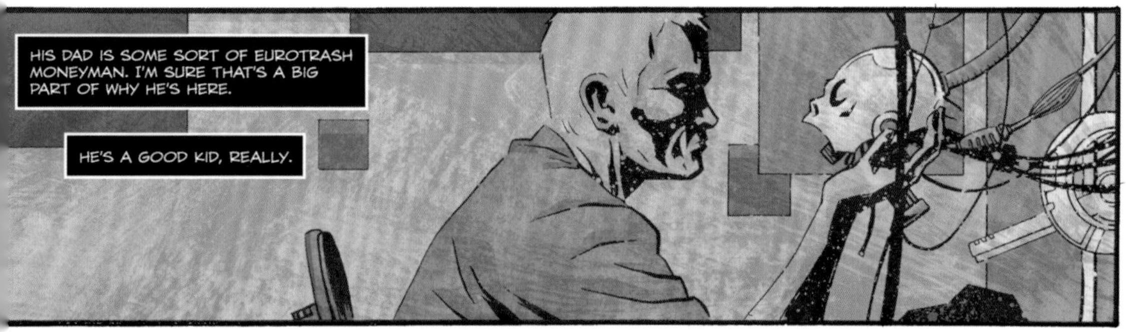
HIS DAD IS SOME SORT OF EUROTRASH MONEYMAN. I'M SURE THAT'S A BIG PART OF WHY HE'S HERE.
HE'S A GOOD KID, REALLY.

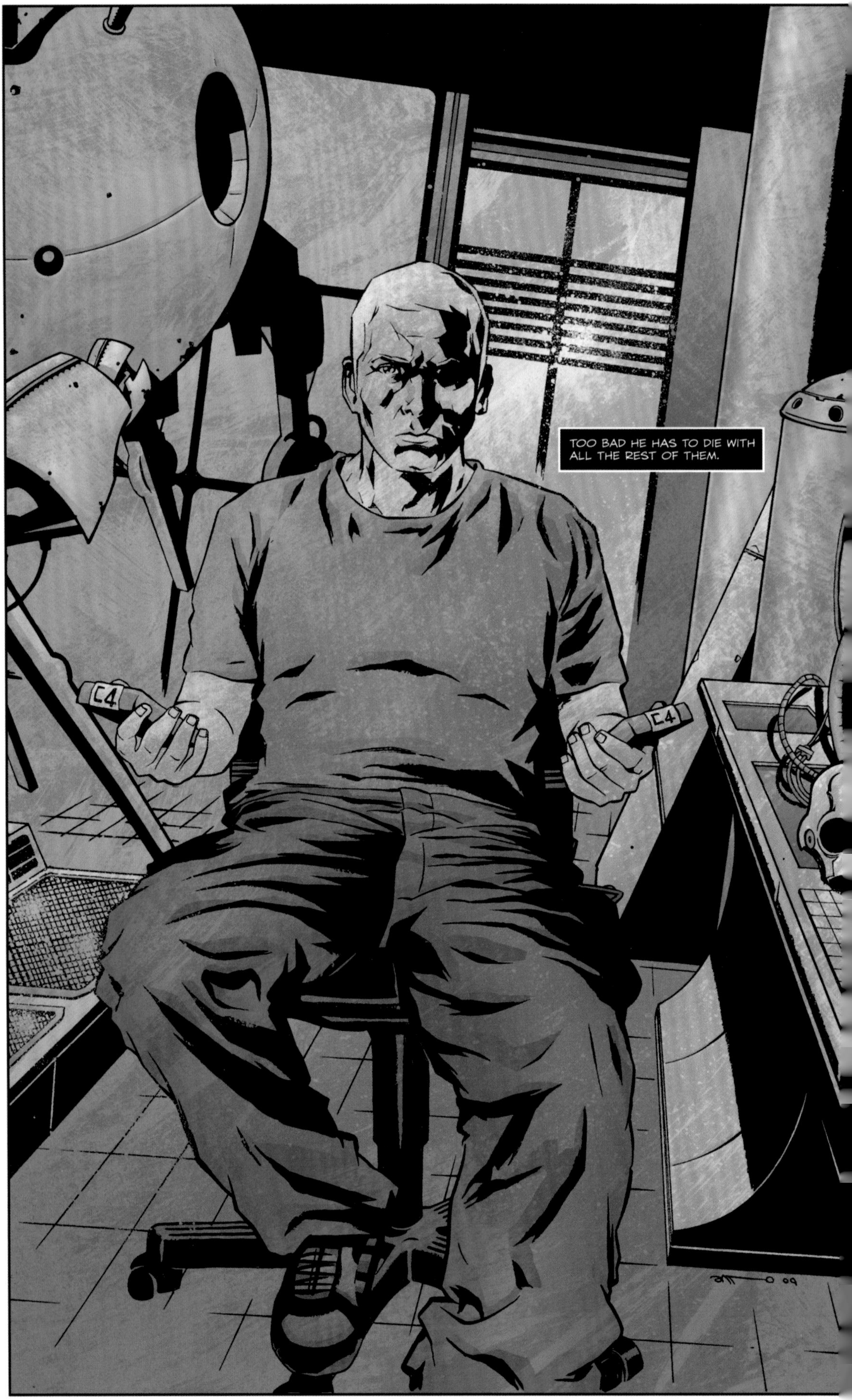
TOO BAD HE HAS TO DIE WITH ALL THE REST OF THEM.
C4
C4

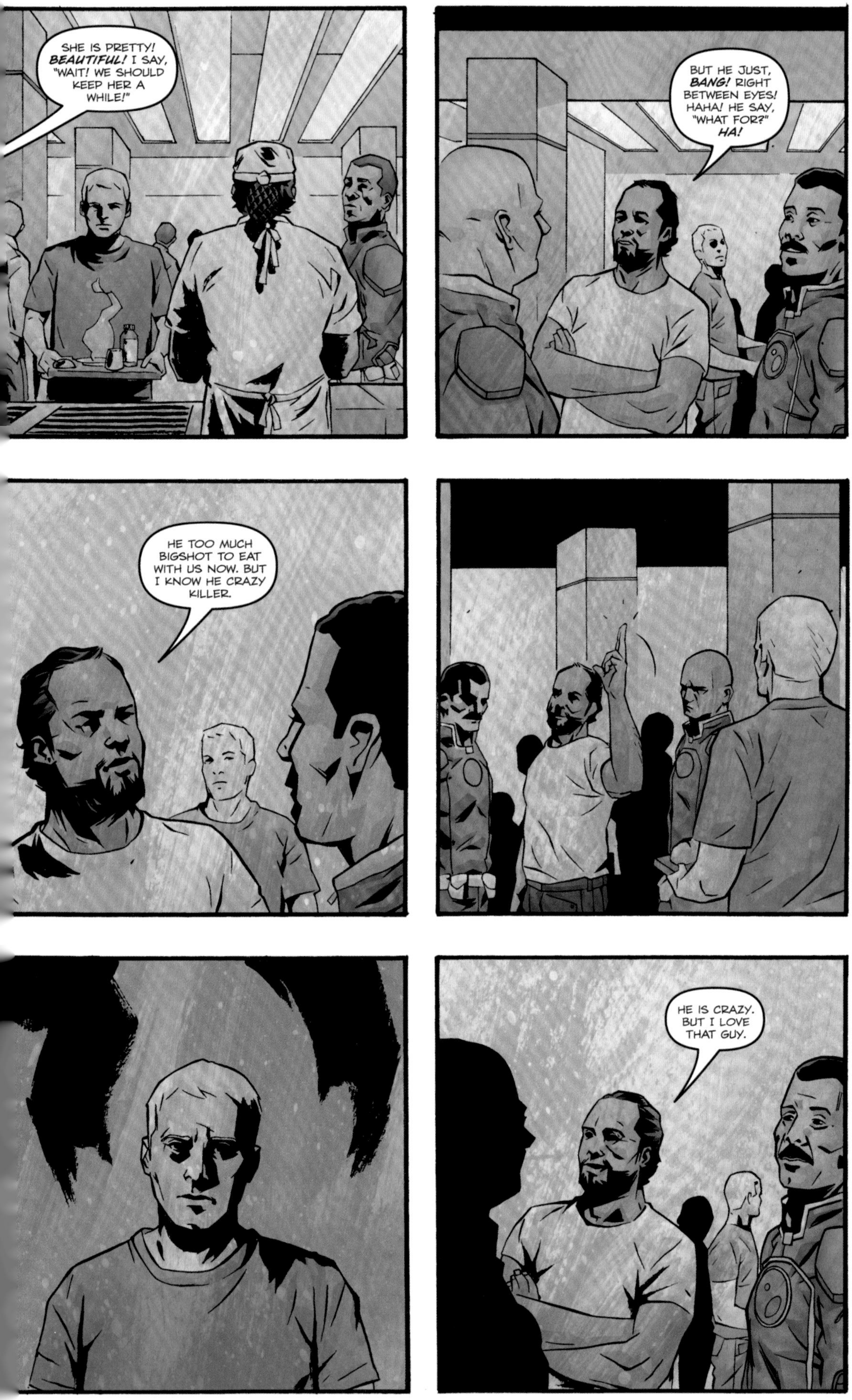
SHE IS PRETTY! **BEAUTIFUL!** I SAY, "WAIT! WE SHOULD KEEP HER A WHILE!"
BUT HE JUST, **BANG!** RIGHT BETWEEN EYES! HAHA! HE SAY, "WHAT FOR?" **HA!**
HE TOO MUCH BIGSHOT TO EAT WITH US NOW. BUT I KNOW HE CRAZY KILLER.
HE IS CRAZY. BUT I LOVE THAT GUY.

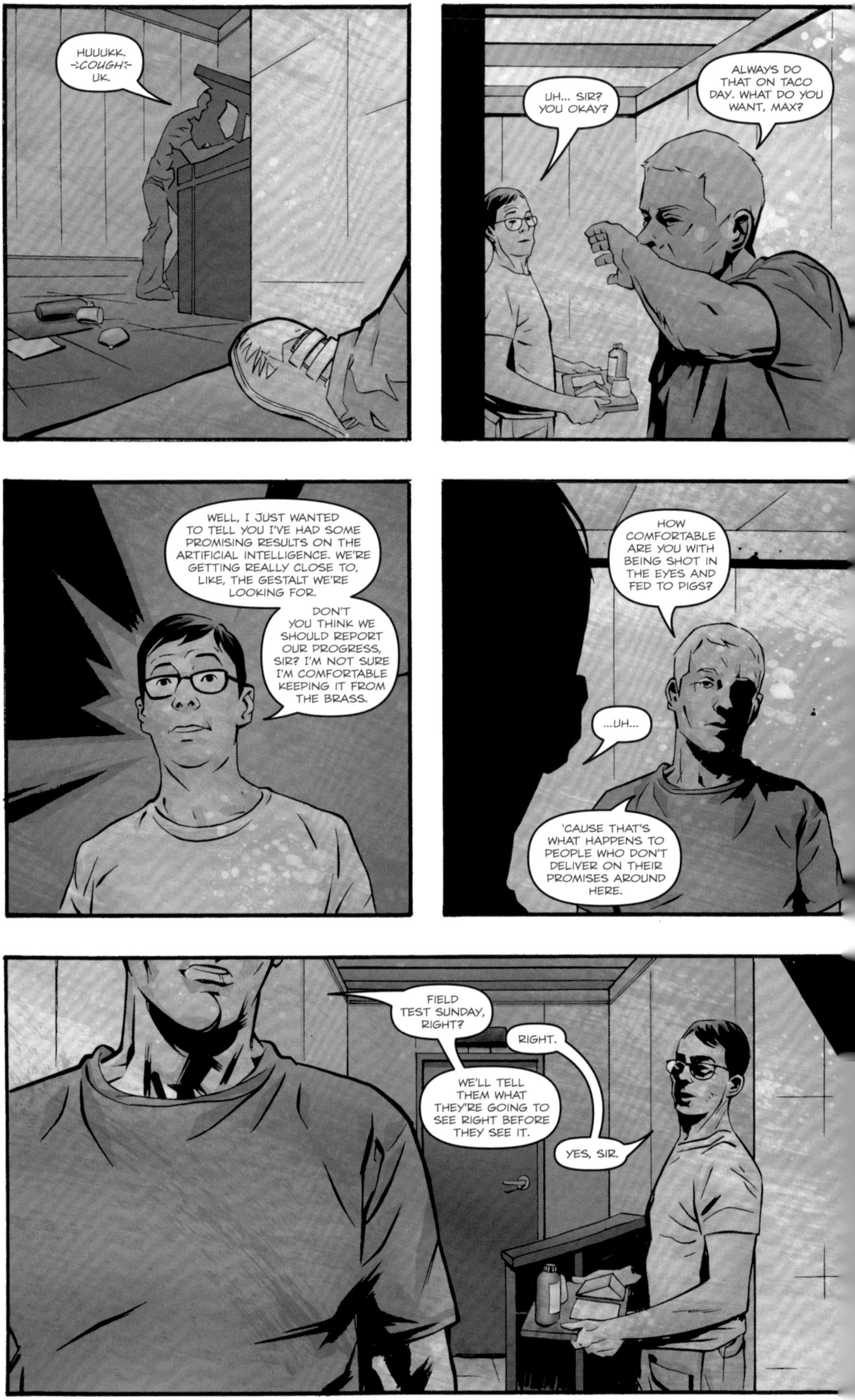

HUUUKK. -:-COUGH-:- UK.
UH... SIR? YOU OKAY?
ALWAYS DO THAT ON TACO DAY. WHAT DO YOU WANT, MAX?
WELL, I JUST WANTED TO TELL YOU I'VE HAD SOME PROMISING RESULTS ON THE ARTIFICIAL INTELLIGENCE. WE'RE GETTING REALLY CLOSE TO, LIKE, THE GESTALT WE'RE LOOKING FOR.
DON'T YOU THINK WE SHOULD REPORT OUR PROGRESS, SIR? I'M NOT SURE I'M COMFORTABLE KEEPING IT FROM THE BRASS.
HOW COMFORTABLE ARE YOU WITH BEING SHOT IN THE EYES AND FED TO PIGS?
...UH...
'CAUSE THAT'S WHAT HAPPENS TO PEOPLE WHO DON'T DELIVER ON THEIR PROMISES AROUND HERE.
FIELD TEST SUNDAY, RIGHT?
RIGHT.
WE'LL TELL THEM WHAT THEY'RE GOING TO SEE RIGHT BEFORE THEY SEE IT.
YES, SIR.

HERE'S WHAT I'VE FIGURED OUT SO FAR.

HATCHET MEN LIKE ME, OR THAT IDIOT SEMYON, GET SENT OUT ON HORRIBLE MERCENARY MISSIONS TO BLOW UP FEDERAL RESERVES OR BREAK MANIACS OUT OF PRISON OR ASSASSINATE ARCHDUKES OR WHATEVER. BASICALLY WHATEVER IT TAKES TO DESTABILIZE DEVELOPING NATIONS.

THEN, AFTER WE'VE STIRRED UP ALL KINDS OF MAYHEM, COBRA COMES IN UNDER THE GUISE OF GOD KNOWS HOW MANY SHELL COMPANIES AND WE HIRE OUT OUR PRIVATE ARMY. OUR *CRIMSON GUARD.*

THE MORE CHAOS WE CAUSE, THE LESS FAITH THE PEOPLE HAVE IN THEIR OWN MILITARY. AND THE MORE GUARDSMEN THEY HIRE. AND SOON, WE'RE THE SUPREME MILITARY FORCE IN THEIR NATION.

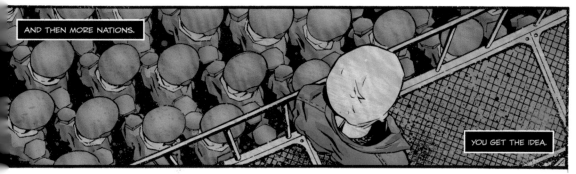

AND THEN MORE NATIONS.

YOU GET THE IDEA.

THE PROJECT THEY HAVE ME HEADING IS THEIR NEXT PHASE IN PRIVATE MILITARY. BATTALION AUTOMATION TACTICS.

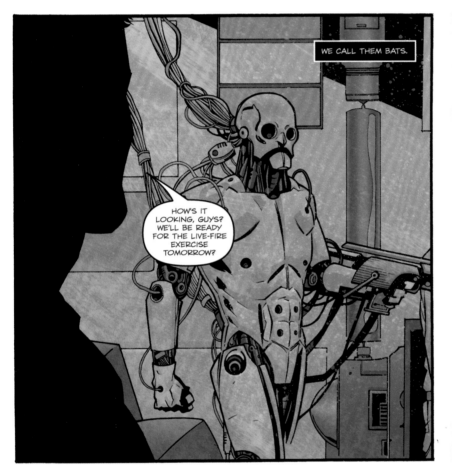

WE CALL THEM BATS.

HOW'S IT LOOKING, GUYS? WE'LL BE READY FOR THE LIVE-FIRE EXERCISE TOMORROW?

YES, SIR!

CHEAPER THAN PEOPLE. DON'T HAVE TO FEED OR HOUSE THEM. TOUGH. NEVER GET TIRED. AND THEY'LL NEVER BURN YOU FOR SOMEONE WHO PAYS THEM MORE.

GOOD.

ONLY ONE PROBLEM.

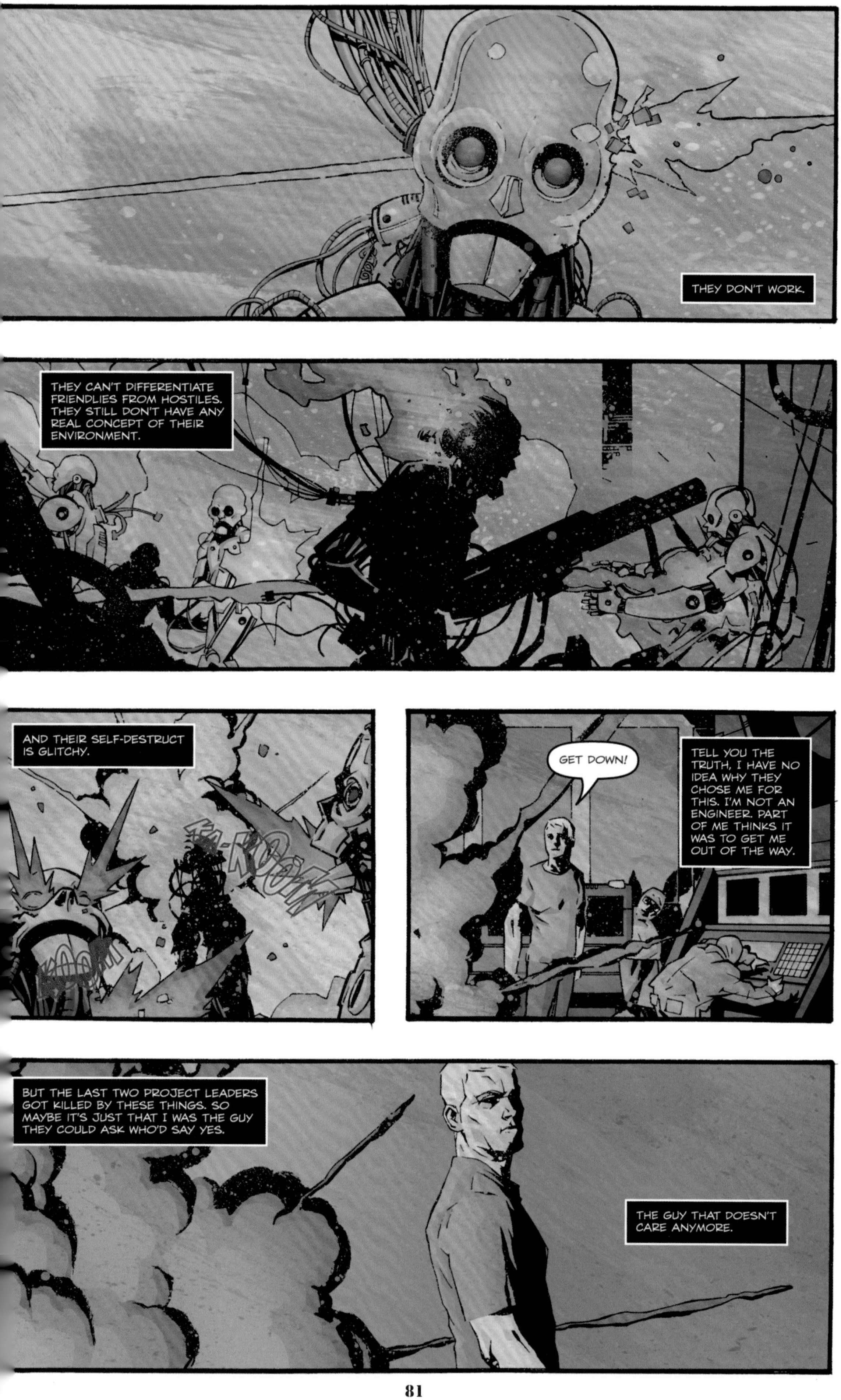
THEY DON'T WORK.
THEY CAN'T DIFFERENTIATE FRIENDLIES FROM HOSTILES. THEY STILL DON'T HAVE ANY REAL CONCEPT OF THEIR ENVIRONMENT.
AND THEIR SELF-DESTRUCT IS GLITCHY.
GET DOWN!
TELL YOU THE TRUTH, I HAVE NO IDEA WHY THEY CHOSE ME FOR THIS. I'M NOT AN ENGINEER. PART OF ME THINKS IT WAS TO GET ME OUT OF THE WAY.
BUT THE LAST TWO PROJECT LEADERS GOT KILLED BY THESE THINGS. SO MAYBE IT'S JUST THAT I WAS THE GUY THEY COULD ASK WHO'D SAY YES.
THE GUY THAT DOESN'T CARE ANYMORE.

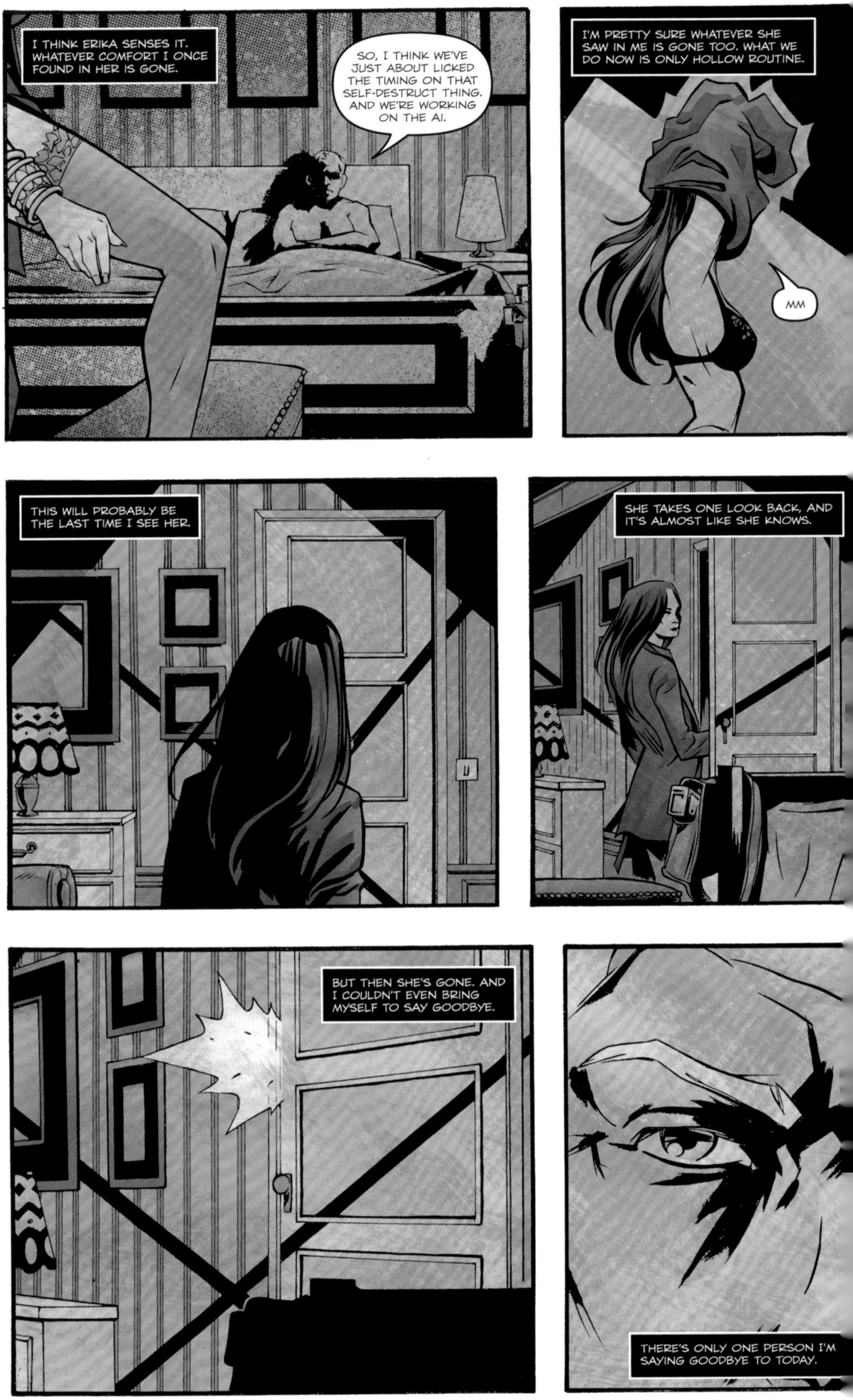
I THINK ERIKA SENSES IT. WHATEVER COMFORT I ONCE FOUND IN HER IS GONE.
SO, I THINK WE'VE JUST ABOUT LICKED THE TIMING ON THAT SELF-DESTRUCT THING. AND WE'RE WORKING ON THE AI.
I'M PRETTY SURE WHATEVER SHE SAW IN ME IS GONE TOO. WHAT WE DO NOW IS ONLY HOLLOW ROUTINE.
MM
THIS WILL PROBABLY BE THE LAST TIME I SEE HER.
SHE TAKES ONE LOOK BACK, AND IT'S ALMOST LIKE SHE KNOWS.
BUT THEN SHE'S GONE. AND I COULDN'T EVEN BRING MYSELF TO SAY GOODBYE.
THERE'S ONLY ONE PERSON I'M SAYING GOODBYE TO TODAY.

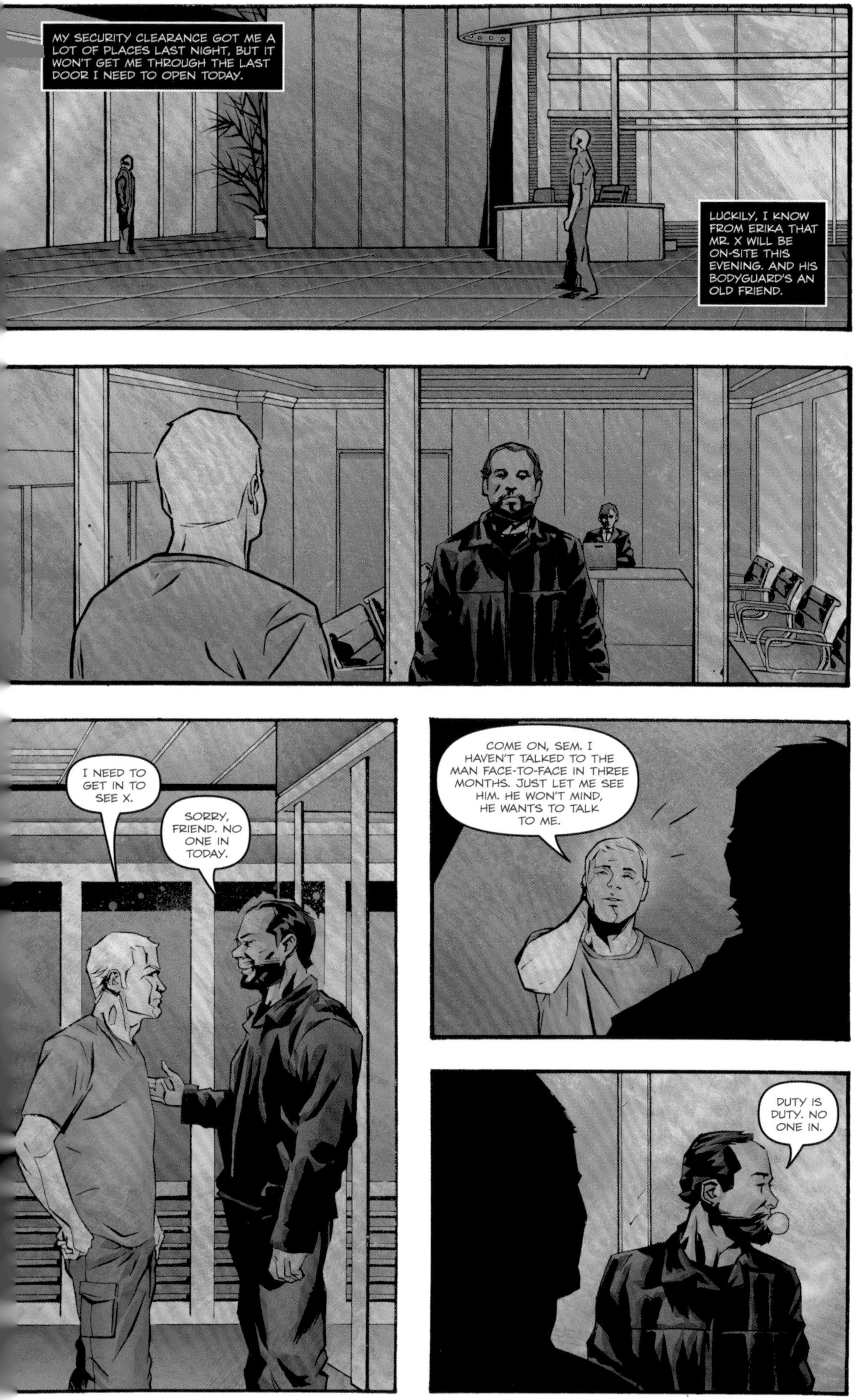

MY SECURITY CLEARANCE GOT ME A LOT OF PLACES LAST NIGHT, BUT IT WON'T GET ME THROUGH THE LAST DOOR I NEED TO OPEN TODAY.
LUCKILY, I KNOW FROM ERIKA THAT MR. X WILL BE ON-SITE THIS EVENING. AND HIS BODYGUARD'S AN OLD FRIEND.
I NEED TO GET IN TO SEE X.
SORRY, FRIEND. NO ONE IN TODAY.
COME ON, SEM. I HAVEN'T TALKED TO THE MAN FACE-TO-FACE IN THREE MONTHS. JUST LET ME SEE HIM. HE WON'T MIND, HE WANTS TO TALK TO ME.
DUTY IS DUTY. NO ONE IN.

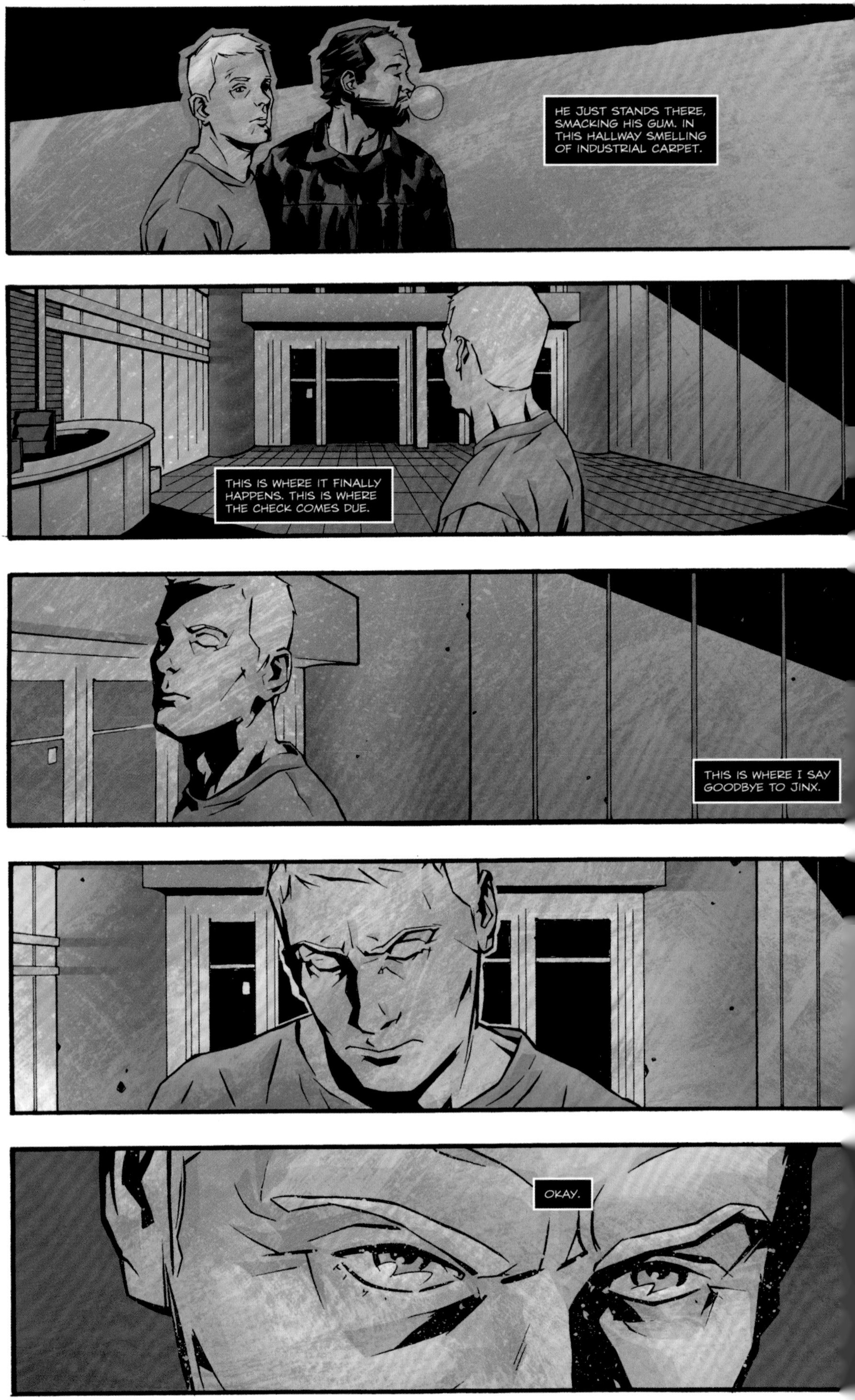
HE JUST STANDS THERE, SMACKING HIS GUM. IN THIS HALLWAY SMELLING OF INDUSTRIAL CARPET.
THIS IS WHERE IT FINALLY HAPPENS. THIS IS WHERE THE CHECK COMES DUE.
THIS IS WHERE I SAY GOODBYE TO JINX.
OKAY.

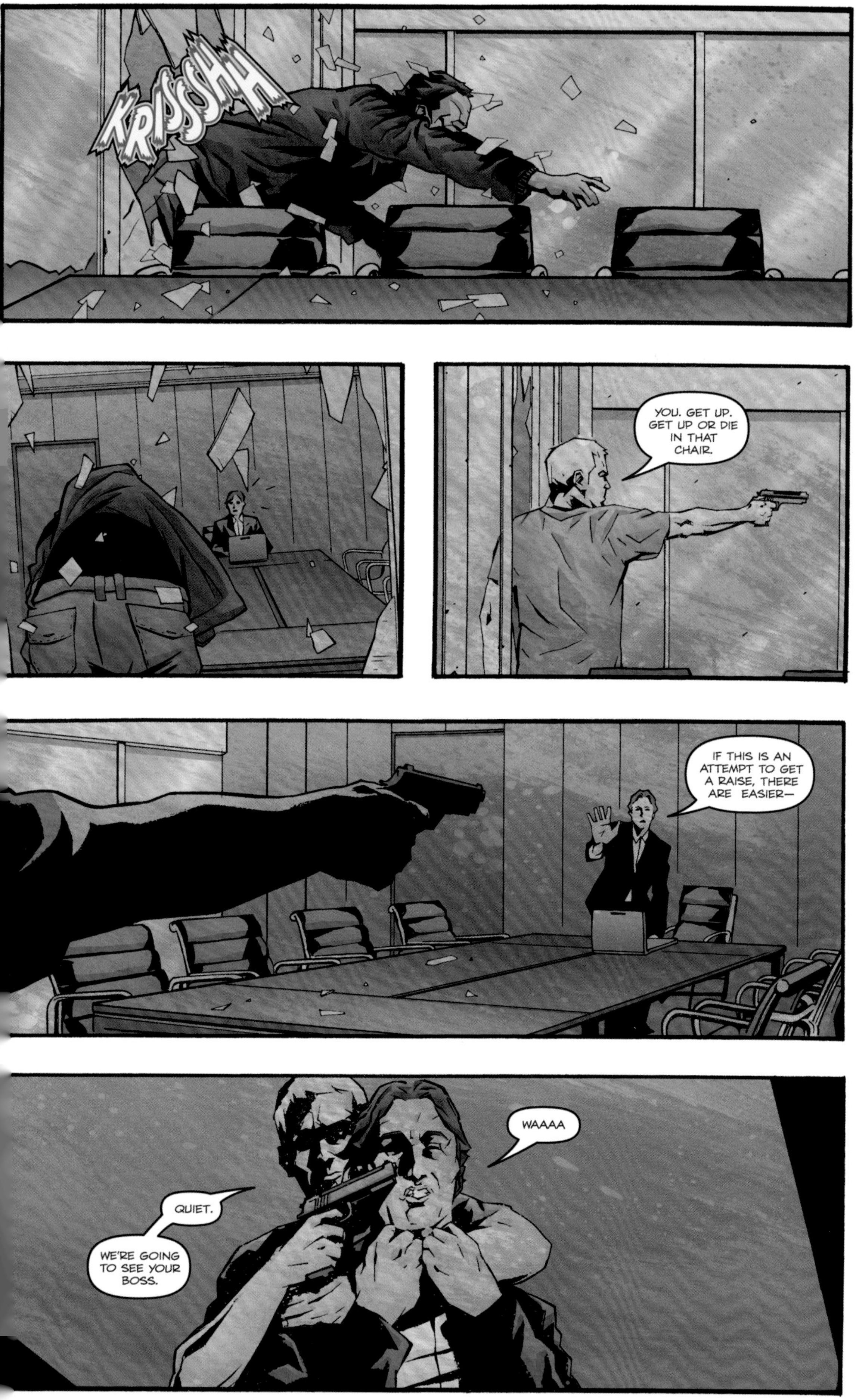
KRISSSHH
YOU. GET UP. GET UP OR DIE IN THAT CHAIR.
IF THIS IS AN ATTEMPT TO GET A RAISE, THERE ARE EASIER—
WAAAA
QUIET.
WE'RE GOING TO SEE YOUR BOSS.

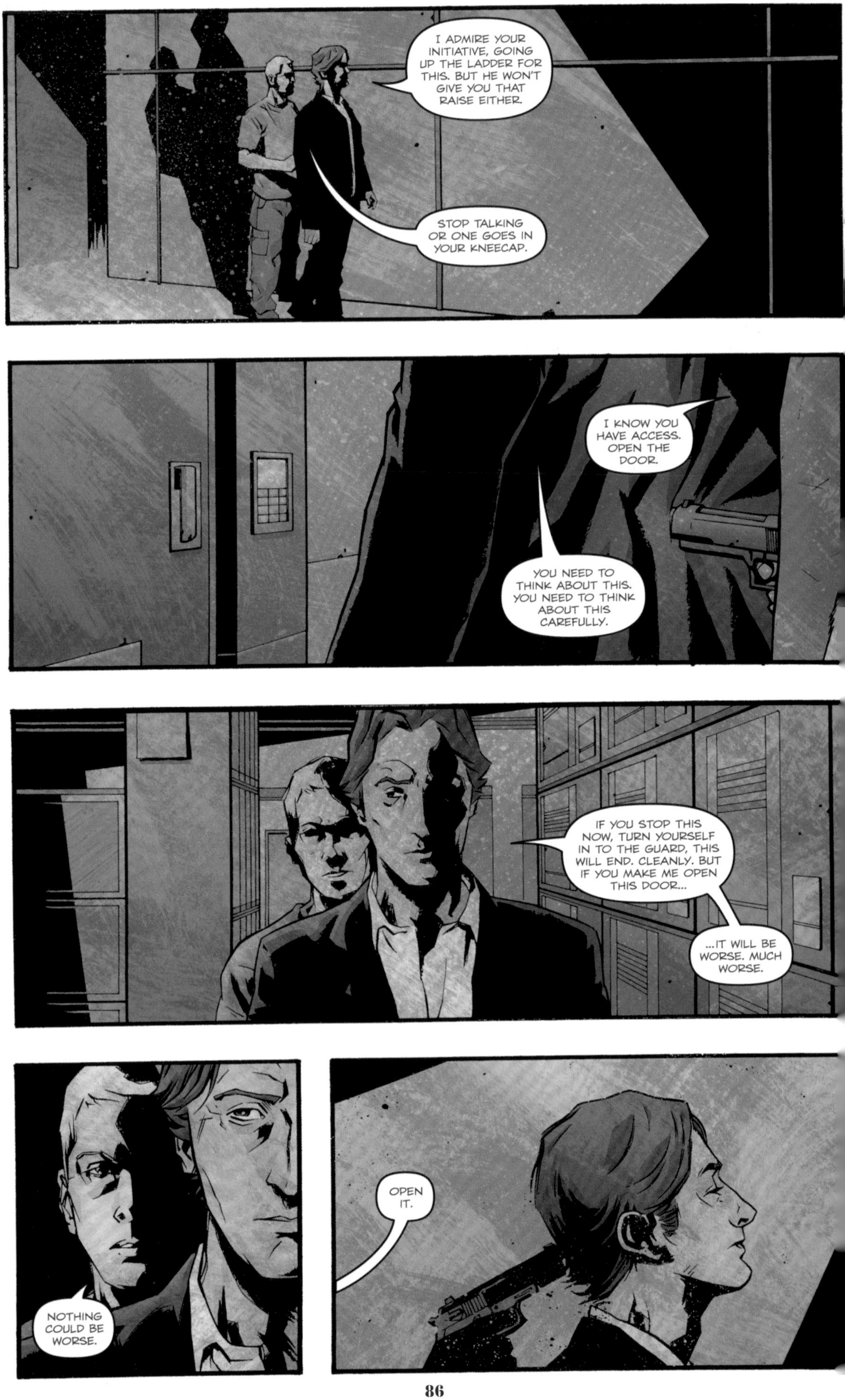
I ADMIRE YOUR INITIATIVE, GOING UP THE LADDER FOR THIS. BUT HE WON'T GIVE YOU THAT RAISE EITHER.
STOP TALKING OR ONE GOES IN YOUR KNEECAP.
I KNOW YOU HAVE ACCESS. OPEN THE DOOR.
YOU NEED TO THINK ABOUT THIS. YOU NEED TO THINK ABOUT THIS CAREFULLY.
IF YOU STOP THIS NOW, TURN YOURSELF IN TO THE GUARD, THIS WILL END. CLEANLY. BUT IF YOU MAKE ME OPEN THIS DOOR...
...IT WILL BE WORSE. MUCH WORSE.
NOTHING COULD BE WORSE.
OPEN IT.

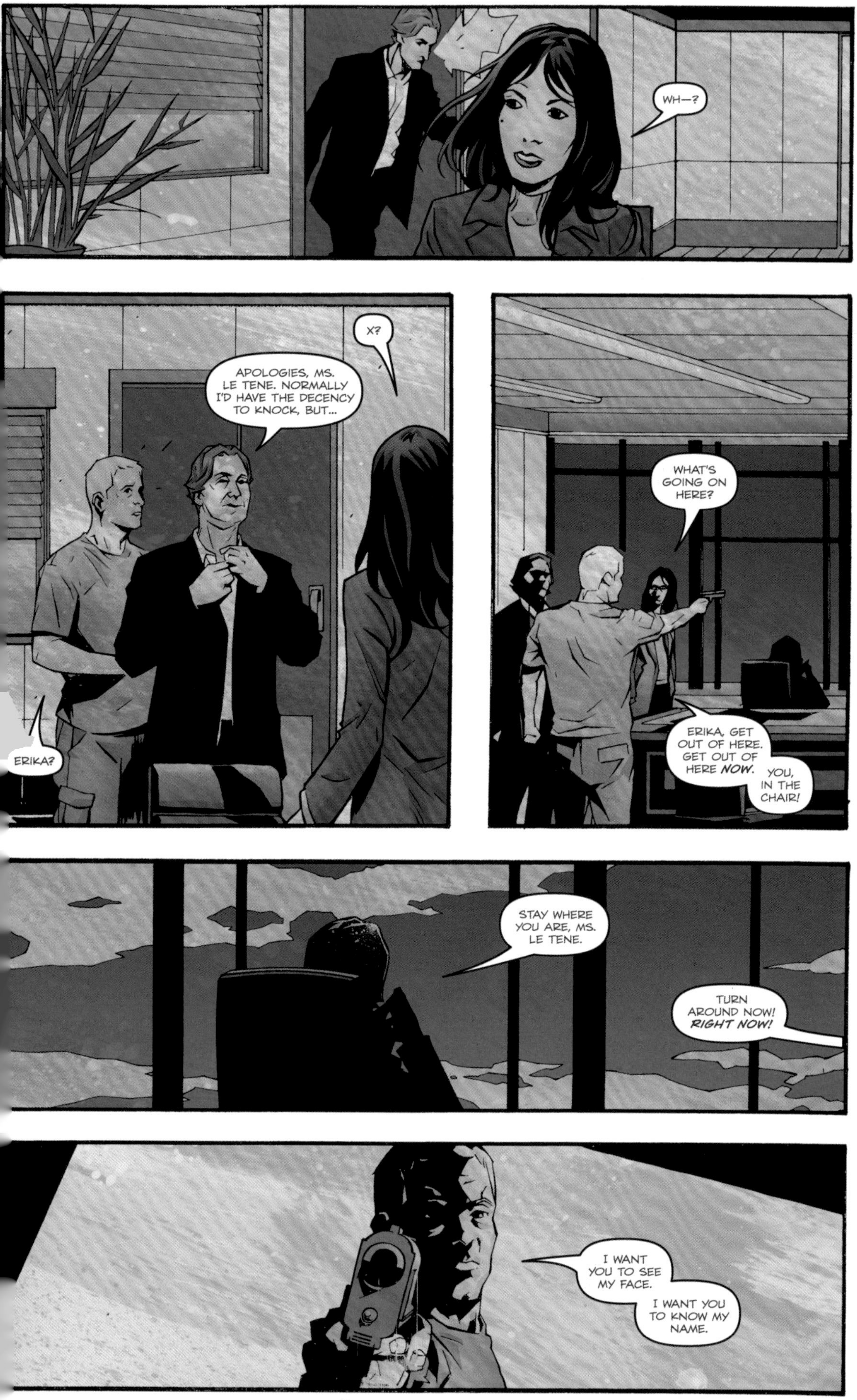
WH—?
APOLOGIES, MS. LE TENE. NORMALLY I'D HAVE THE DECENCY TO KNOCK, BUT...
X?
ERIKA?
WHAT'S GOING ON HERE?
ERIKA, GET OUT OF HERE. GET OUT OF HERE *NOW*.
YOU, IN THE CHAIR!
STAY WHERE YOU ARE, MS. LE TENE.
TURN AROUND NOW! *RIGHT NOW!*
I WANT YOU TO SEE MY FACE.
I WANT YOU TO KNOW MY NAME.

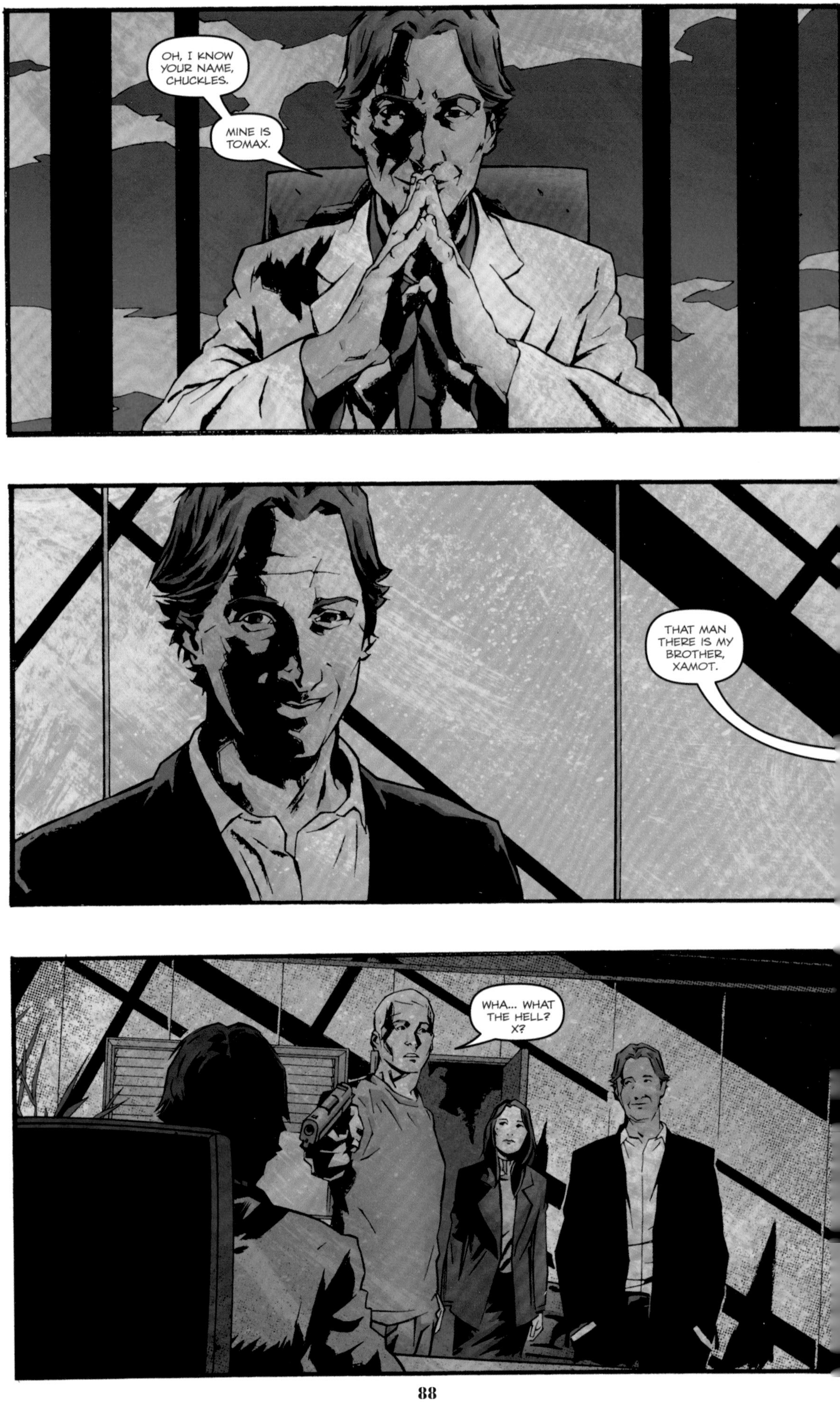
OH, I KNOW YOUR NAME, CHUCKLES.
MINE IS TOMAX.
THAT MAN THERE IS MY BROTHER, XAMOT.
WHA... WHAT THE HELL? X?

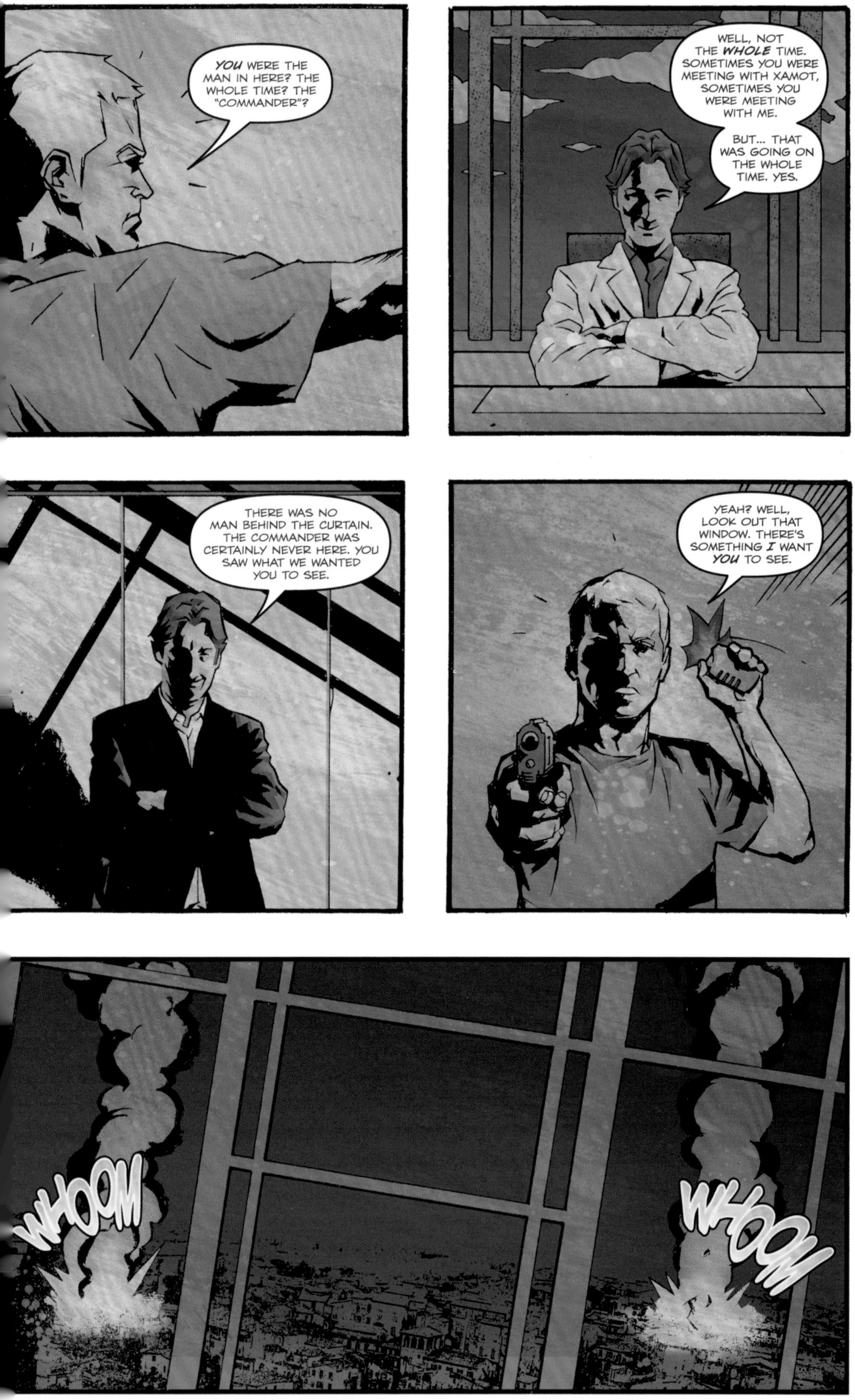

*YOU* WERE THE MAN IN HERE? THE WHOLE TIME? THE "COMMANDER"?
WELL, NOT THE ***WHOLE*** TIME. SOMETIMES YOU WERE MEETING WITH XAMOT, SOMETIMES YOU WERE MEETING WITH ME.
BUT... THAT WAS GOING ON THE WHOLE TIME. YES.
THERE WAS NO MAN BEHIND THE CURTAIN. THE COMMANDER WAS CERTAINLY NEVER HERE. YOU SAW WHAT WE WANTED YOU TO SEE.
YEAH? WELL, LOOK OUT THAT WINDOW. THERE'S SOMETHING *I* WANT *YOU* TO SEE.
WHOOM
WHOOM

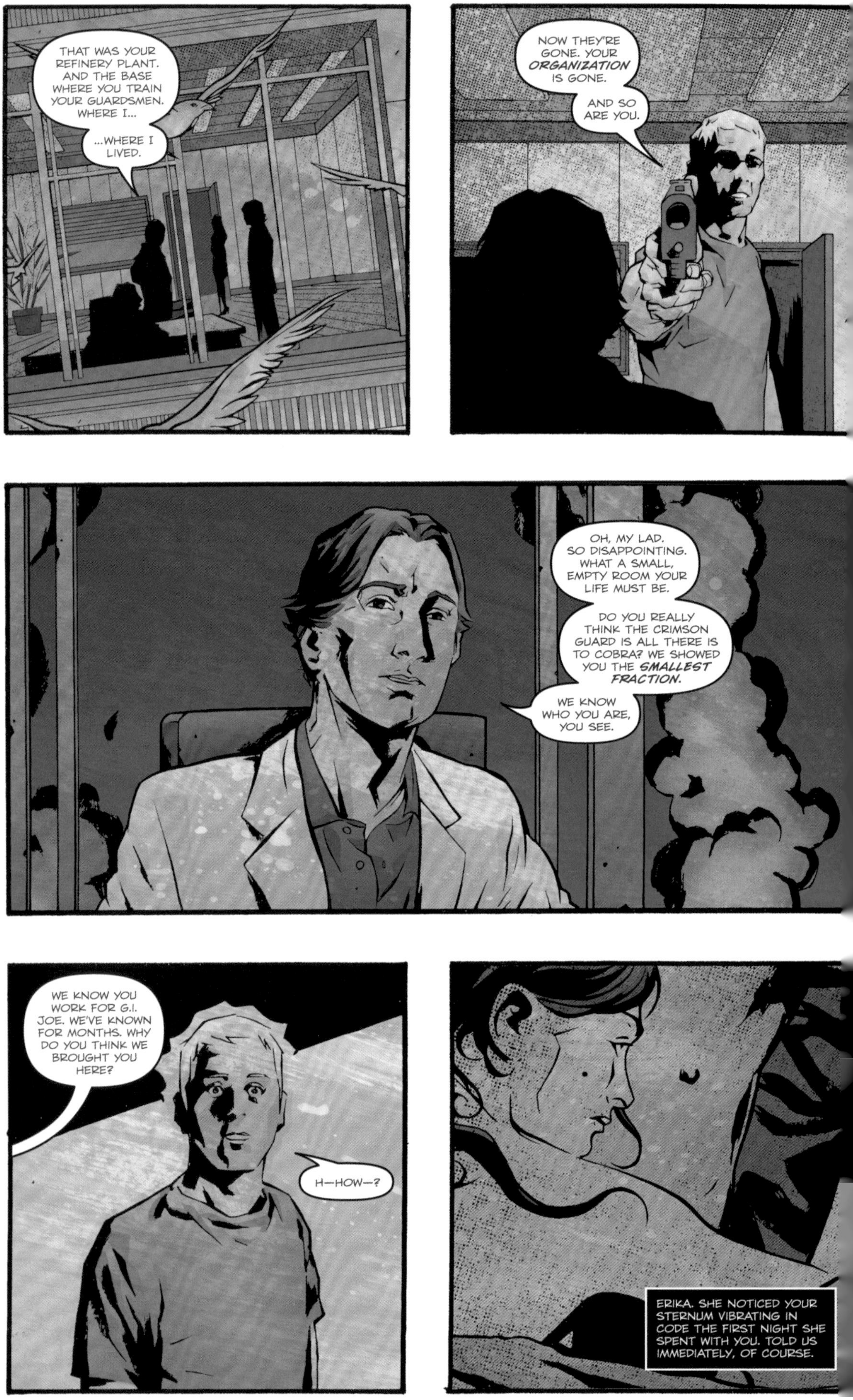
THAT WAS YOUR REFINERY PLANT. AND THE BASE WHERE YOU TRAIN YOUR GUARDSMEN. WHERE I...
...WHERE I LIVED.
NOW THEY'RE GONE. YOUR ORGANIZATION IS GONE.
AND SO ARE YOU.
OH, MY LAD. SO DISAPPOINTING. WHAT A SMALL, EMPTY ROOM YOUR LIFE MUST BE.
DO YOU REALLY THINK THE CRIMSON GUARD IS ALL THERE IS TO COBRA? WE SHOWED YOU THE SMALLEST FRACTION.
WE KNOW WHO YOU ARE, YOU SEE.
WE KNOW YOU WORK FOR G.I. JOE. WE'VE KNOWN FOR MONTHS. WHY DO YOU THINK WE BROUGHT YOU HERE?
H—HOW—?
ERIKA. SHE NOTICED YOUR STERNUM VIBRATING IN CODE THE FIRST NIGHT SHE SPENT WITH YOU. TOLD US IMMEDIATELY, OF COURSE.

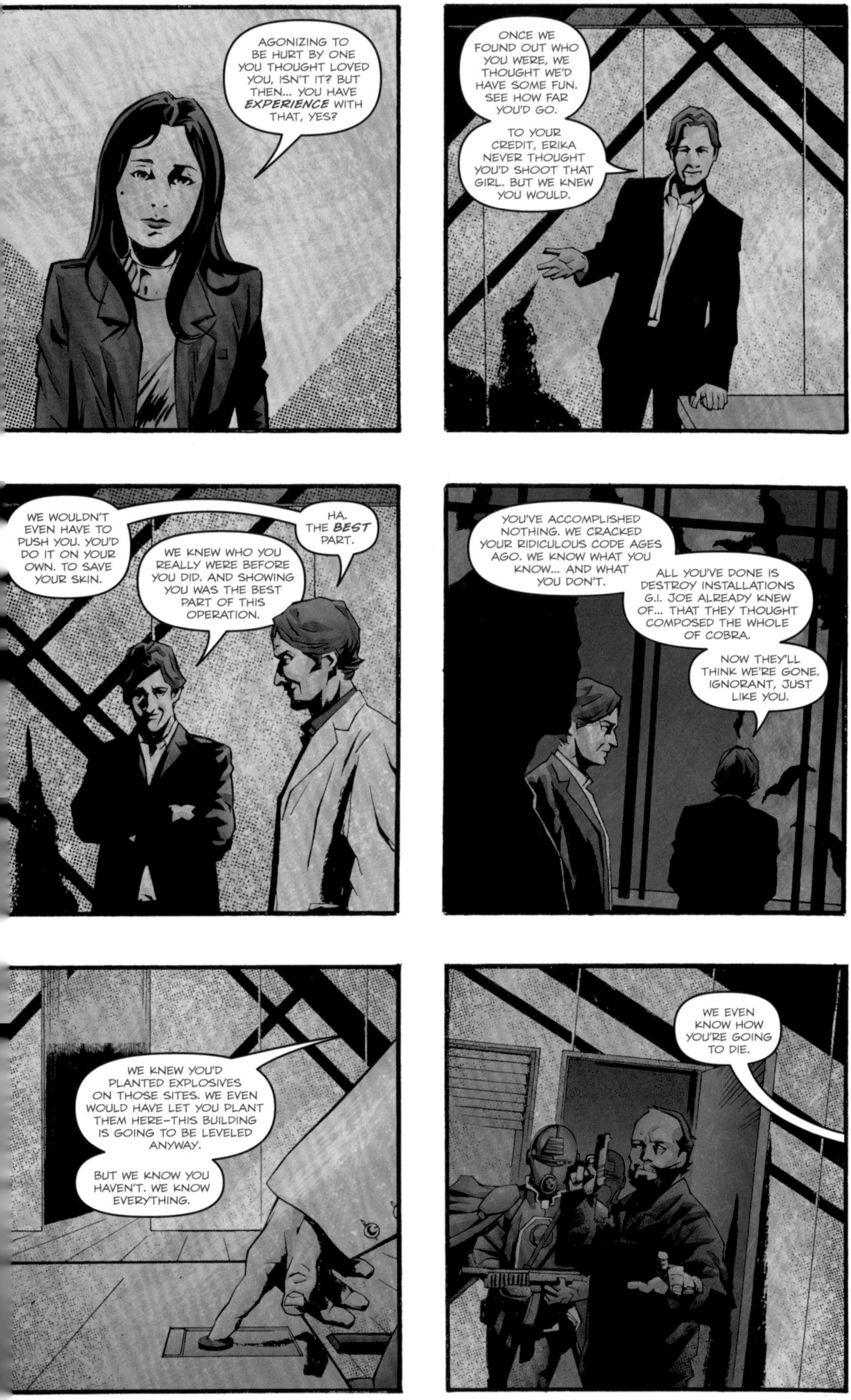
AGONIZING TO BE HURT BY ONE YOU THOUGHT LOVED YOU, ISN'T IT? BUT THEN... YOU HAVE EXPERIENCE WITH THAT, YES?
ONCE WE FOUND OUT WHO YOU WERE, WE THOUGHT WE'D HAVE SOME FUN. SEE HOW FAR YOU'D GO.
TO YOUR CREDIT, ERIKA NEVER THOUGHT YOU'D SHOOT THAT GIRL. BUT WE KNEW YOU WOULD.
WE WOULDN'T EVEN HAVE TO PUSH YOU. YOU'D DO IT ON YOUR OWN. TO SAVE YOUR SKIN.
WE KNEW WHO YOU REALLY WERE BEFORE YOU DID. AND SHOWING YOU WAS THE BEST PART OF THIS OPERATION.
HA. THE BEST PART.
YOU'VE ACCOMPLISHED NOTHING. WE CRACKED YOUR RIDICULOUS CODE AGES AGO. WE KNOW WHAT YOU KNOW... AND WHAT YOU DON'T.
ALL YOU'VE DONE IS DESTROY INSTALLATIONS G.I. JOE ALREADY KNEW OF... THAT THEY THOUGHT COMPOSED THE WHOLE OF COBRA.
NOW THEY'LL THINK WE'RE GONE. IGNORANT, JUST LIKE YOU.
WE KNEW YOU'D PLANTED EXPLOSIVES ON THOSE SITES. WE EVEN WOULD HAVE LET YOU PLANT THEM HERE–THIS BUILDING IS GOING TO BE LEVELED ANYWAY.
BUT WE KNOW YOU HAVEN'T. WE KNOW EVERYTHING.
WE EVEN KNOW HOW YOU'RE GOING TO DIE.

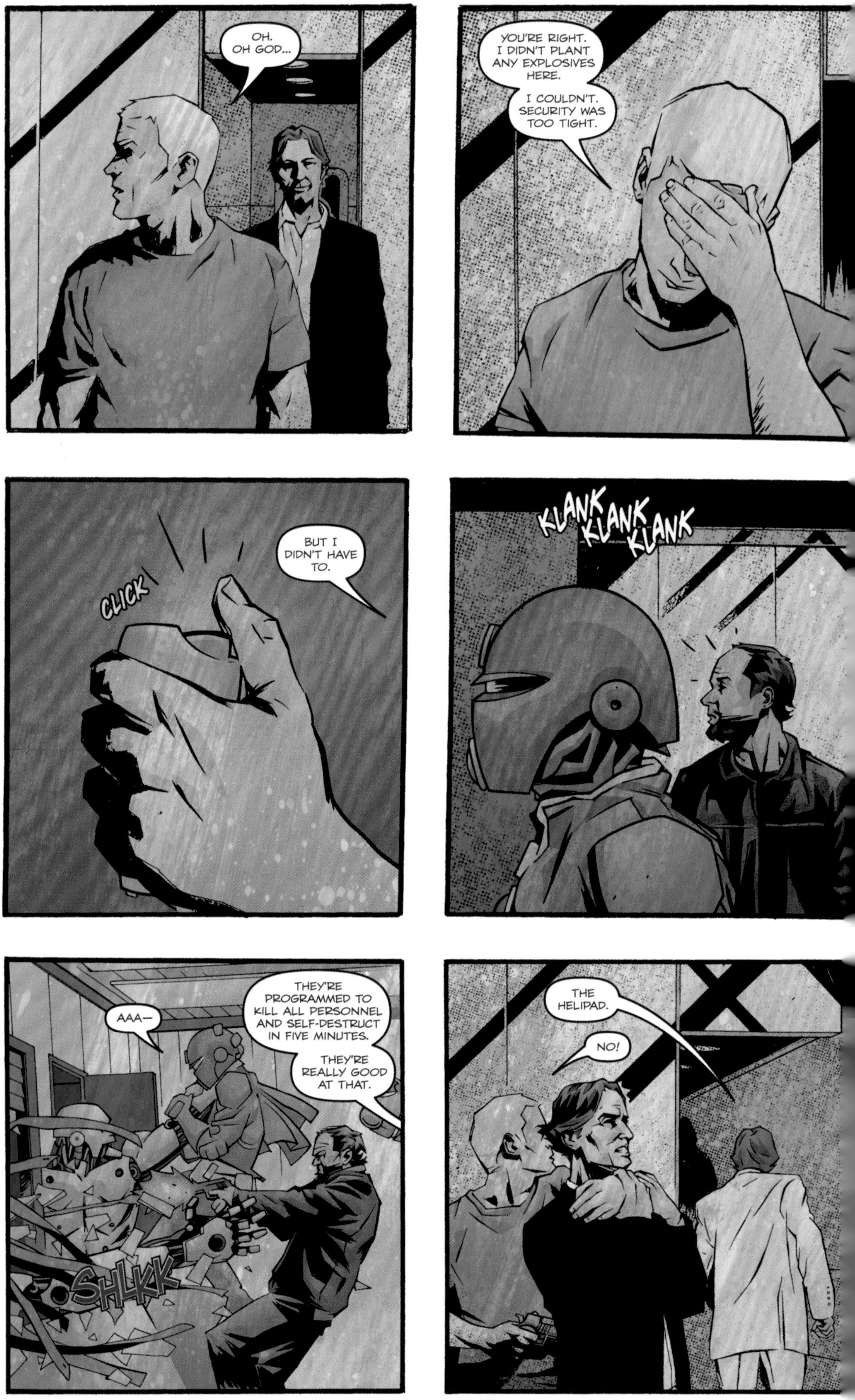
OH. OH GOD...
YOU'RE RIGHT. I DIDN'T PLANT ANY EXPLOSIVES HERE.
I COULDN'T. SECURITY WAS TOO TIGHT.
CLICK
BUT I DIDN'T HAVE TO.
KLANK KLANK KLANK
AAA—
THEY'RE PROGRAMMED TO KILL ALL PERSONNEL AND SELF-DESTRUCT IN FIVE MINUTES.
THEY'RE REALLY GOOD AT THAT.
SHLKK
THE HELIPAD.
NO!

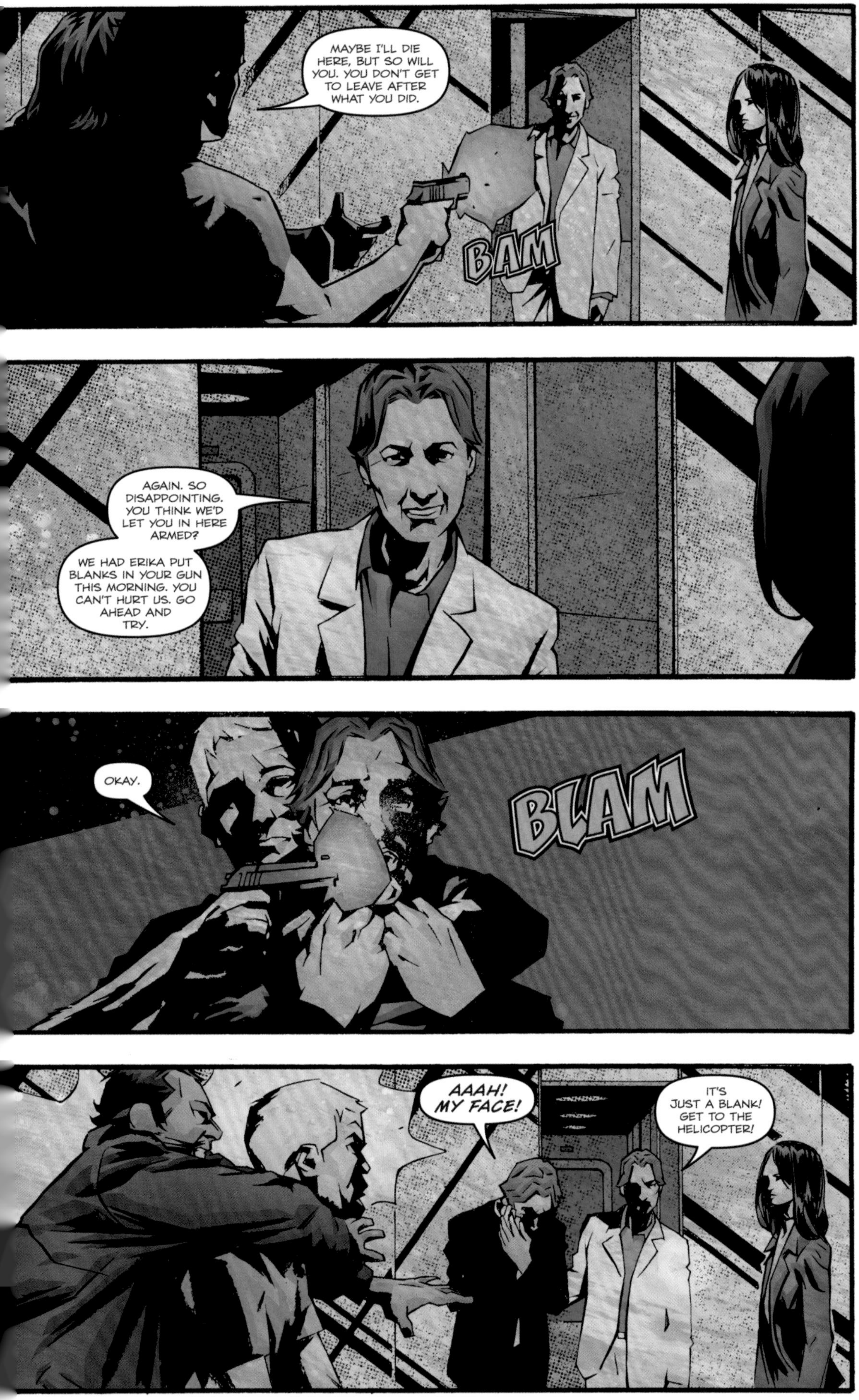
MAYBE I'LL DIE HERE, BUT SO WILL YOU. YOU DON'T GET TO LEAVE AFTER WHAT YOU DID.
BAM
AGAIN. SO DISAPPOINTING. YOU THINK WE'D LET YOU IN HERE ARMED?
WE HAD ERIKA PUT BLANKS IN YOUR GUN THIS MORNING. YOU CAN'T HURT US. GO AHEAD AND TRY.
OKAY.
BLAM
AAAH! MY FACE!
IT'S JUST A BLANK! GET TO THE HELICOPTER!

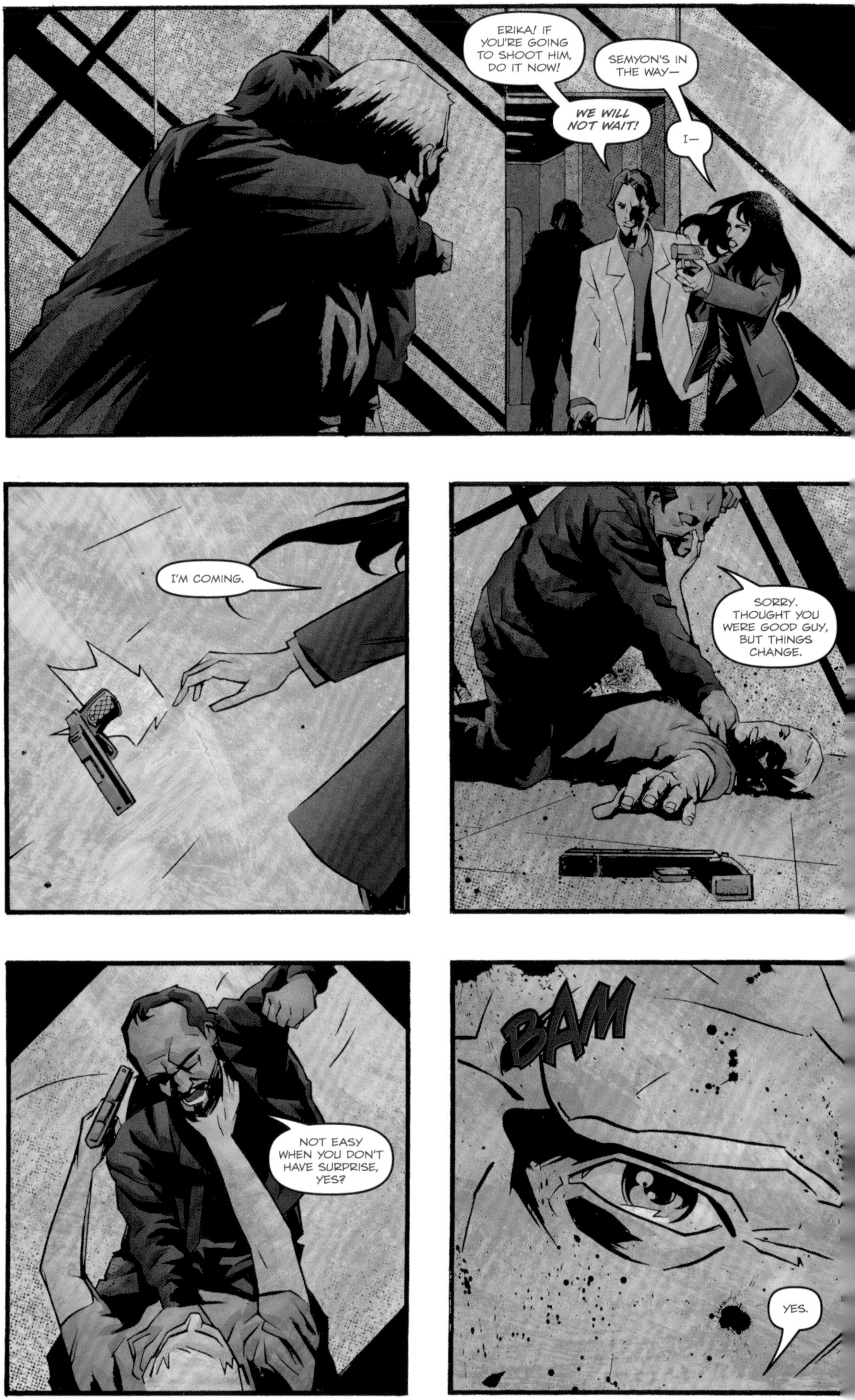
ERIKA! IF YOU'RE GOING TO SHOOT HIM, DO IT NOW!
WE WILL NOT WAIT!
SEMYON'S IN THE WAY—
I—
I'M COMING.
SORRY. THOUGHT YOU WERE GOOD GUY, BUT THINGS CHANGE.
NOT EASY WHEN YOU DON'T HAVE SURPRISE, YES?
BAM
YES.

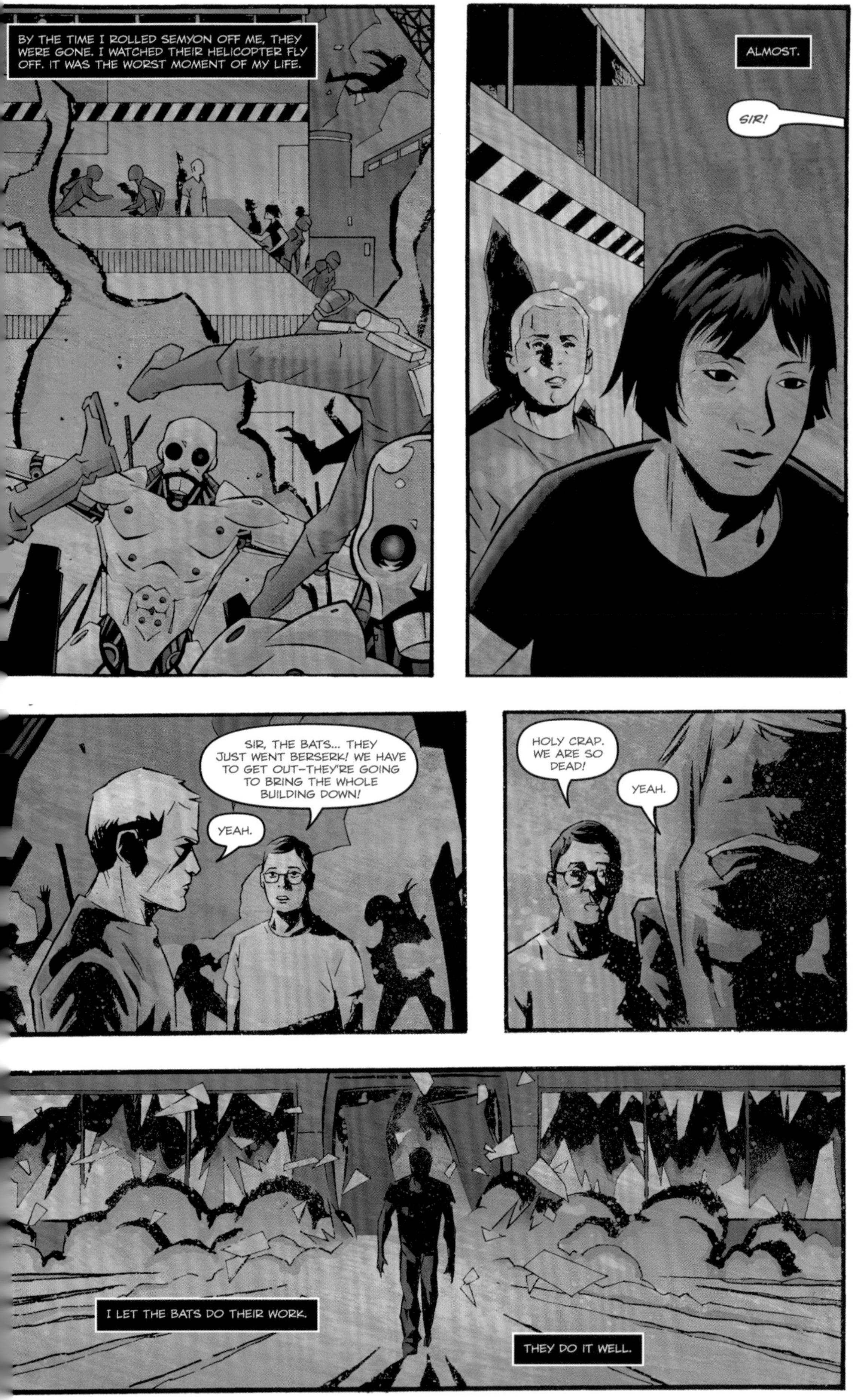
BY THE TIME I ROLLED SEMYON OFF ME, THEY WERE GONE. I WATCHED THEIR HELICOPTER FLY OFF. IT WAS THE WORST MOMENT OF MY LIFE.
ALMOST.
SIR!
SIR, THE BATS... THEY JUST WENT BERSERK! WE HAVE TO GET OUT–THEY'RE GOING TO BRING THE WHOLE BUILDING DOWN!
YEAH.
HOLY CRAP. WE ARE SO DEAD!
YEAH.
I LET THE BATS DO THEIR WORK.
THEY DO IT WELL.

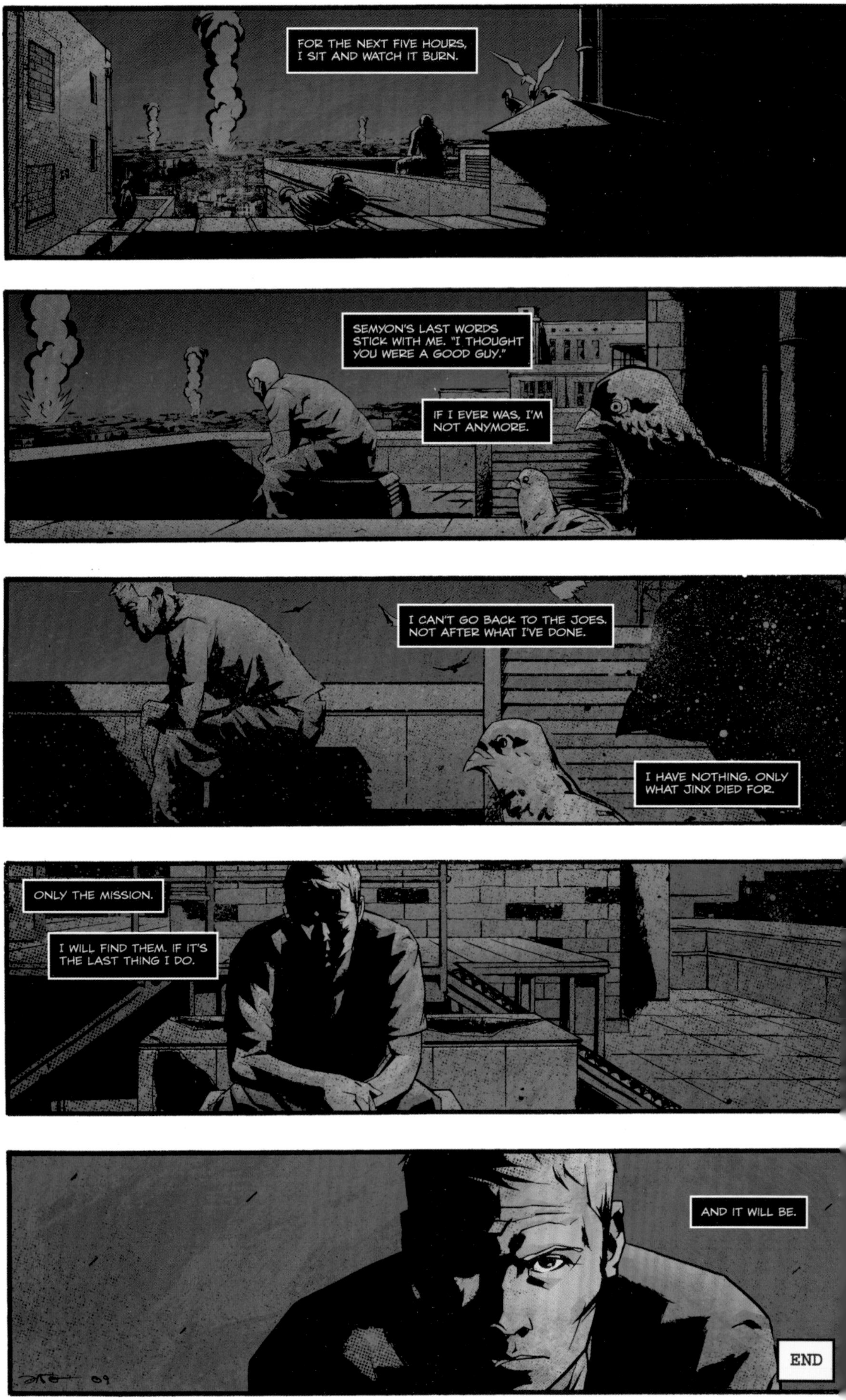
FOR THE NEXT FIVE HOURS, I SIT AND WATCH IT BURN.
SEMYON'S LAST WORDS STICK WITH ME. "I THOUGHT YOU WERE A GOOD GUY."
IF I EVER WAS, I'M NOT ANYMORE.
I CAN'T GO BACK TO THE JOES. NOT AFTER WHAT I'VE DONE.
I HAVE NOTHING. ONLY WHAT JINX DIED FOR.
ONLY THE MISSION.
I WILL FIND THEM. IF IT'S THE LAST THING I DO.
AND IT WILL BE.
END

TOMAX & XAMOT SPECIAL

# G.I. JOE SPECIAL COBRA

WRITER....MIKE COSTA

ARTIST....ANTONIO FUSO

COLORIST....LOVERN KINDZIERSKI

LETTERS....ROBBIE ROBBINS

ASSISTANT EDITOR....CARLOS GUZMAN

ASSOCIATE EDITOR....DENTON TIPTON

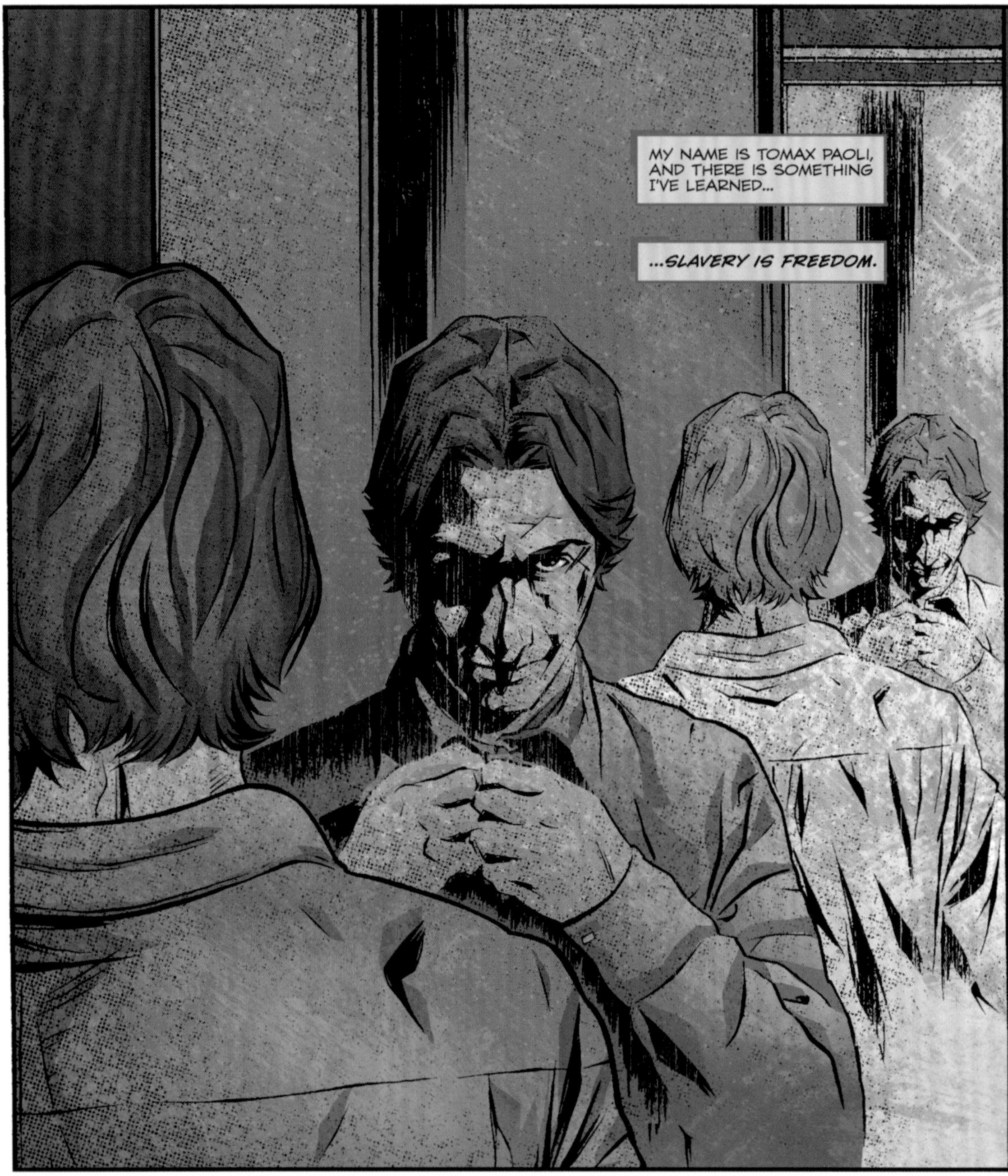
MY NAME IS TOMAX PAOLI, AND THERE IS SOMETHING I'VE LEARNED...
...SLAVERY IS FREEDOM.

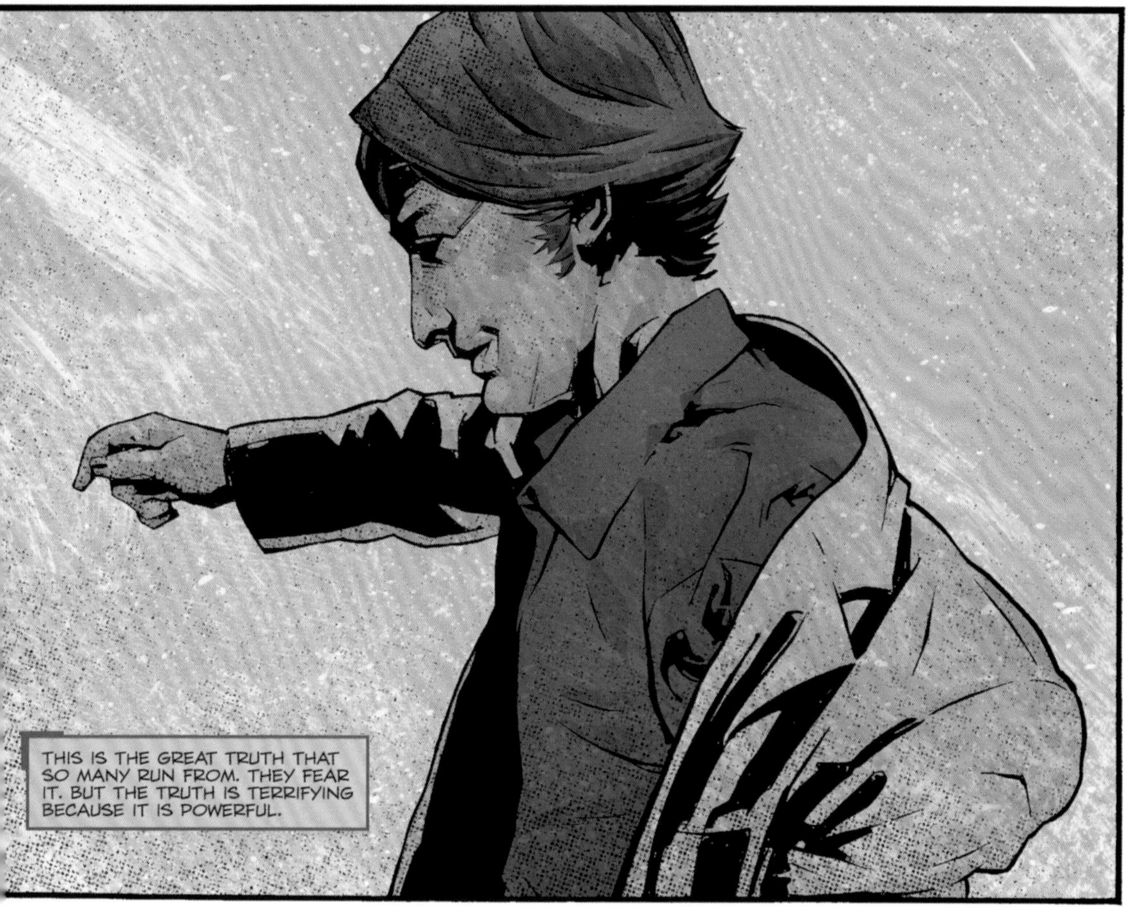
THIS IS THE GREAT TRUTH THAT SO MANY RUN FROM. THEY FEAR IT. BUT THE TRUTH IS TERRIFYING BECAUSE IT IS POWERFUL.

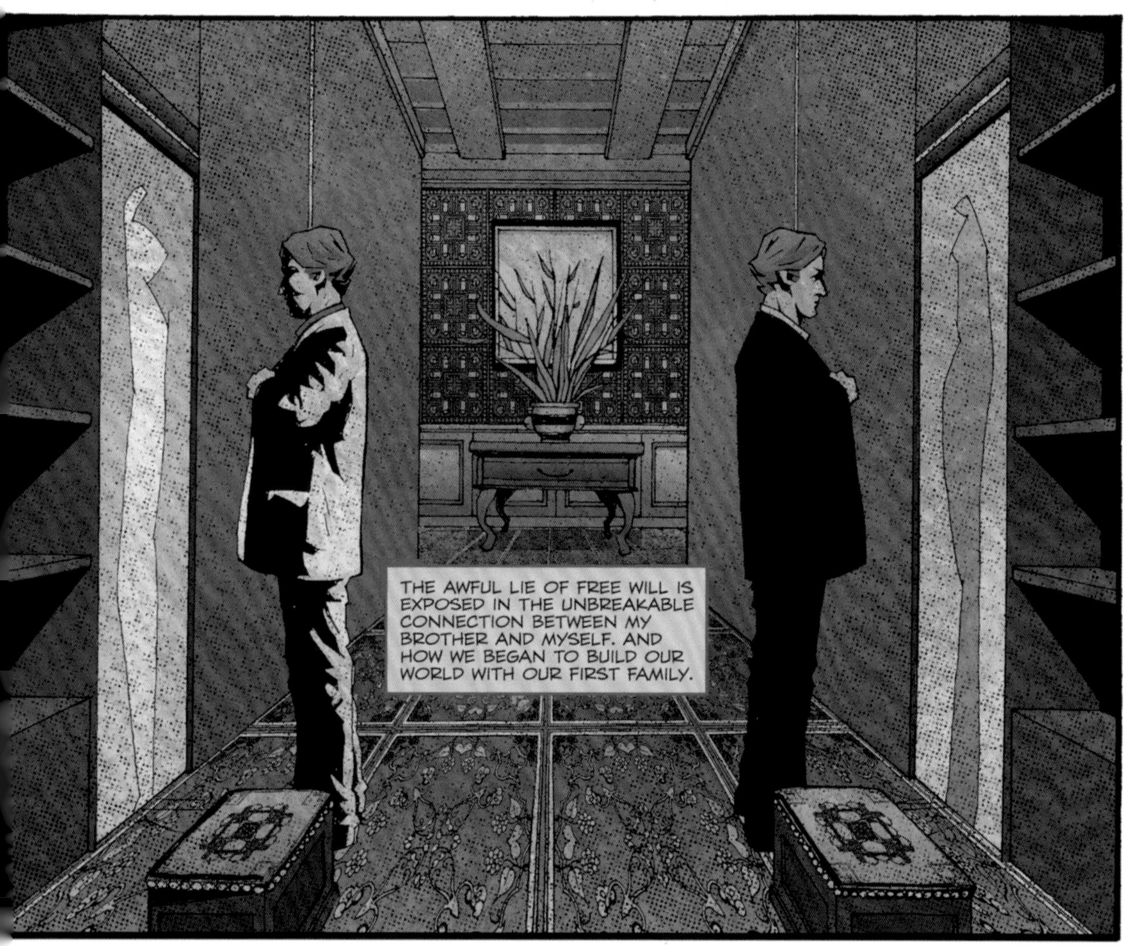
THE AWFUL LIE OF FREE WILL IS EXPOSED IN THE UNBREAKABLE CONNECTION BETWEEN MY BROTHER AND MYSELF. AND HOW WE BEGAN TO BUILD OUR WORLD WITH OUR FIRST FAMILY.

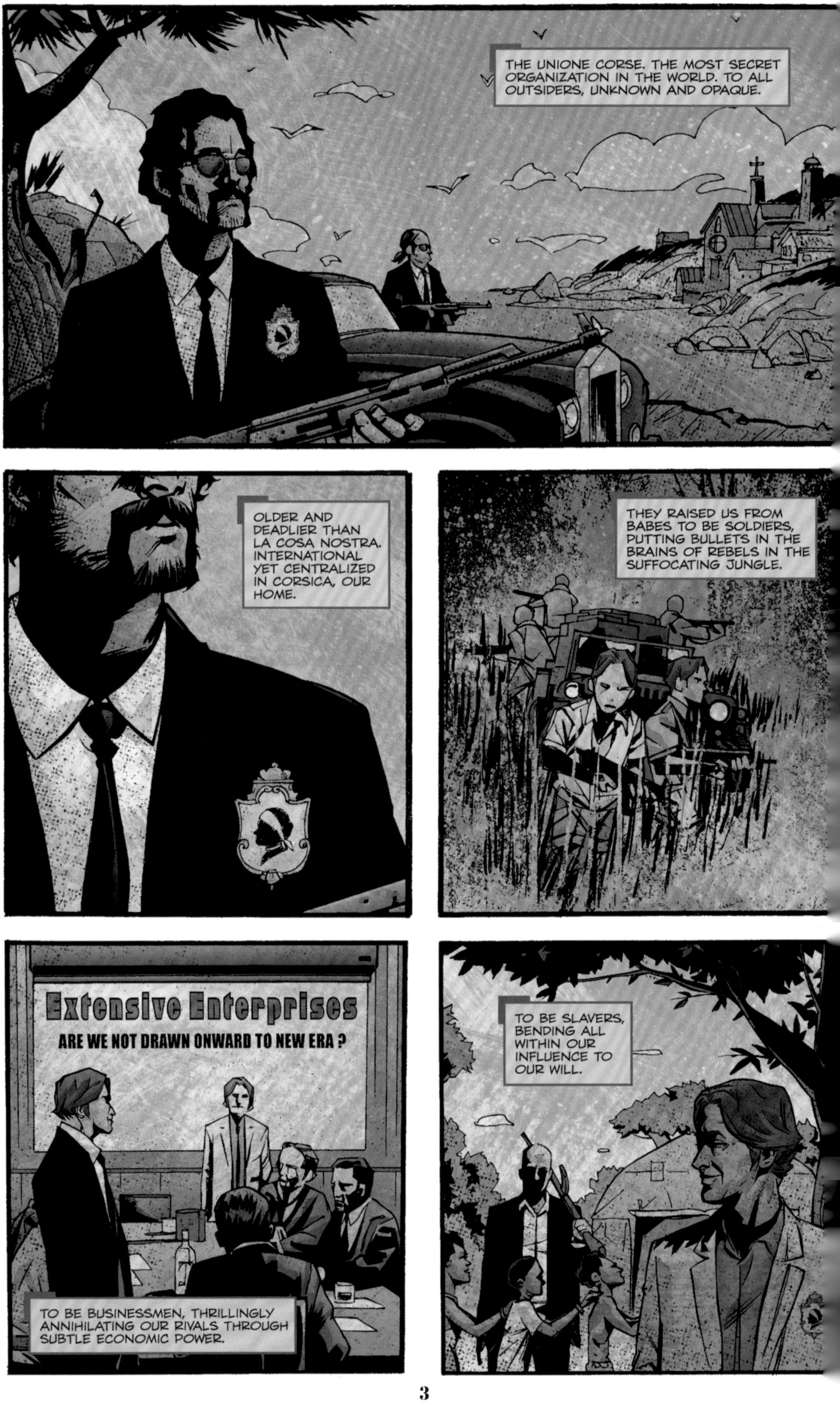
THE UNIONE CORSE. THE MOST SECRET ORGANIZATION IN THE WORLD. TO ALL OUTSIDERS, UNKNOWN AND OPAQUE.
OLDER AND DEADLIER THAN LA COSA NOSTRA. INTERNATIONAL YET CENTRALIZED IN CORSICA, OUR HOME.
THEY RAISED US FROM BABES TO BE SOLDIERS, PUTTING BULLETS IN THE BRAINS OF REBELS IN THE SUFFOCATING JUNGLE.
Extensive Enterprises
ARE WE NOT DRAWN ONWARD TO NEW ERA ?
TO BE BUSINESSMEN, THRILLINGLY ANNIHILATING OUR RIVALS THROUGH SUBTLE ECONOMIC POWER.
TO BE SLAVERS, BENDING ALL WITHIN OUR INFLUENCE TO OUR WILL.

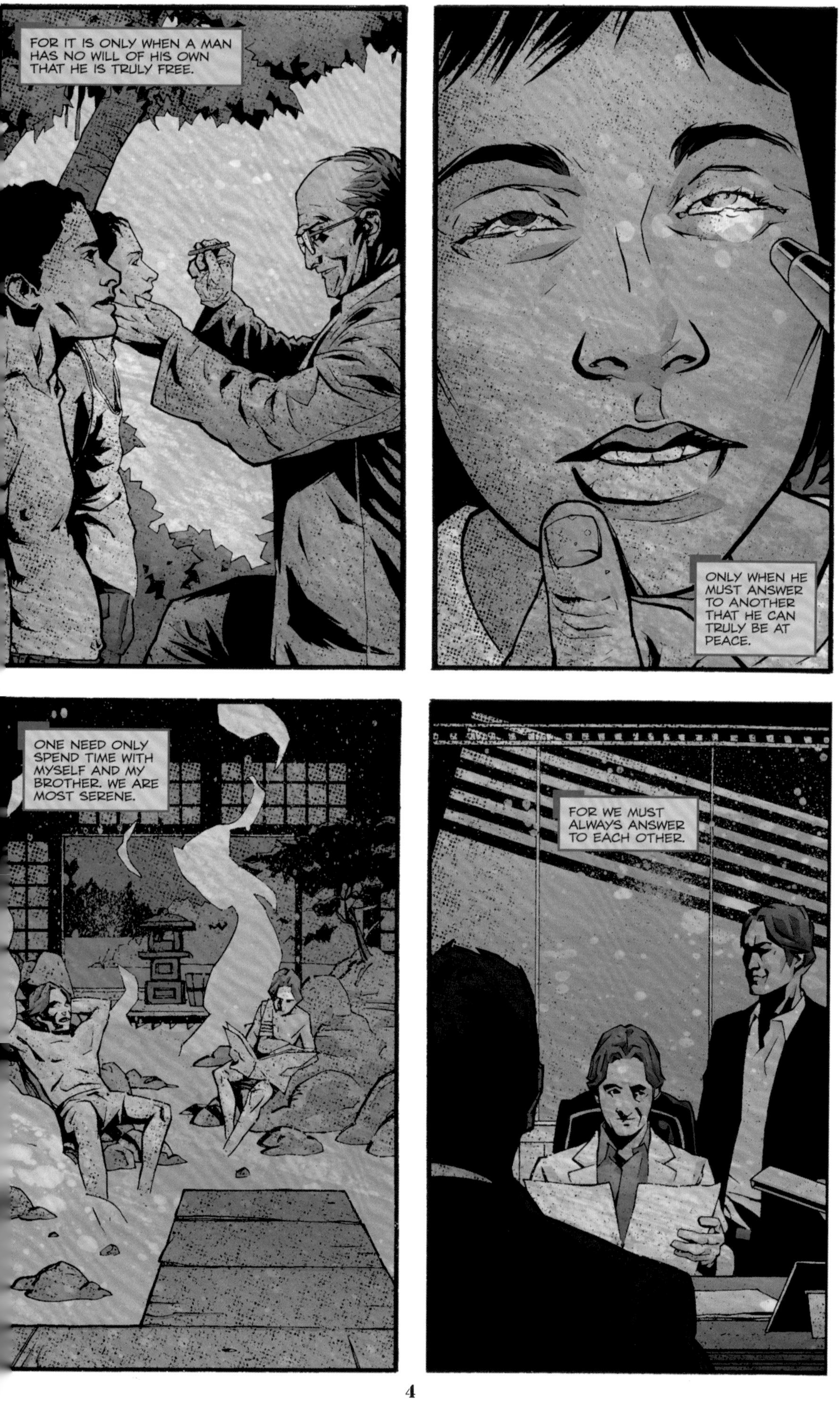
FOR IT IS ONLY WHEN A MAN HAS NO WILL OF HIS OWN THAT HE IS TRULY FREE.
ONLY WHEN HE MUST ANSWER TO ANOTHER THAT HE CAN TRULY BE AT PEACE.
ONE NEED ONLY SPEND TIME WITH MYSELF AND MY BROTHER. WE ARE MOST SERENE.
FOR WE MUST ALWAYS ANSWER TO EACH OTHER.

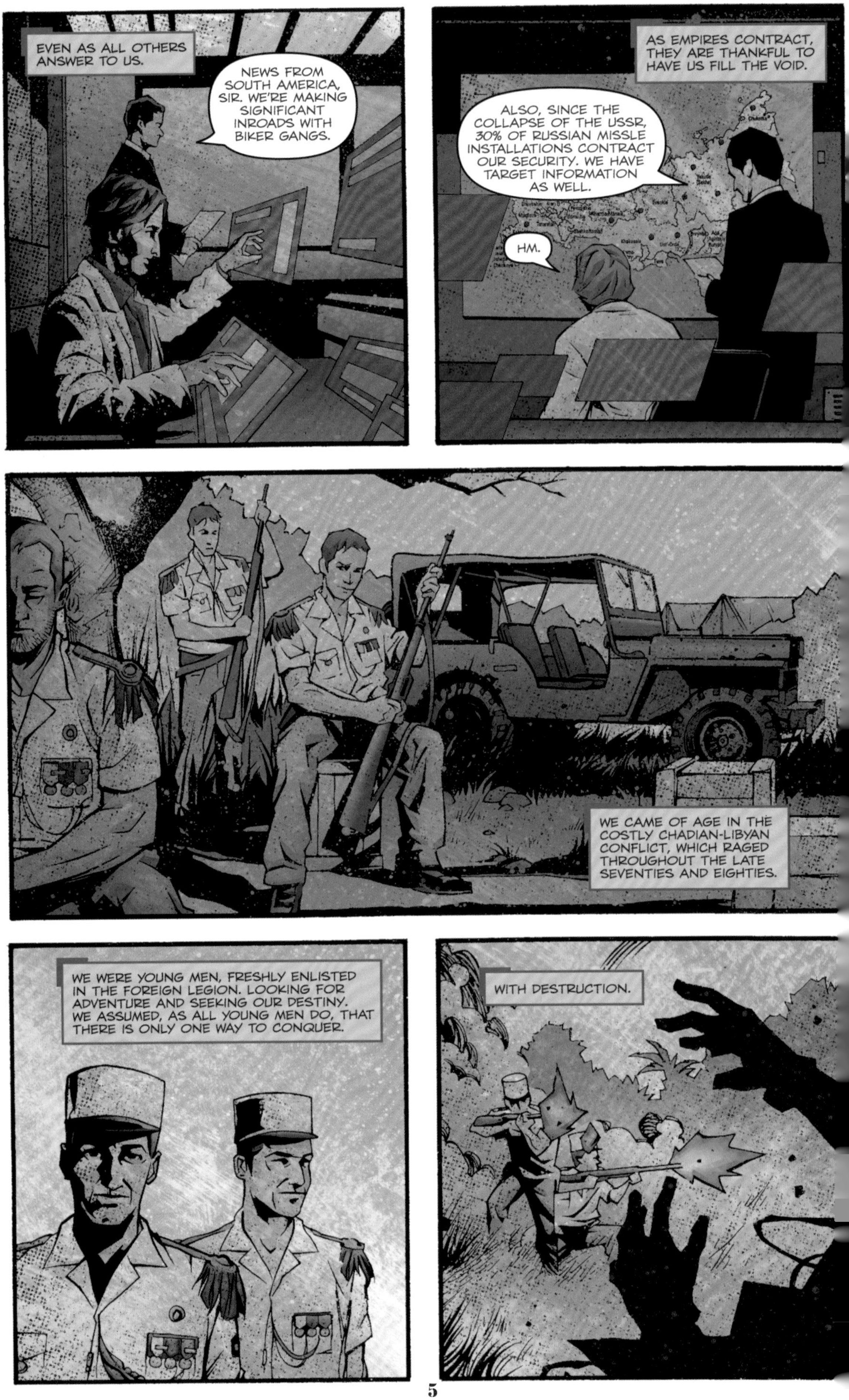
EVEN AS ALL OTHERS ANSWER TO US.
NEWS FROM SOUTH AMERICA, SIR. WE'RE MAKING SIGNIFICANT INROADS WITH BIKER GANGS.
AS EMPIRES CONTRACT, THEY ARE THANKFUL TO HAVE US FILL THE VOID.
ALSO, SINCE THE COLLAPSE OF THE USSR, 30% OF RUSSIAN MISSLE INSTALLATIONS CONTRACT OUR SECURITY. WE HAVE TARGET INFORMATION AS WELL.
HM.
WE CAME OF AGE IN THE COSTLY CHADIAN-LIBYAN CONFLICT, WHICH RAGED THROUGHOUT THE LATE SEVENTIES AND EIGHTIES.
WE WERE YOUNG MEN, FRESHLY ENLISTED IN THE FOREIGN LEGION. LOOKING FOR ADVENTURE AND SEEKING OUR DESTINY. WE ASSUMED, AS ALL YOUNG MEN DO, THAT THERE IS ONLY ONE WAY TO CONQUER.
WITH DESTRUCTION.

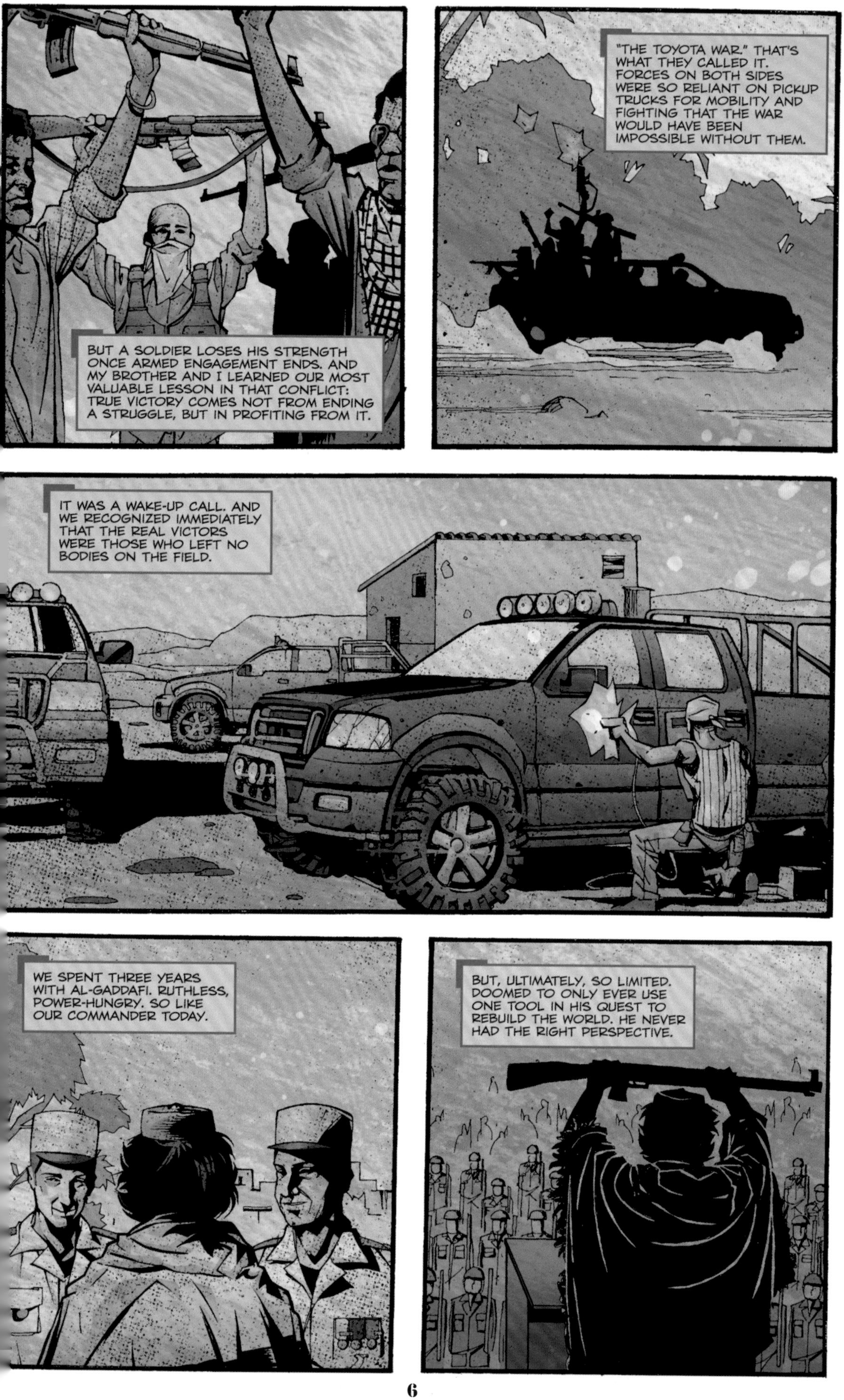
BUT A SOLDIER LOSES HIS STRENGTH ONCE ARMED ENGAGEMENT ENDS. AND MY BROTHER AND I LEARNED OUR MOST VALUABLE LESSON IN THAT CONFLICT: TRUE VICTORY COMES NOT FROM ENDING A STRUGGLE, BUT IN PROFITING FROM IT.
"THE TOYOTA WAR." THAT'S WHAT THEY CALLED IT. FORCES ON BOTH SIDES WERE SO RELIANT ON PICKUP TRUCKS FOR MOBILITY AND FIGHTING THAT THE WAR WOULD HAVE BEEN IMPOSSIBLE WITHOUT THEM.
IT WAS A WAKE-UP CALL. AND WE RECOGNIZED IMMEDIATELY THAT THE REAL VICTORS WERE THOSE WHO LEFT NO BODIES ON THE FIELD.
WE SPENT THREE YEARS WITH AL-GADDAFI. RUTHLESS, POWER-HUNGRY. SO LIKE OUR COMMANDER TODAY.
BUT, ULTIMATELY, SO LIMITED. DOOMED TO ONLY EVER USE ONE TOOL IN HIS QUEST TO REBUILD THE WORLD. HE NEVER HAD THE RIGHT PERSPECTIVE.

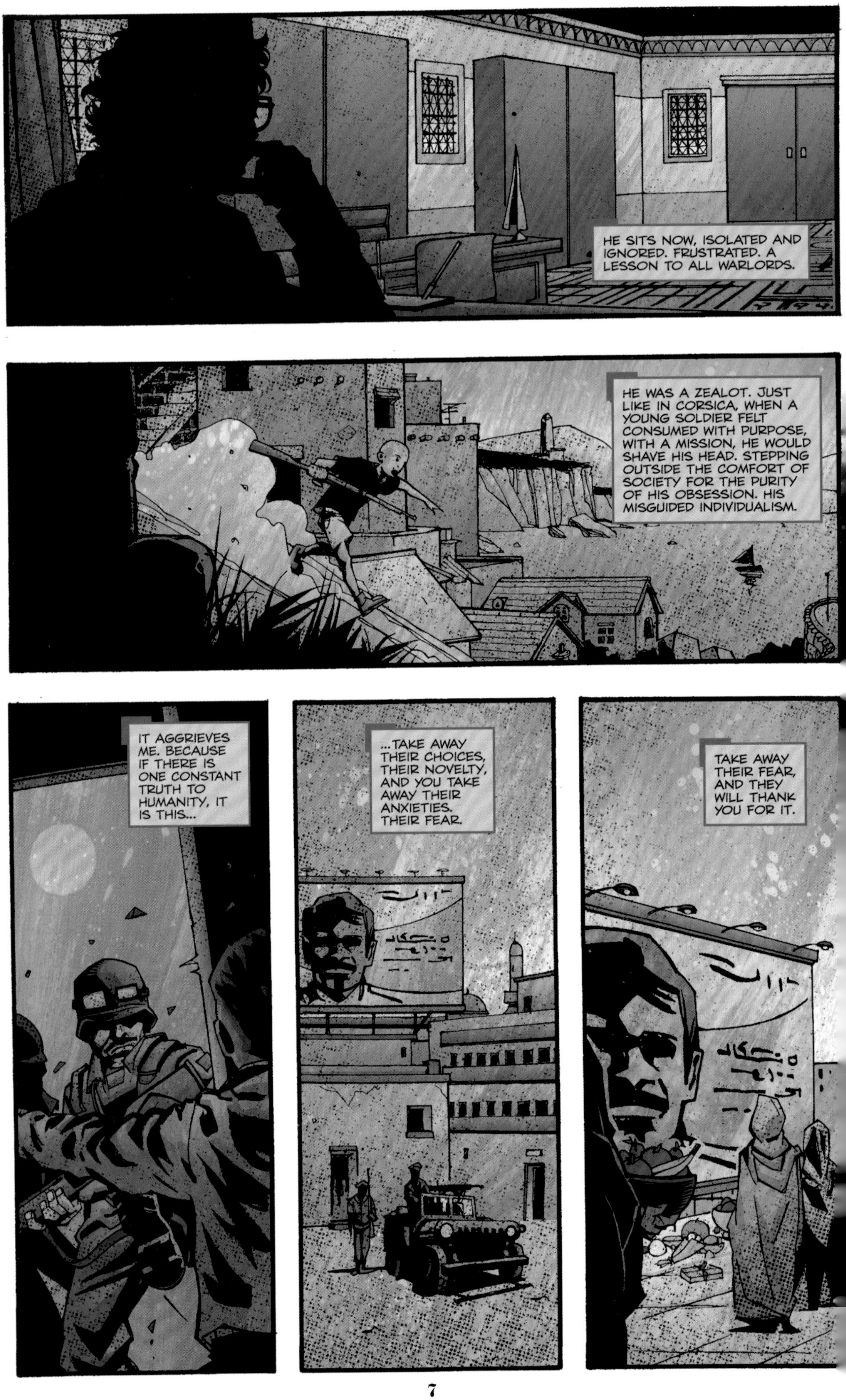
HE SITS NOW, ISOLATED AND IGNORED. FRUSTRATED. A LESSON TO ALL WARLORDS.
HE WAS A ZEALOT. JUST LIKE IN CORSICA, WHEN A YOUNG SOLDIER FELT CONSUMED WITH PURPOSE, WITH A MISSION, HE WOULD SHAVE HIS HEAD. STEPPING OUTSIDE THE COMFORT OF SOCIETY FOR THE PURITY OF HIS OBSESSION. HIS MISGUIDED INDIVIDUALISM.
IT AGGRIEVES ME. BECAUSE IF THERE IS ONE CONSTANT TRUTH TO HUMANITY, IT IS THIS...
...TAKE AWAY THEIR CHOICES, THEIR NOVELTY, AND YOU TAKE AWAY THEIR ANXIETIES. THEIR FEAR.
TAKE AWAY THEIR FEAR, AND THEY WILL THANK YOU FOR IT.

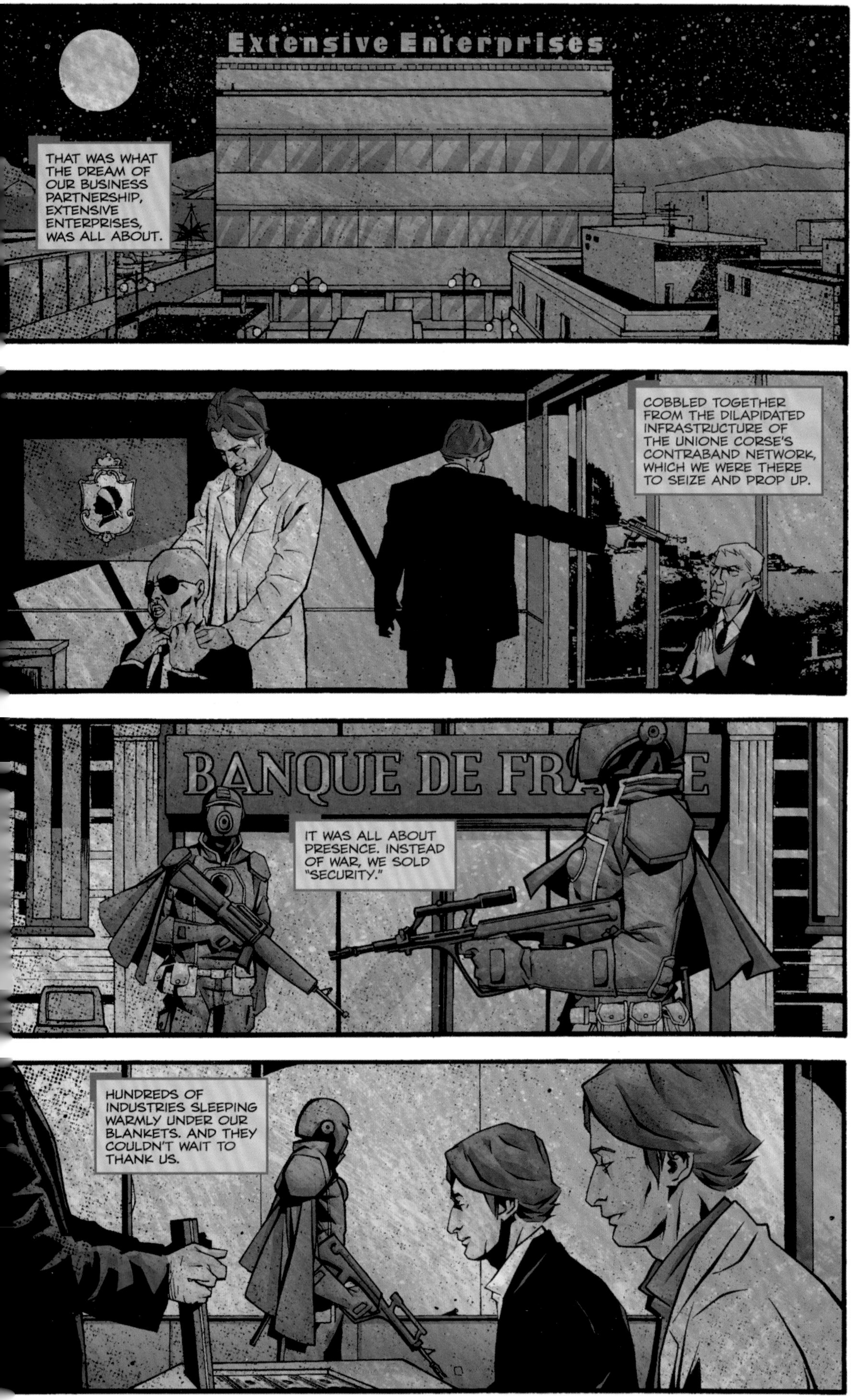
Extensive Enterprises
THAT WAS WHAT THE DREAM OF OUR BUSINESS PARTNERSHIP, EXTENSIVE ENTERPRISES, WAS ALL ABOUT.
COBBLED TOGETHER FROM THE DILAPIDATED INFRASTRUCTURE OF THE UNIONE CORSE'S CONTRABAND NETWORK, WHICH WE WERE THERE TO SEIZE AND PROP UP.
BANQUE DE FRA E
IT WAS ALL ABOUT PRESENCE. INSTEAD OF WAR, WE SOLD "SECURITY."
HUNDREDS OF INDUSTRIES SLEEPING WARMLY UNDER OUR BLANKETS. AND THEY COULDN'T WAIT TO THANK US.

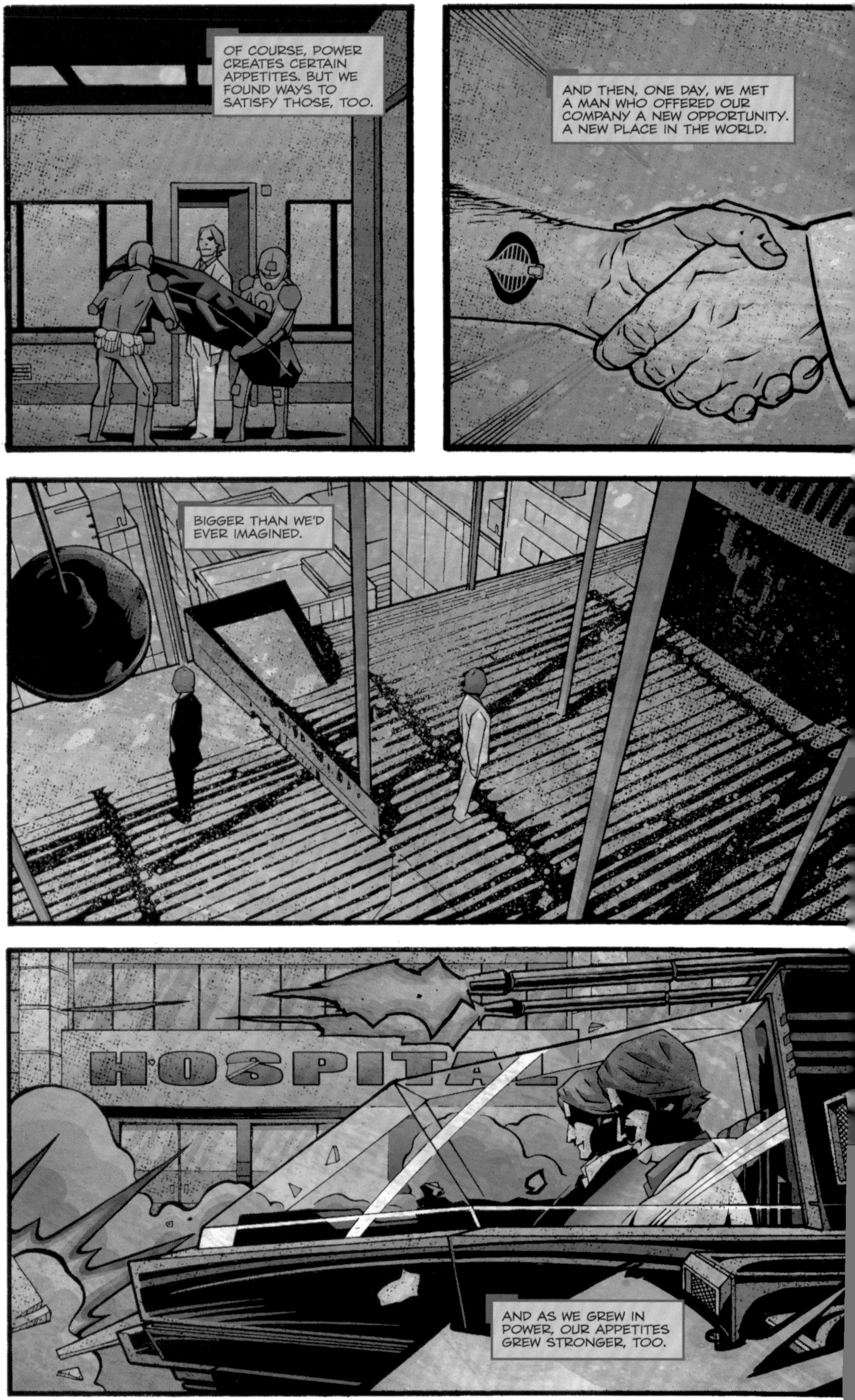
OF COURSE, POWER CREATES CERTAIN APPETITES. BUT WE FOUND WAYS TO SATISFY THOSE, TOO.
AND THEN, ONE DAY, WE MET A MAN WHO OFFERED OUR COMPANY A NEW OPPORTUNITY. A NEW PLACE IN THE WORLD.
BIGGER THAN WE'D EVER IMAGINED.
HOSPITAL
AND AS WE GREW IN POWER, OUR APPETITES GREW STRONGER, TOO.

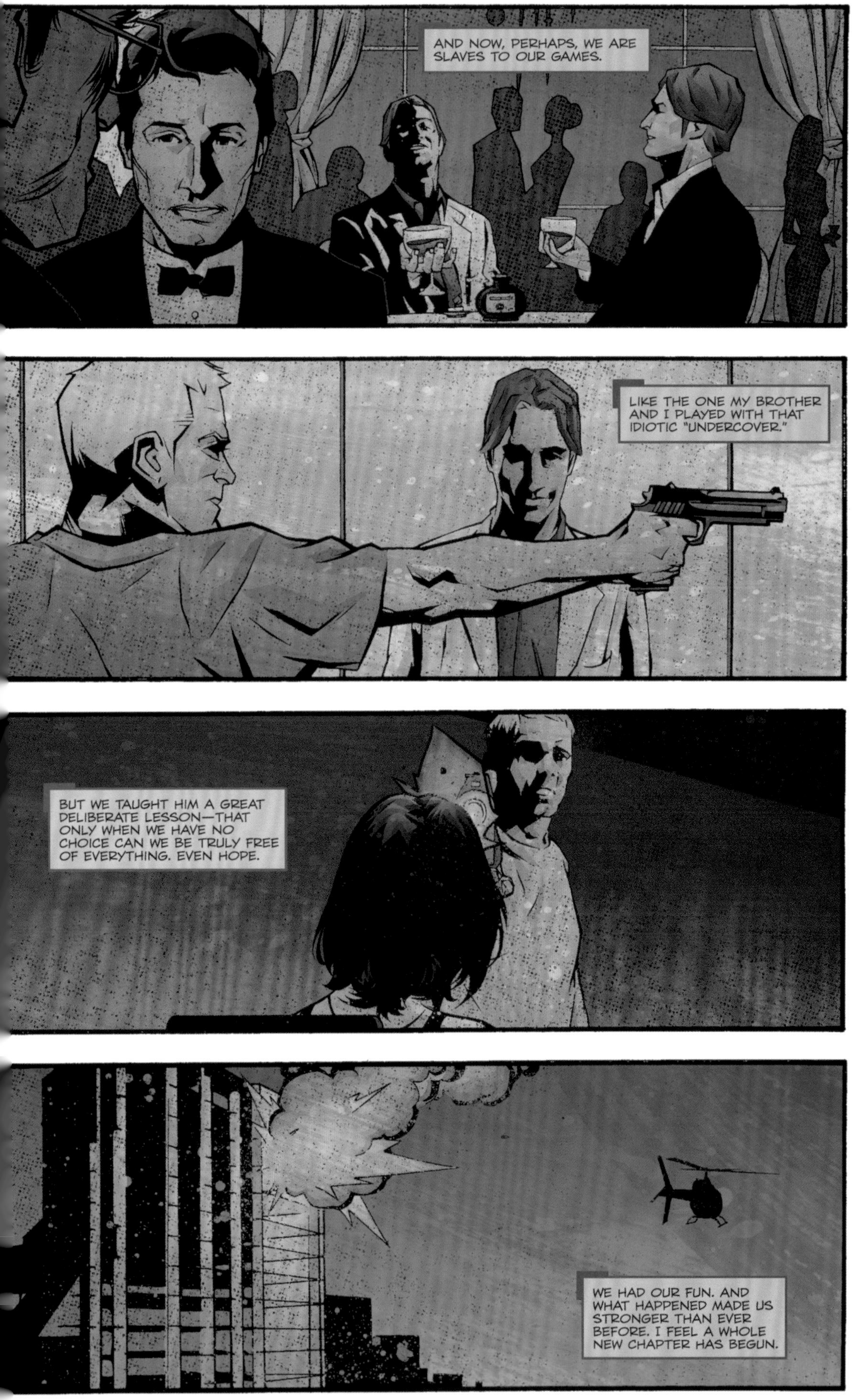
AND NOW, PERHAPS, WE ARE SLAVES TO OUR GAMES.
LIKE THE ONE MY BROTHER AND I PLAYED WITH THAT IDIOTIC "UNDERCOVER."
BUT WE TAUGHT HIM A GREAT DELIBERATE LESSON—THAT ONLY WHEN WE HAVE NO CHOICE CAN WE BE TRULY FREE OF EVERYTHING. EVEN HOPE.
WE HAD OUR FUN. AND WHAT HAPPENED MADE US STRONGER THAN EVER BEFORE. I FEEL A WHOLE NEW CHAPTER HAS BEGUN.

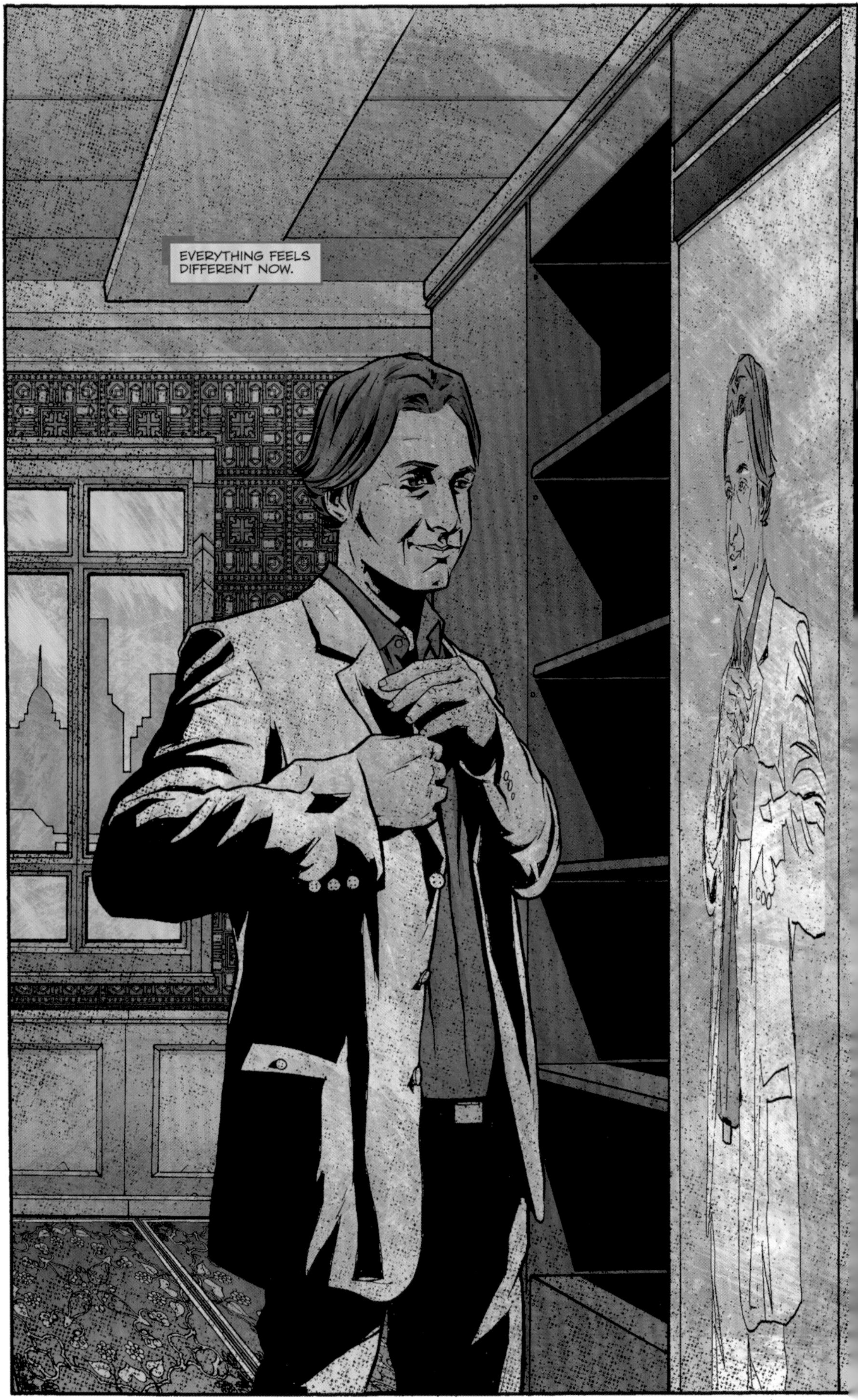
EVERYTHING FEELS DIFFERENT NOW.

Art by Antonio Fuso

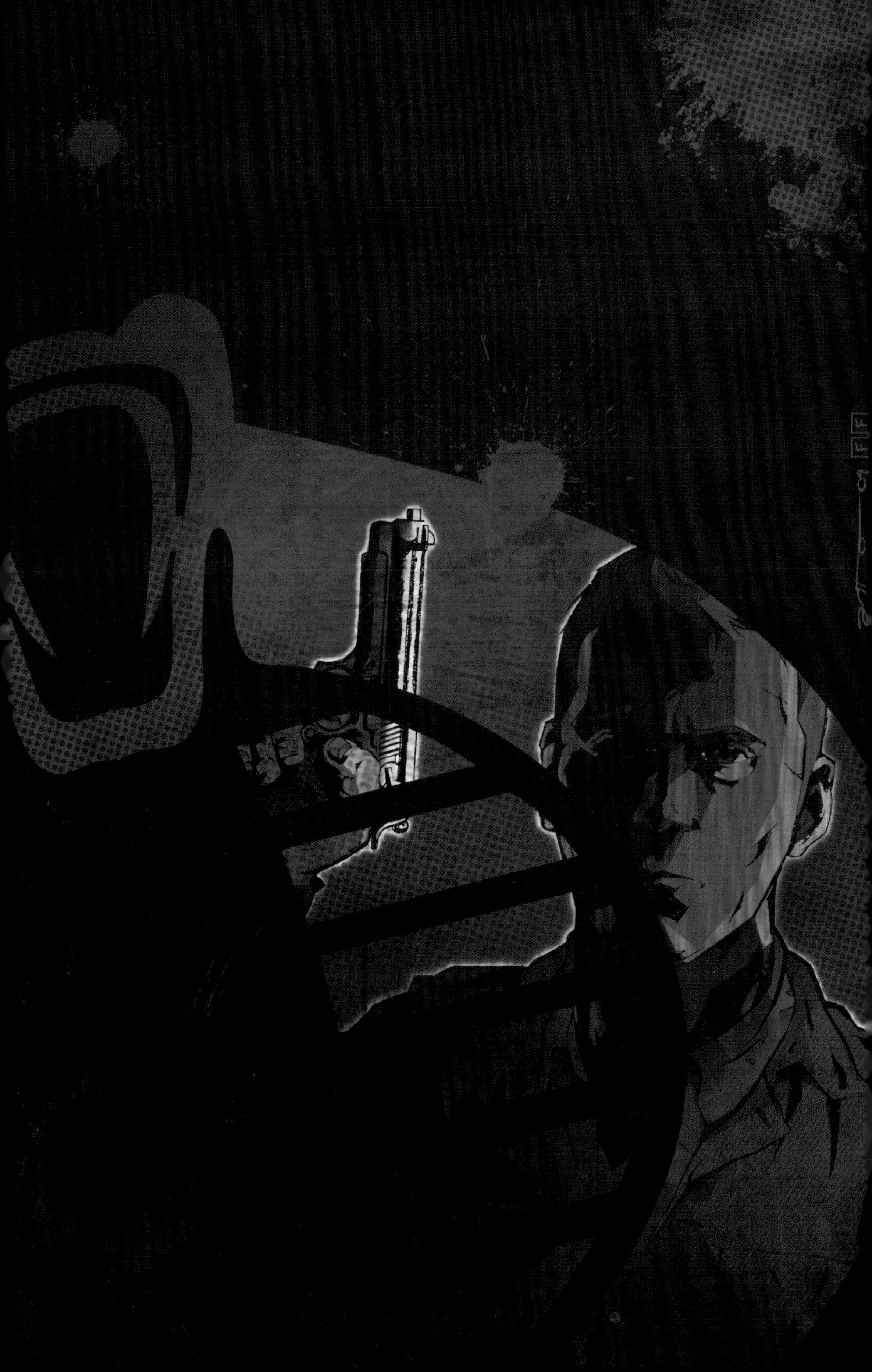

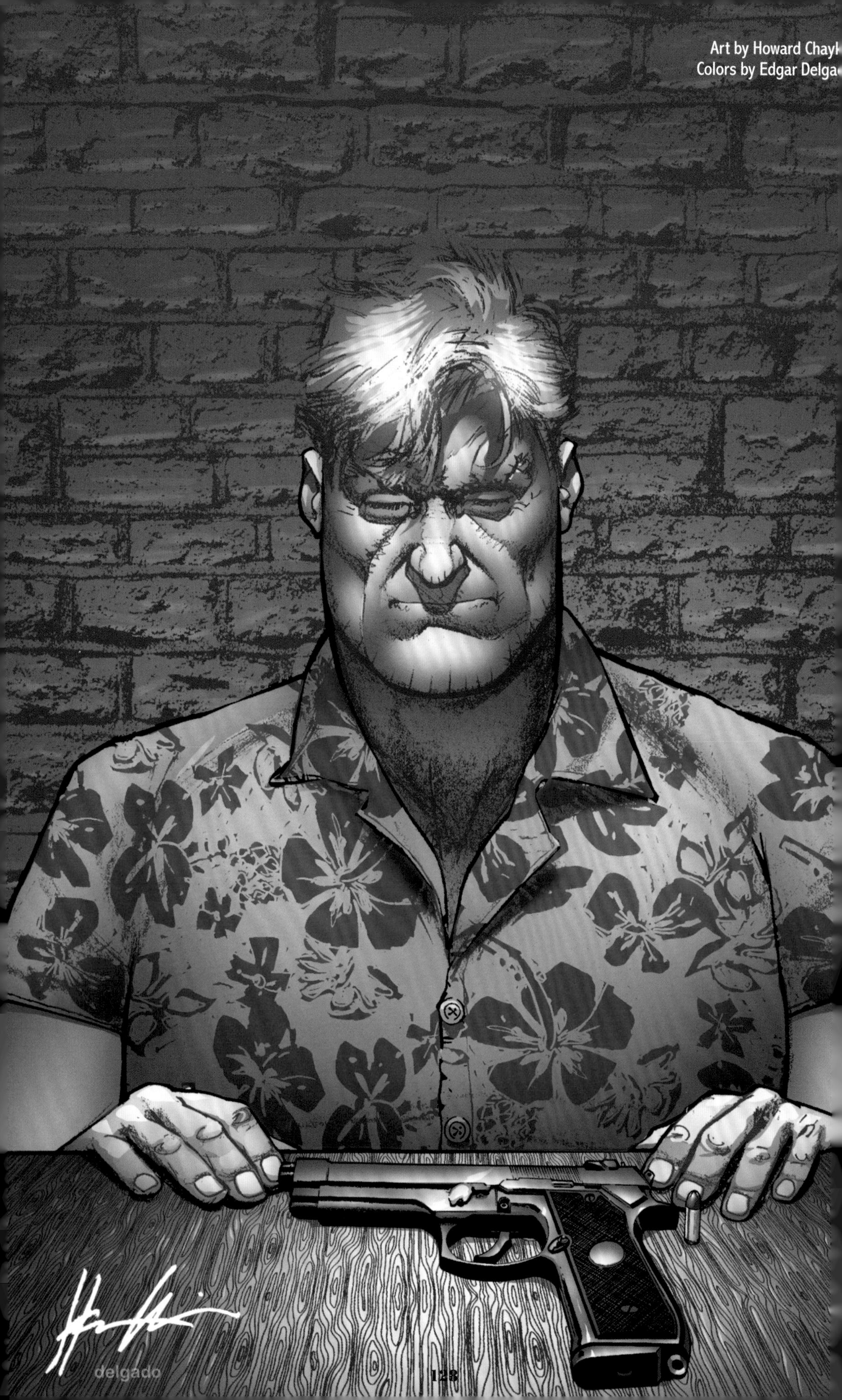
Art by Howard Chayk
Colors by Edgar Delga
delgado

t by Antonio Fuso

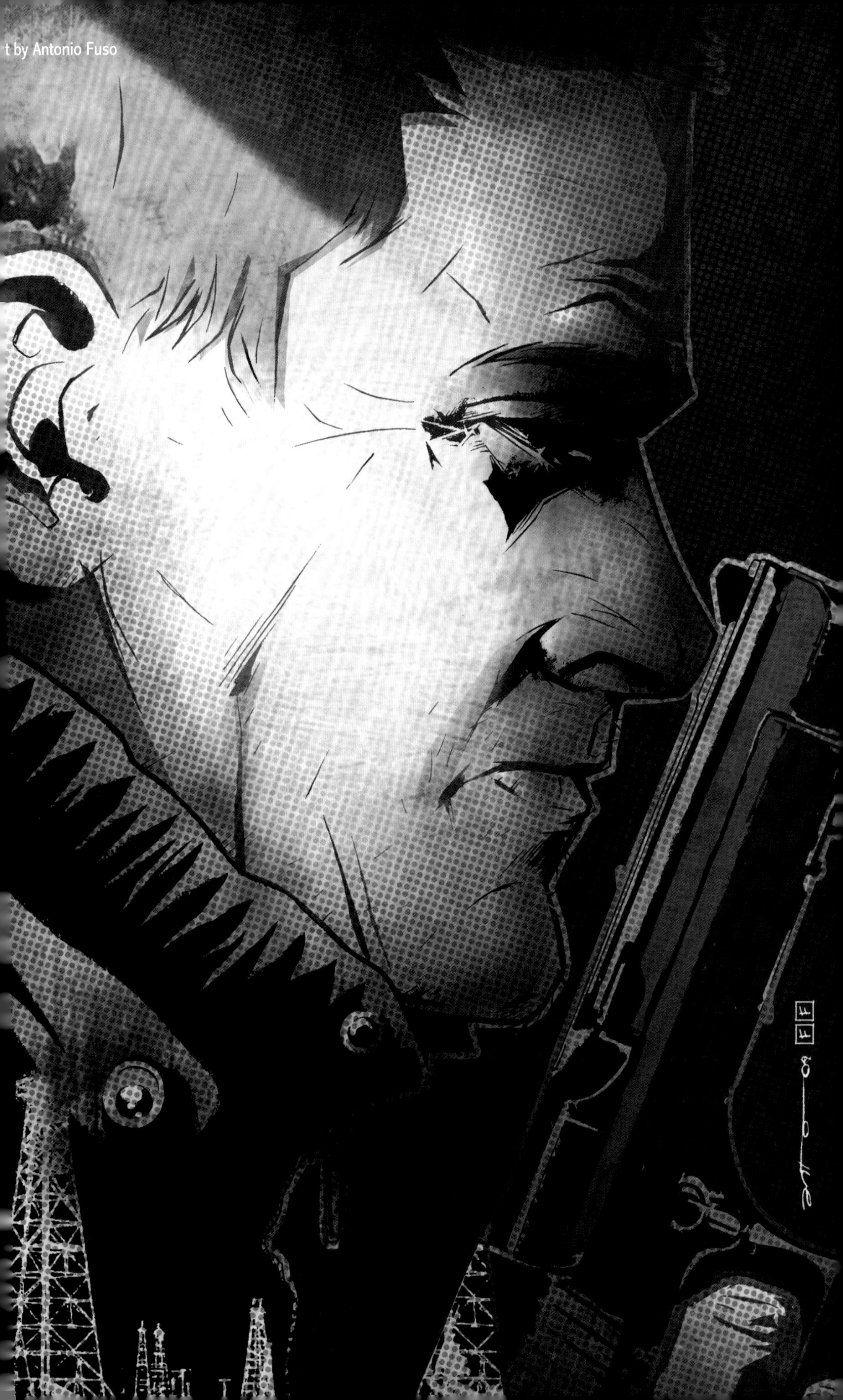

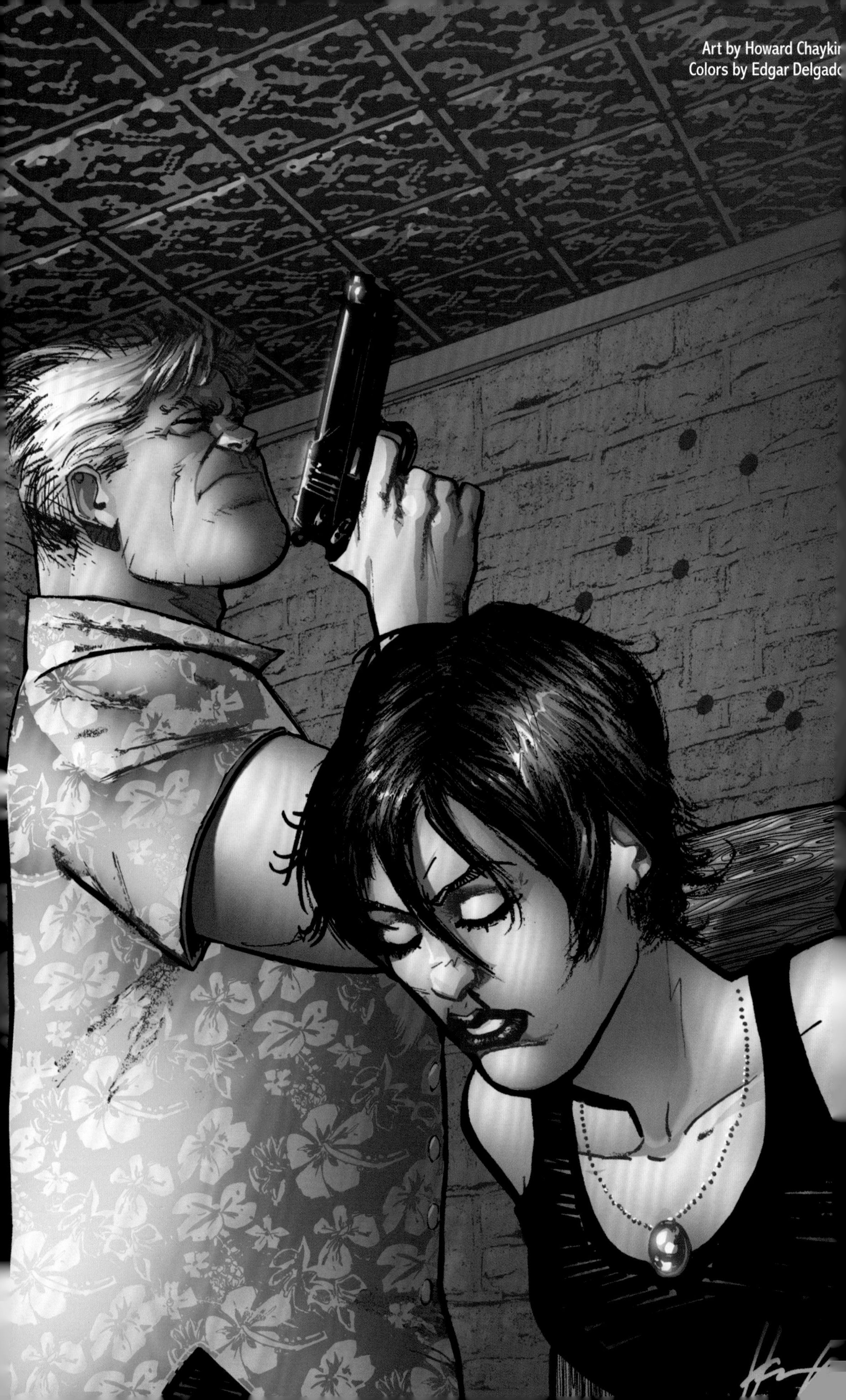
Art by Howard Chaykin
Colors by Edgar Delgado

Art by Antonio Fuso

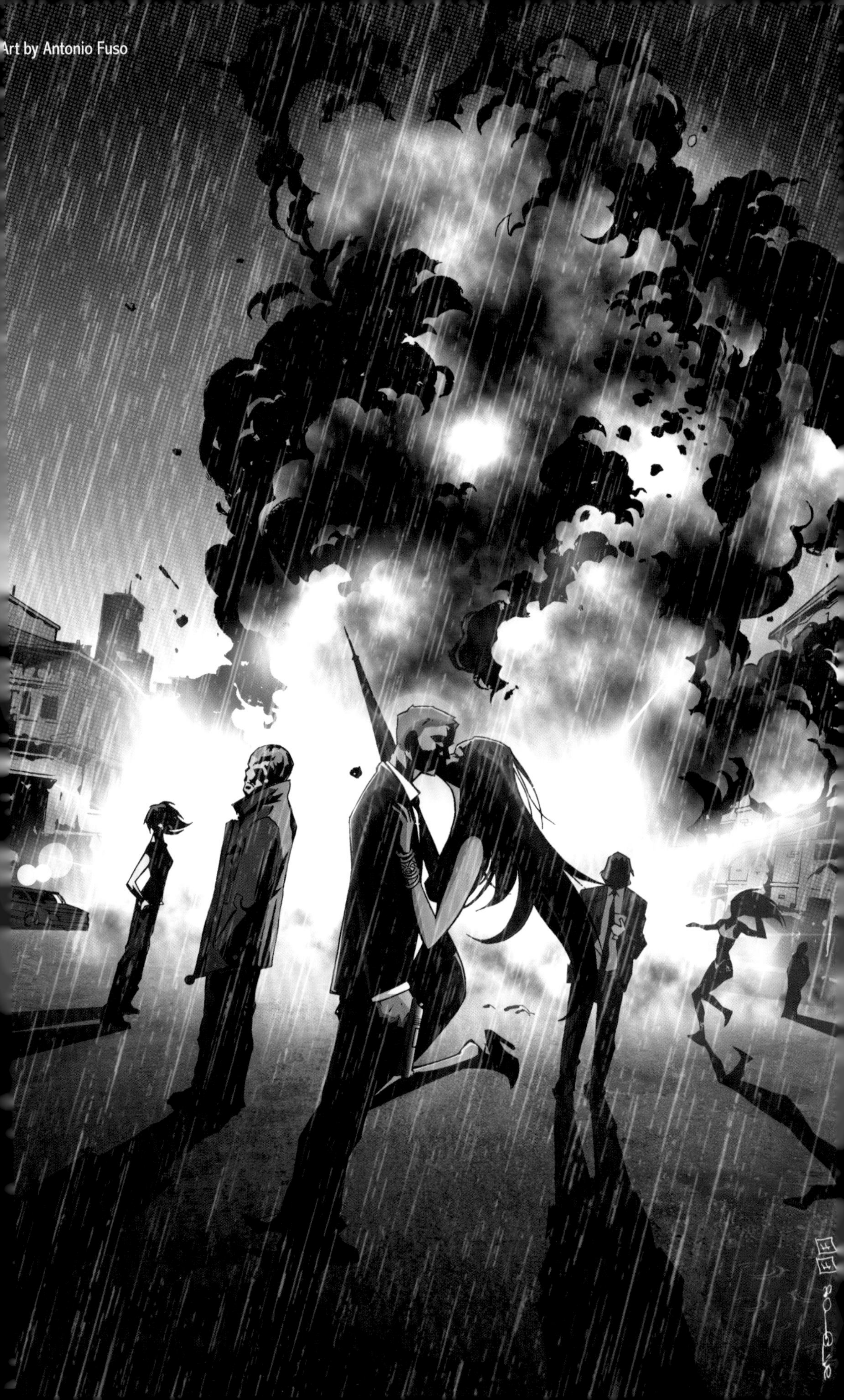

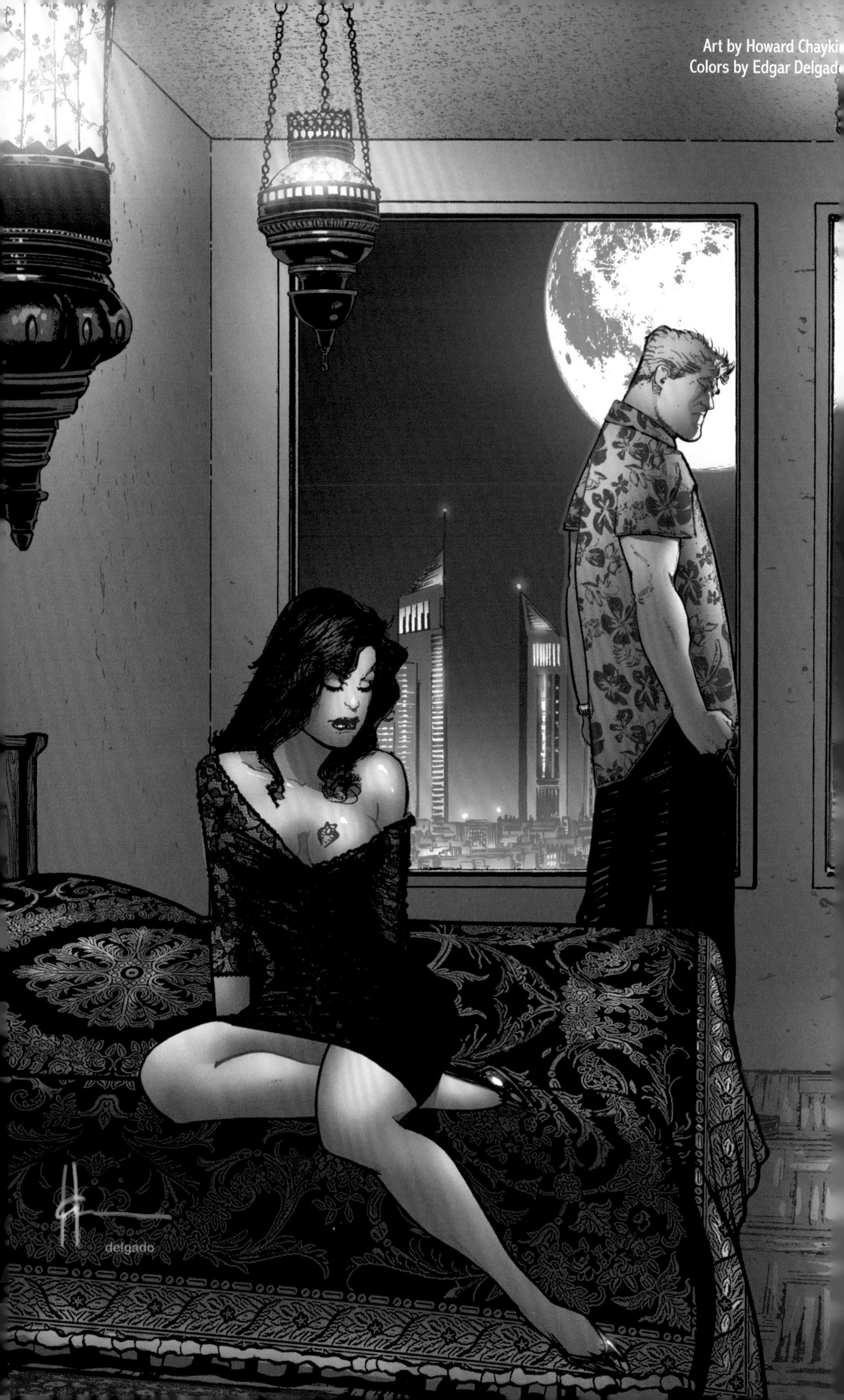
delgado

Art by Howard Chayki
Colors by Edgar Delgad

Art by Antonio Fuso

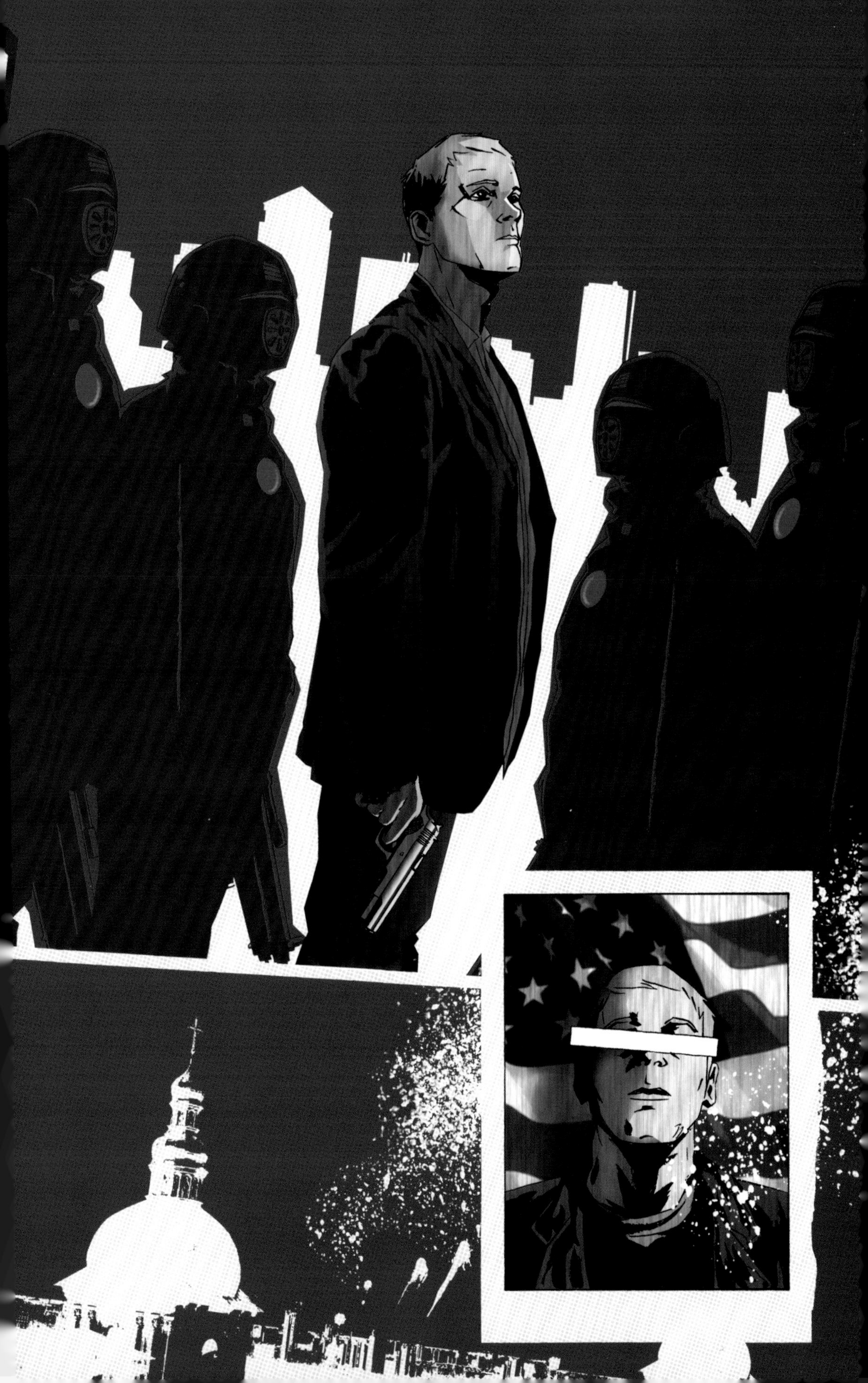

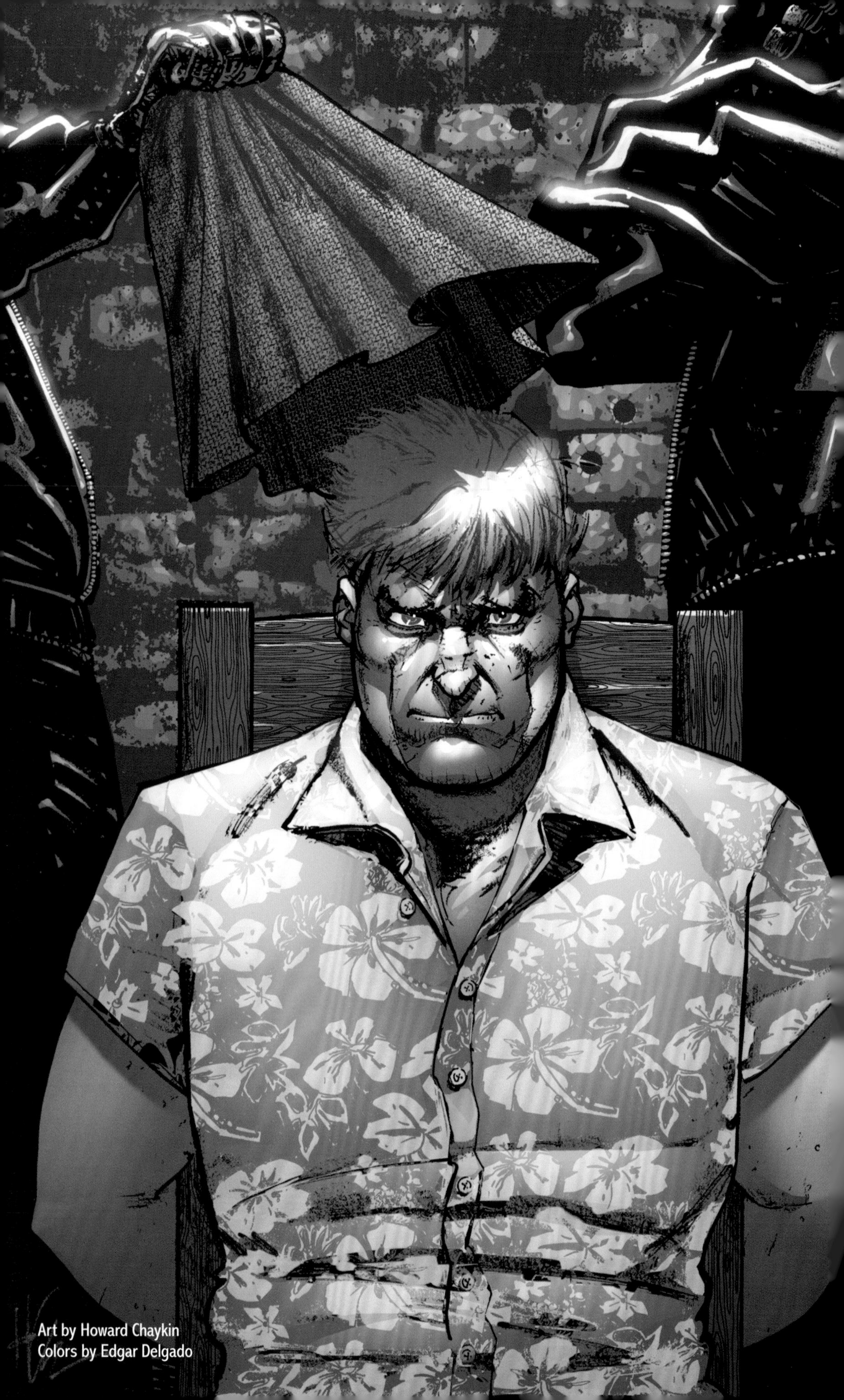

Art by Howard Chaykin
Colors by Edgar Delgado

# ART GALLERY

# G.I. JOE
## COBRA

WRITER....MIKE COSTA

ARTIST....ANTONIO FUSO

COLORIST....LOVERN KINDZIERSKI

LETTERS....ROBBIE ROBBINS

ASSISTANT EDITOR....CARLOS GUZMAN

ASSOCIATE EDITOR....DENTON TIPTON

EDITOR....ANDY SCHMIDT

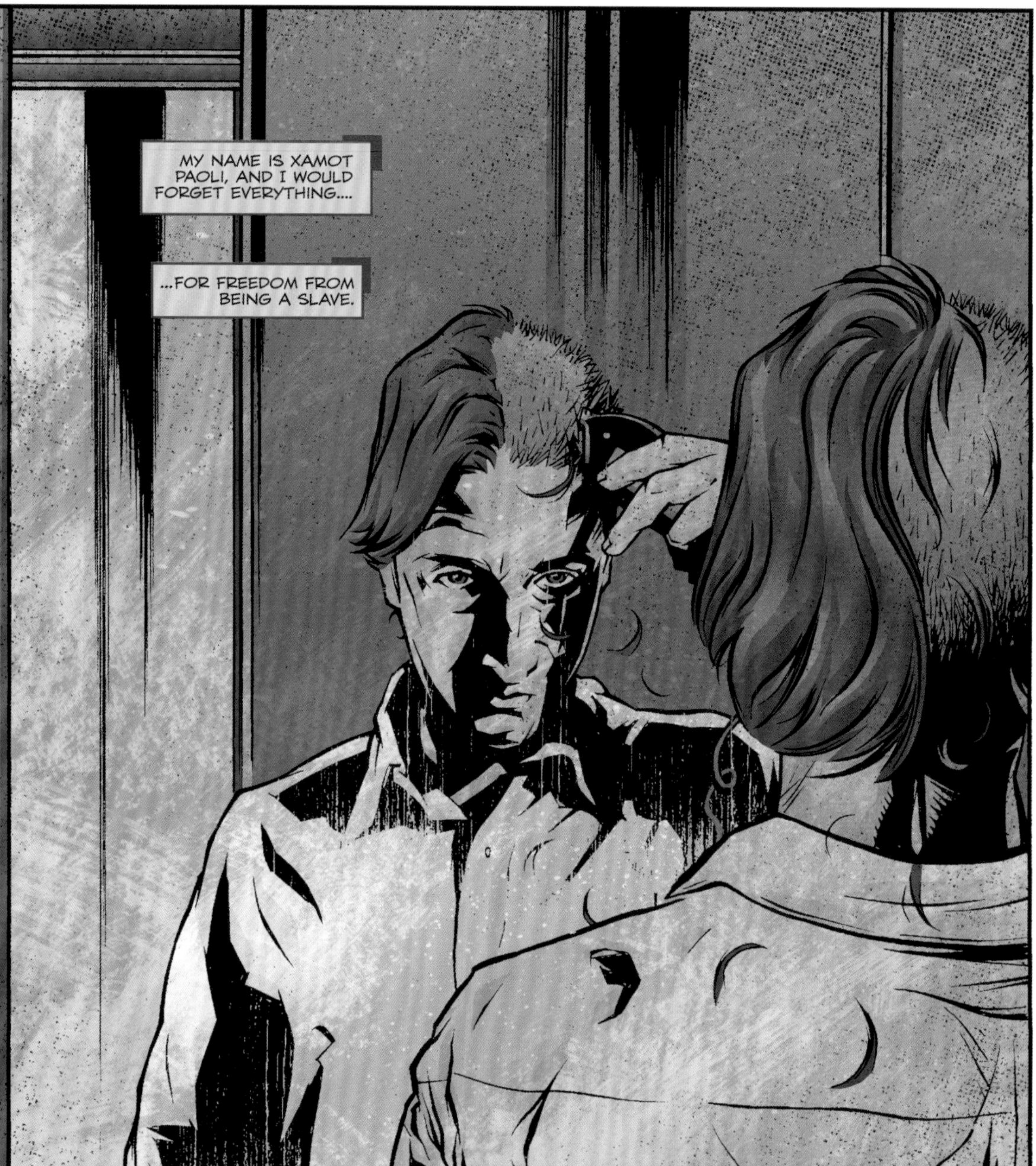
MY NAME IS XAMOT PAOLI, AND I WOULD FORGET EVERYTHING....
...FOR FREEDOM FROM BEING A SLAVE.

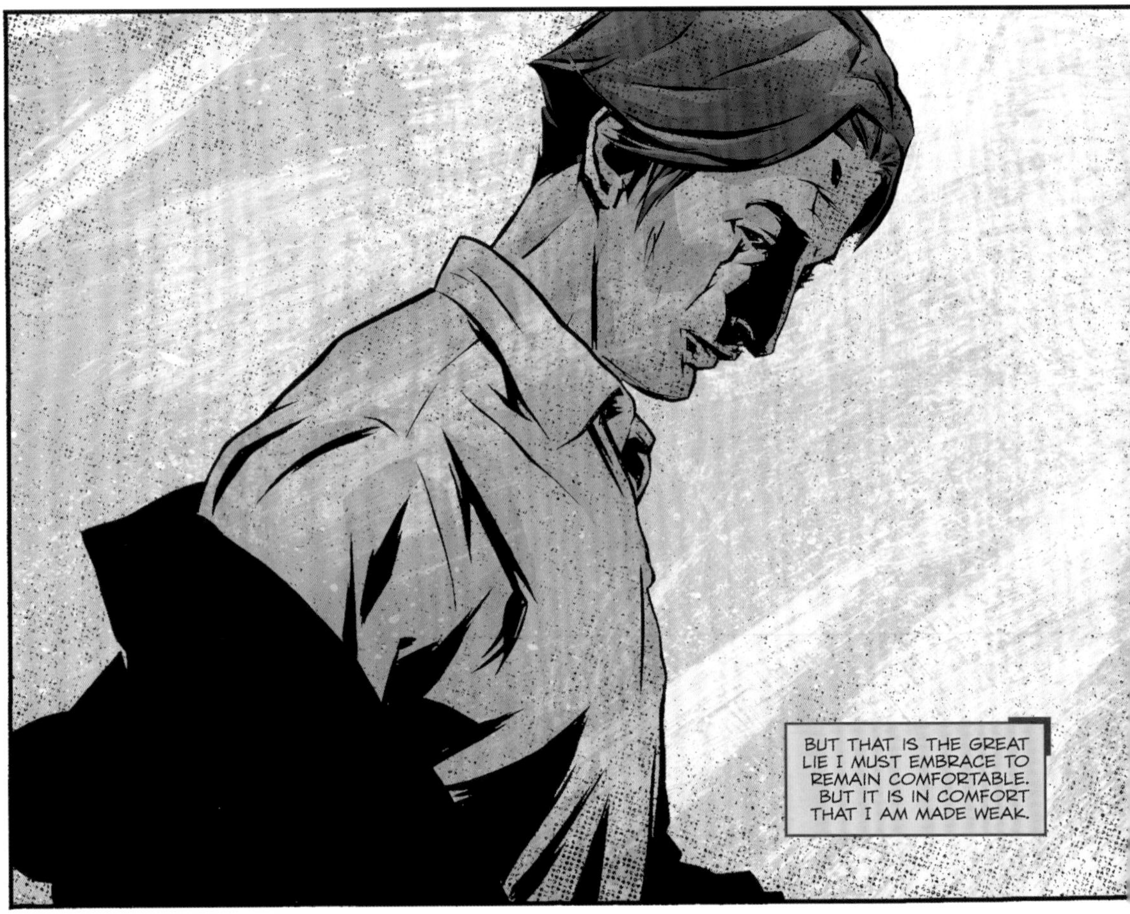
BUT THAT IS THE GREAT LIE I MUST EMBRACE TO REMAIN COMFORTABLE. BUT IT IS IN COMFORT THAT I AM MADE WEAK.

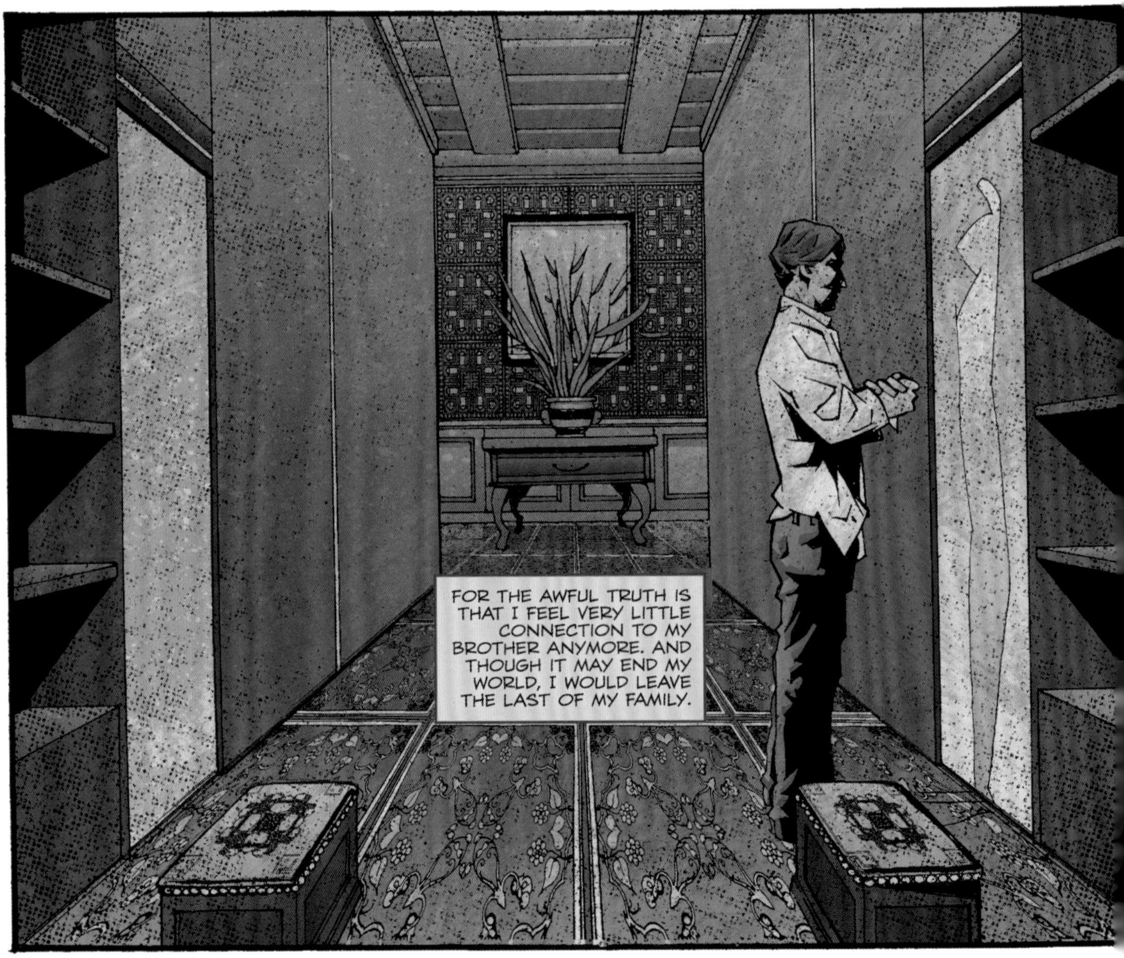
FOR THE AWFUL TRUTH IS THAT I FEEL VERY LITTLE CONNECTION TO MY BROTHER ANYMORE. AND THOUGH IT MAY END MY WORLD, I WOULD LEAVE THE LAST OF MY FAMILY.

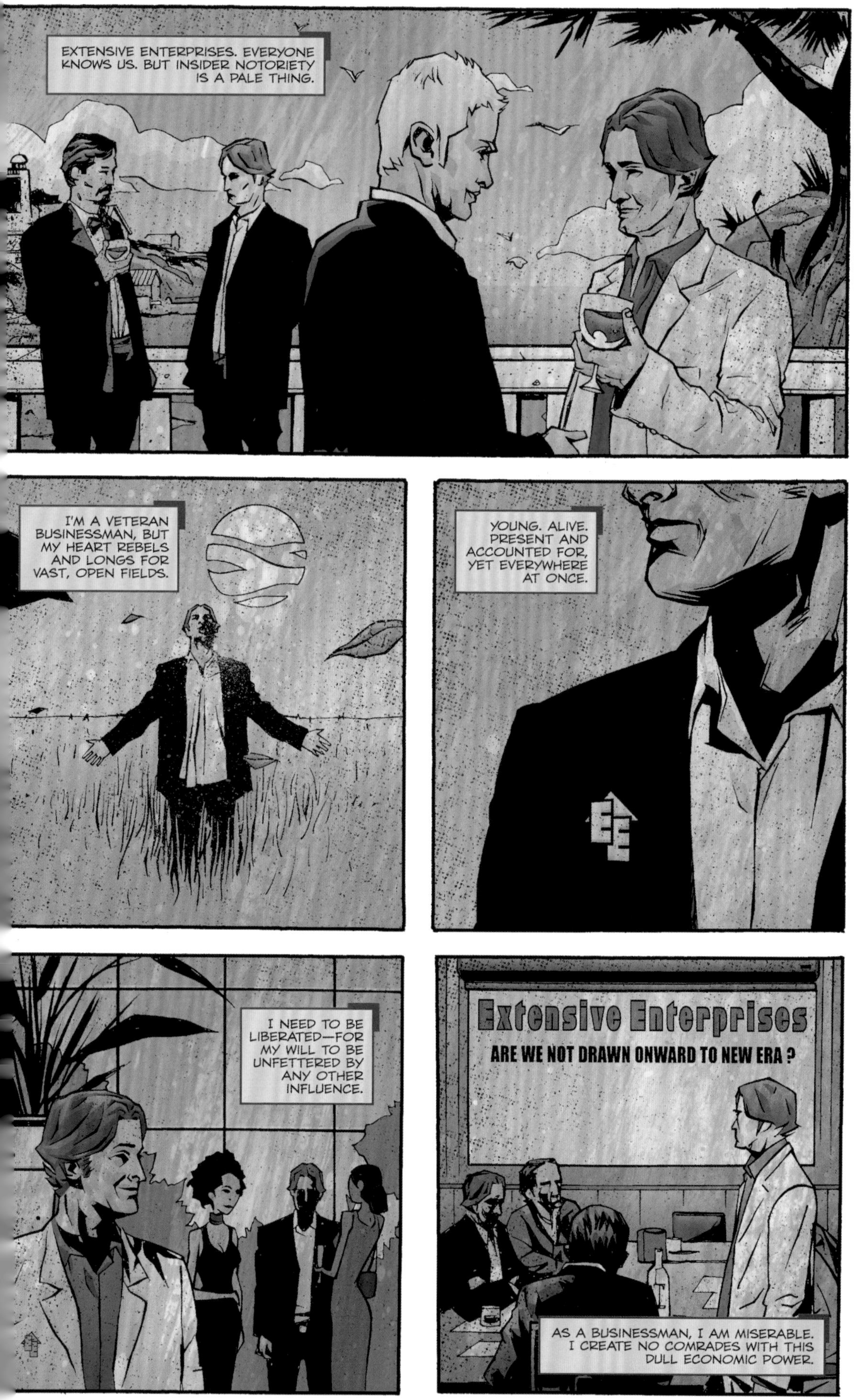
EXTENSIVE ENTERPRISES. EVERYONE KNOWS US. BUT INSIDER NOTORIETY IS A PALE THING.
I'M A VETERAN BUSINESSMAN, BUT MY HEART REBELS AND LONGS FOR VAST, OPEN FIELDS.
YOUNG. ALIVE. PRESENT AND ACCOUNTED FOR, YET EVERYWHERE AT ONCE.
I NEED TO BE LIBERATED—FOR MY WILL TO BE UNFETTERED BY ANY OTHER INFLUENCE.
Extensive Enterprises
ARE WE NOT DRAWN ONWARD TO NEW ERA ?
AS A BUSINESSMAN, I AM MISERABLE. I CREATE NO COMRADES WITH THIS DULL ECONOMIC POWER.

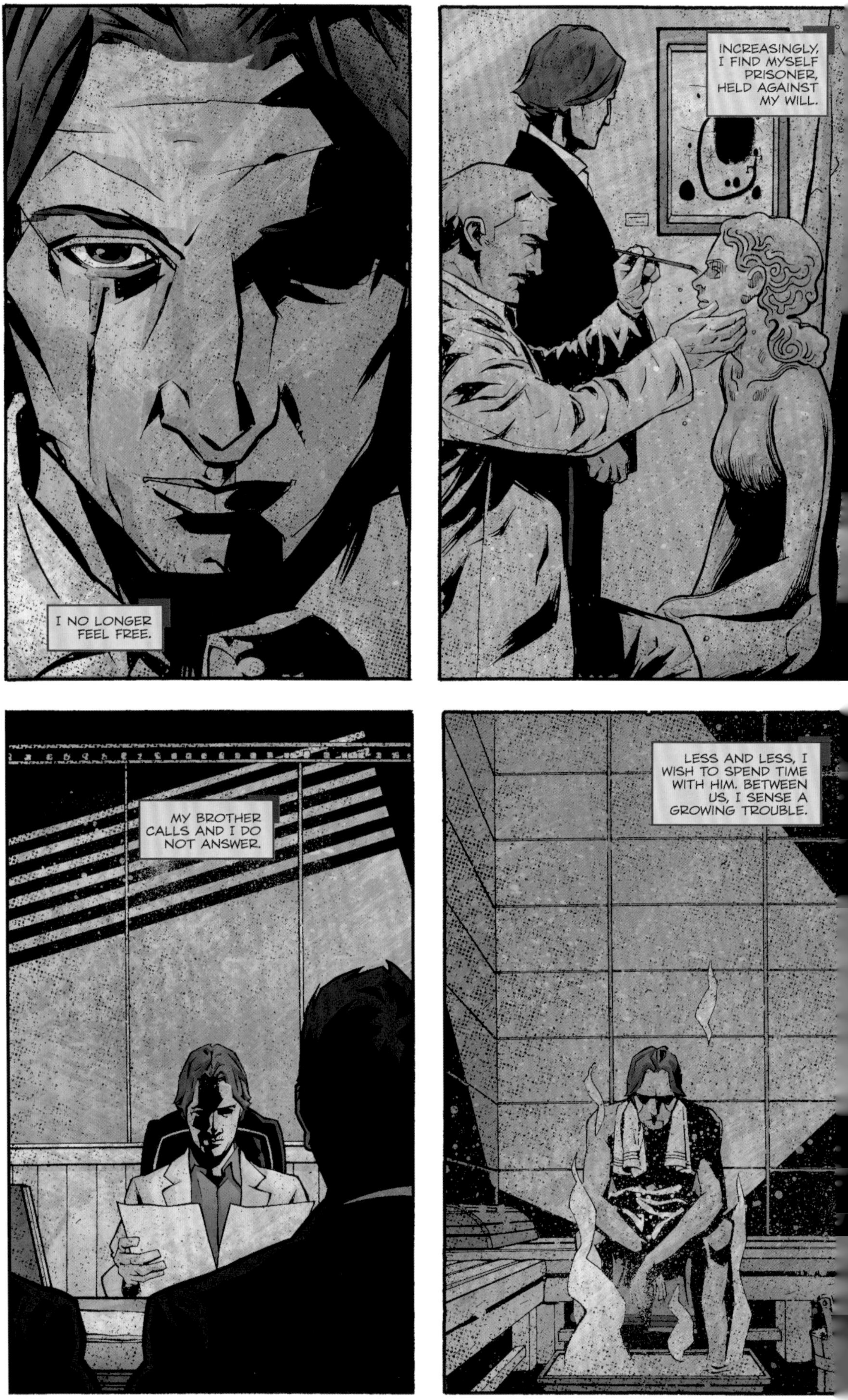
I NO LONGER FEEL FREE.
INCREASINGLY, I FIND MYSELF PRISONER, HELD AGAINST MY WILL.
MY BROTHER CALLS AND I DO NOT ANSWER.
LESS AND LESS, I WISH TO SPEND TIME WITH HIM. BETWEEN US, I SENSE A GROWING TROUBLE.

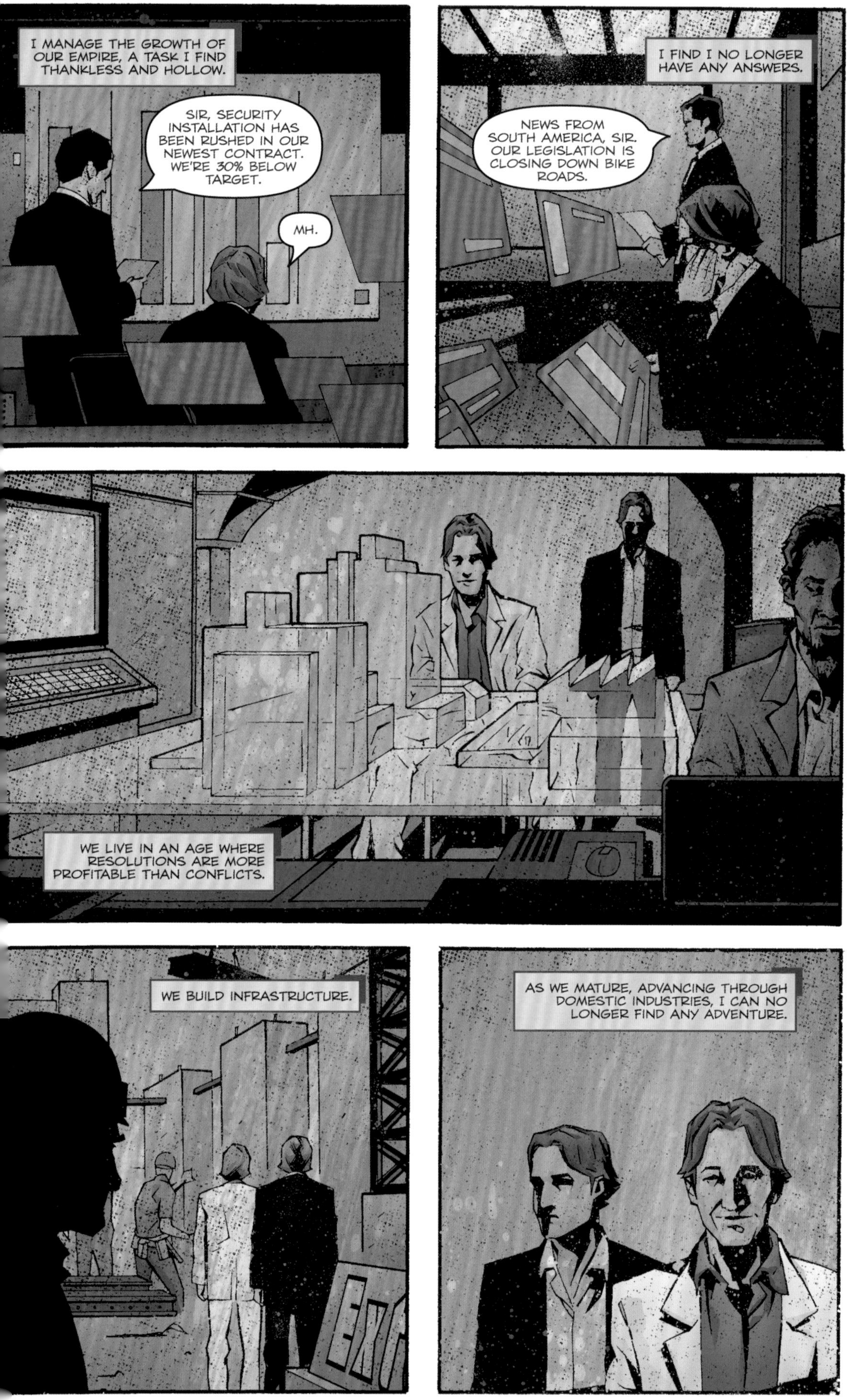

I MANAGE THE GROWTH OF OUR EMPIRE, A TASK I FIND THANKLESS AND HOLLOW.
SIR, SECURITY INSTALLATION HAS BEEN RUSHED IN OUR NEWEST CONTRACT. WE'RE 30% BELOW TARGET.
MH.
I FIND I NO LONGER HAVE ANY ANSWERS.
NEWS FROM SOUTH AMERICA, SIR. OUR LEGISLATION IS CLOSING DOWN BIKE ROADS.
WE LIVE IN AN AGE WHERE RESOLUTIONS ARE MORE PROFITABLE THAN CONFLICTS.
WE BUILD INFRASTRUCTURE.
AS WE MATURE, ADVANCING THROUGH DOMESTIC INDUSTRIES, I CAN NO LONGER FIND ANY ADVENTURE.

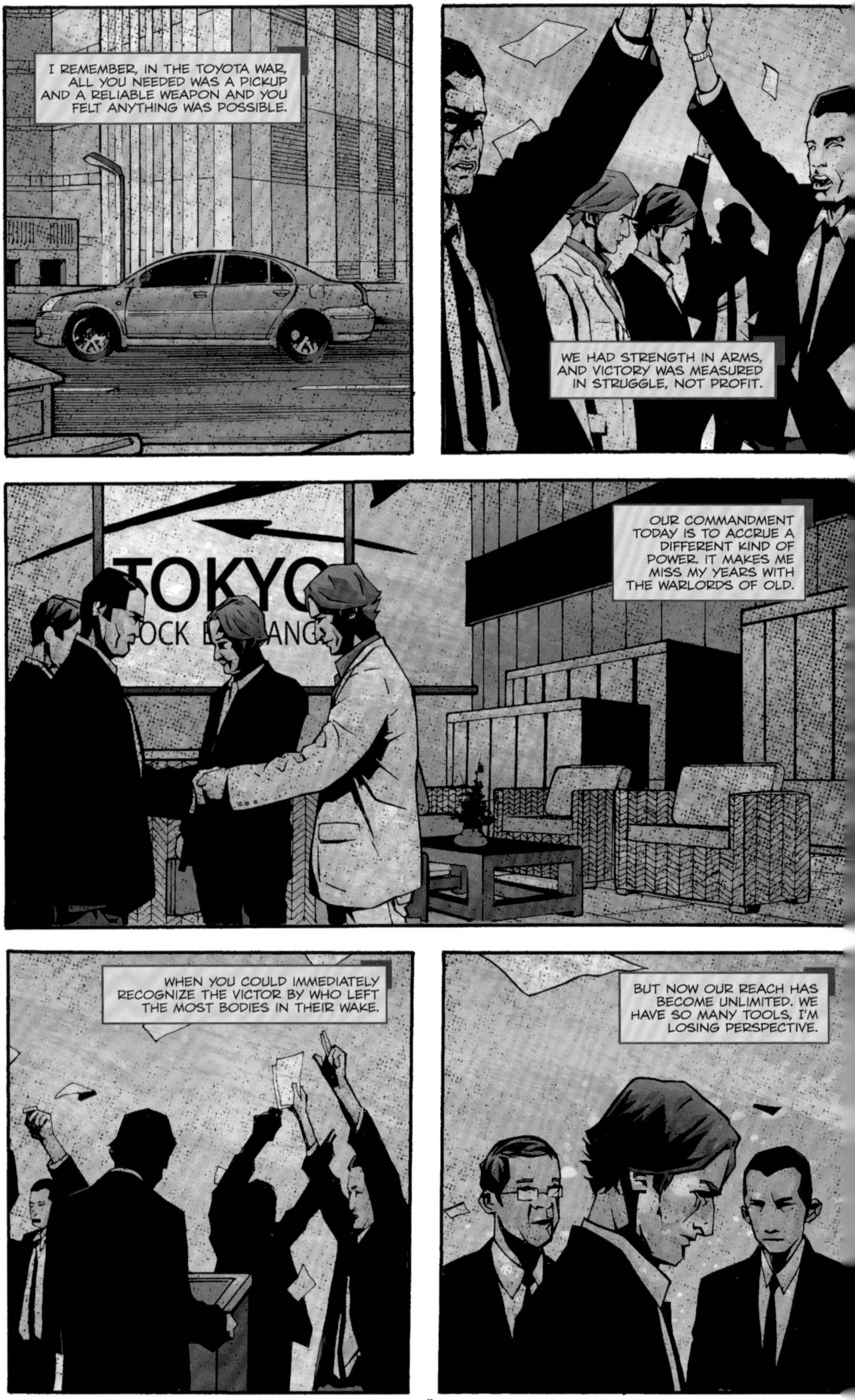
I REMEMBER, IN THE TOYOTA WAR, ALL YOU NEEDED WAS A PICKUP AND A RELIABLE WEAPON AND YOU FELT ANYTHING WAS POSSIBLE.
WE HAD STRENGTH IN ARMS, AND VICTORY WAS MEASURED IN STRUGGLE, NOT PROFIT.
OUR COMMANDMENT TODAY IS TO ACCRUE A DIFFERENT KIND OF POWER. IT MAKES ME MISS MY YEARS WITH THE WARLORDS OF OLD.
WHEN YOU COULD IMMEDIATELY RECOGNIZE THE VICTOR BY WHO LEFT THE MOST BODIES IN THEIR WAKE.
BUT NOW OUR REACH HAS BECOME UNLIMITED. WE HAVE SO MANY TOOLS, I'M LOSING PERSPECTIVE.

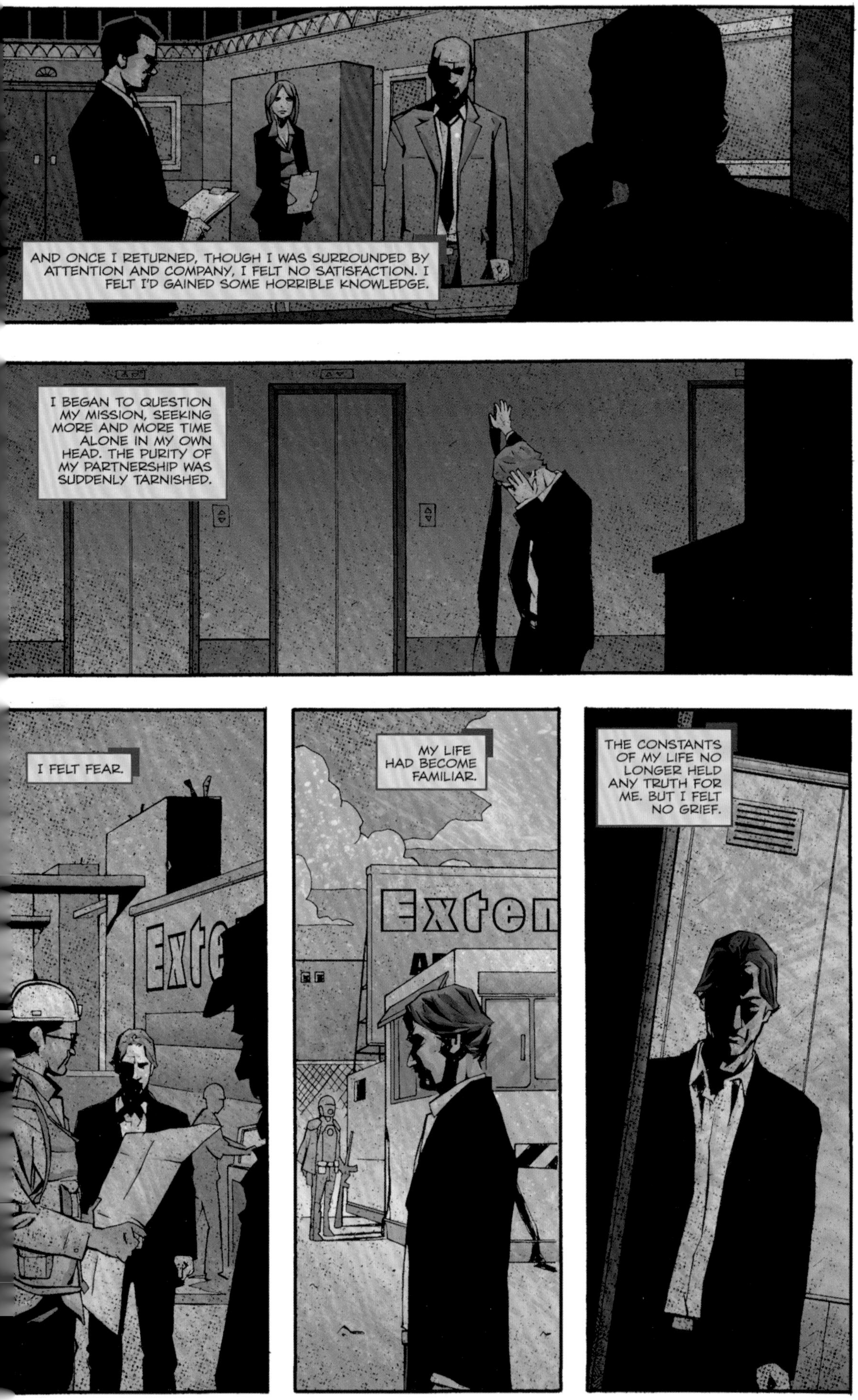
AND ONCE I RETURNED, THOUGH I WAS SURROUNDED BY ATTENTION AND COMPANY, I FELT NO SATISFACTION. I FELT I'D GAINED SOME HORRIBLE KNOWLEDGE.
I BEGAN TO QUESTION MY MISSION, SEEKING MORE AND MORE TIME ALONE IN MY OWN HEAD. THE PURITY OF MY PARTNERSHIP WAS SUDDENLY TARNISHED.
I FELT FEAR.
MY LIFE HAD BECOME FAMILIAR.
THE CONSTANTS OF MY LIFE NO LONGER HELD ANY TRUTH FOR ME. BUT I FELT NO GRIEF.

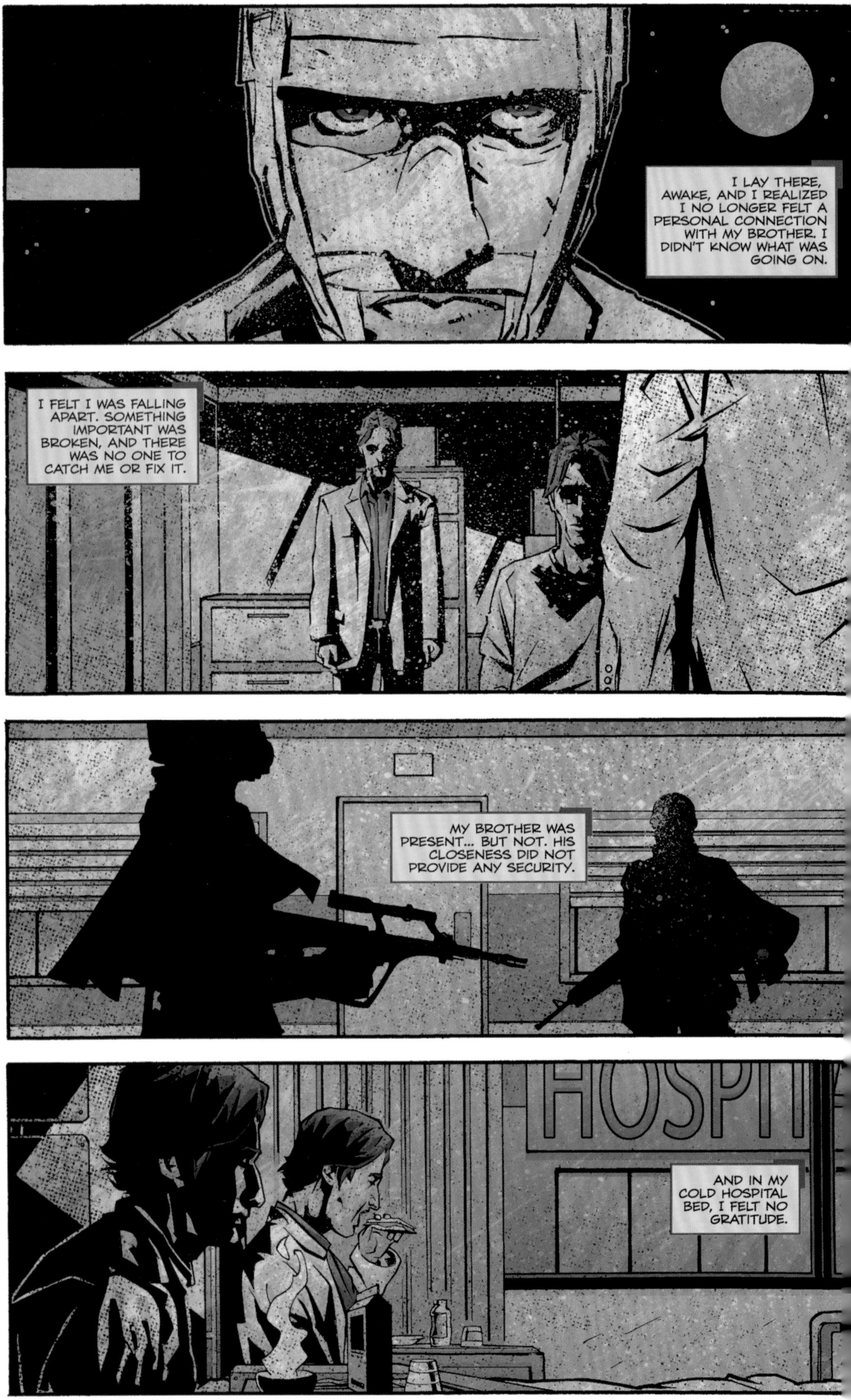
I LAY THERE, AWAKE, AND I REALIZED I NO LONGER FELT A PERSONAL CONNECTION WITH MY BROTHER. I DIDN'T KNOW WHAT WAS GOING ON.
I FELT I WAS FALLING APART. SOMETHING IMPORTANT WAS BROKEN, AND THERE WAS NO ONE TO CATCH ME OR FIX IT.
MY BROTHER WAS PRESENT... BUT NOT. HIS CLOSENESS DID NOT PROVIDE ANY SECURITY.
AND IN MY COLD HOSPITAL BED, I FELT NO GRATITUDE.

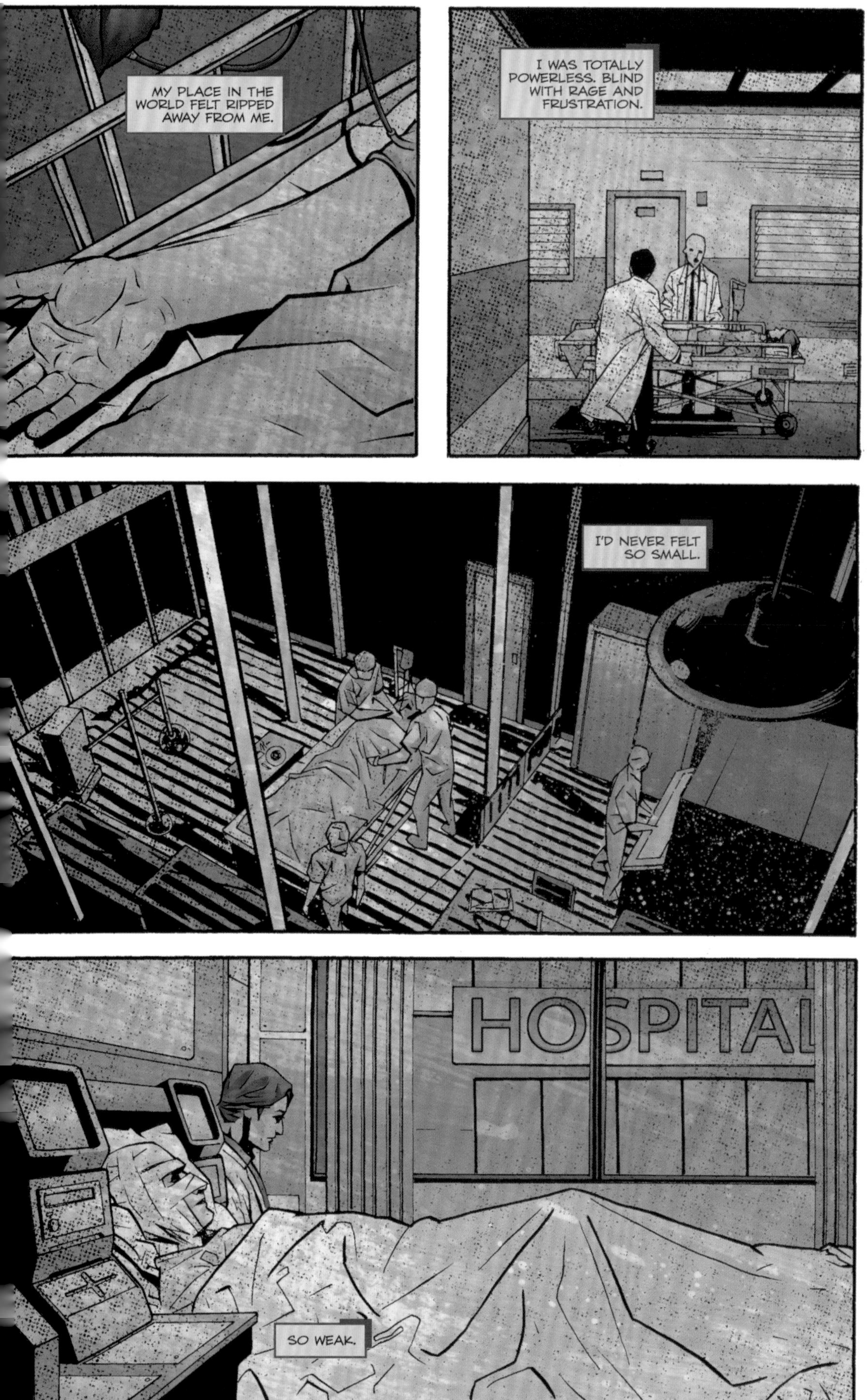
MY PLACE IN THE WORLD FELT RIPPED AWAY FROM ME.
I WAS TOTALLY POWERLESS. BLIND WITH RAGE AND FRUSTRATION.
I'D NEVER FELT SO SMALL.
HOSPITAL
SO WEAK.

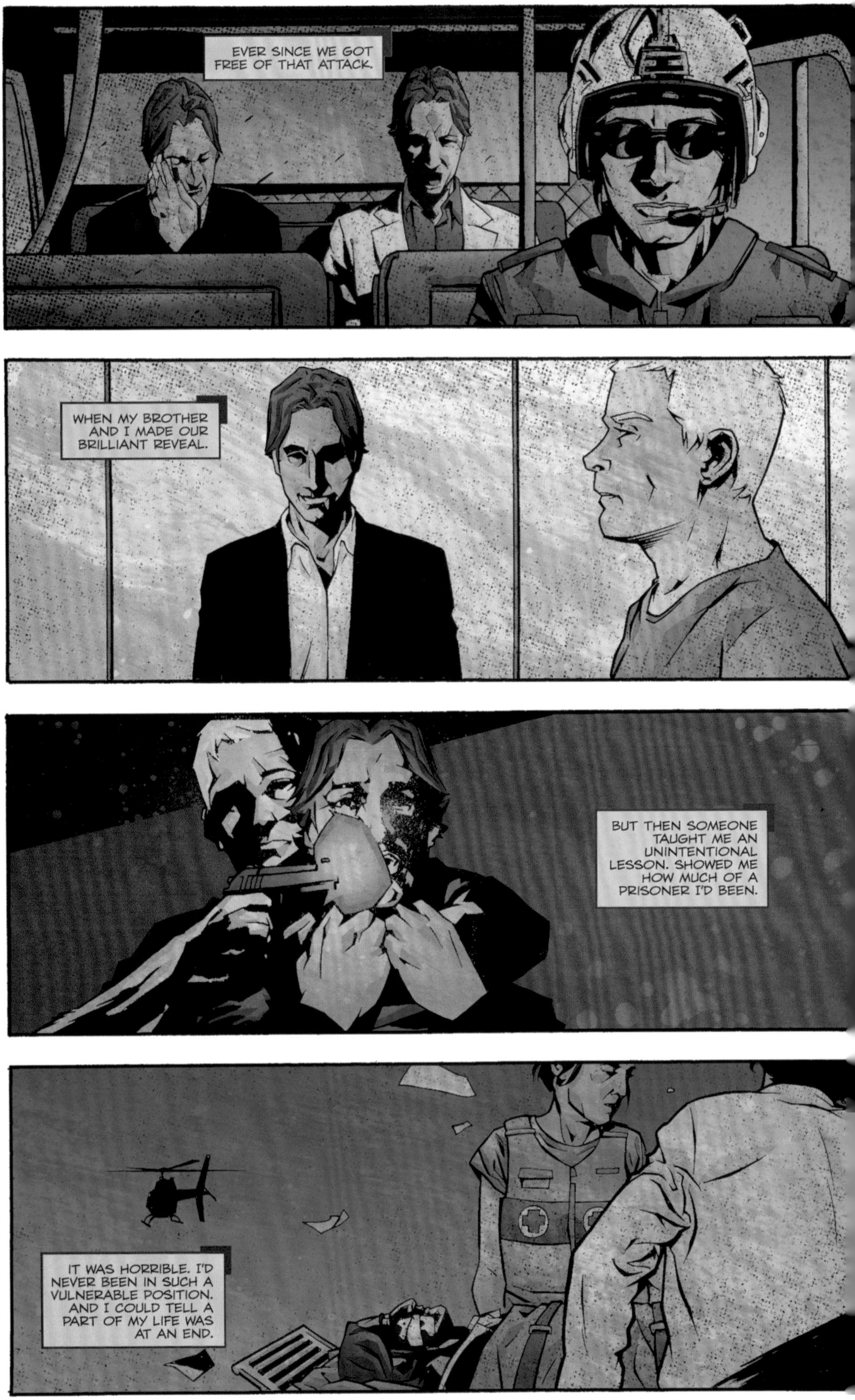
EVER SINCE WE GOT FREE OF THAT ATTACK.
WHEN MY BROTHER AND I MADE OUR BRILLIANT REVEAL.
BUT THEN SOMEONE TAUGHT ME AN UNINTENTIONAL LESSON. SHOWED ME HOW MUCH OF A PRISONER I'D BEEN.
IT WAS HORRIBLE. I'D NEVER BEEN IN SUCH A VULNERABLE POSITION. AND I COULD TELL A PART OF MY LIFE WAS AT AN END.

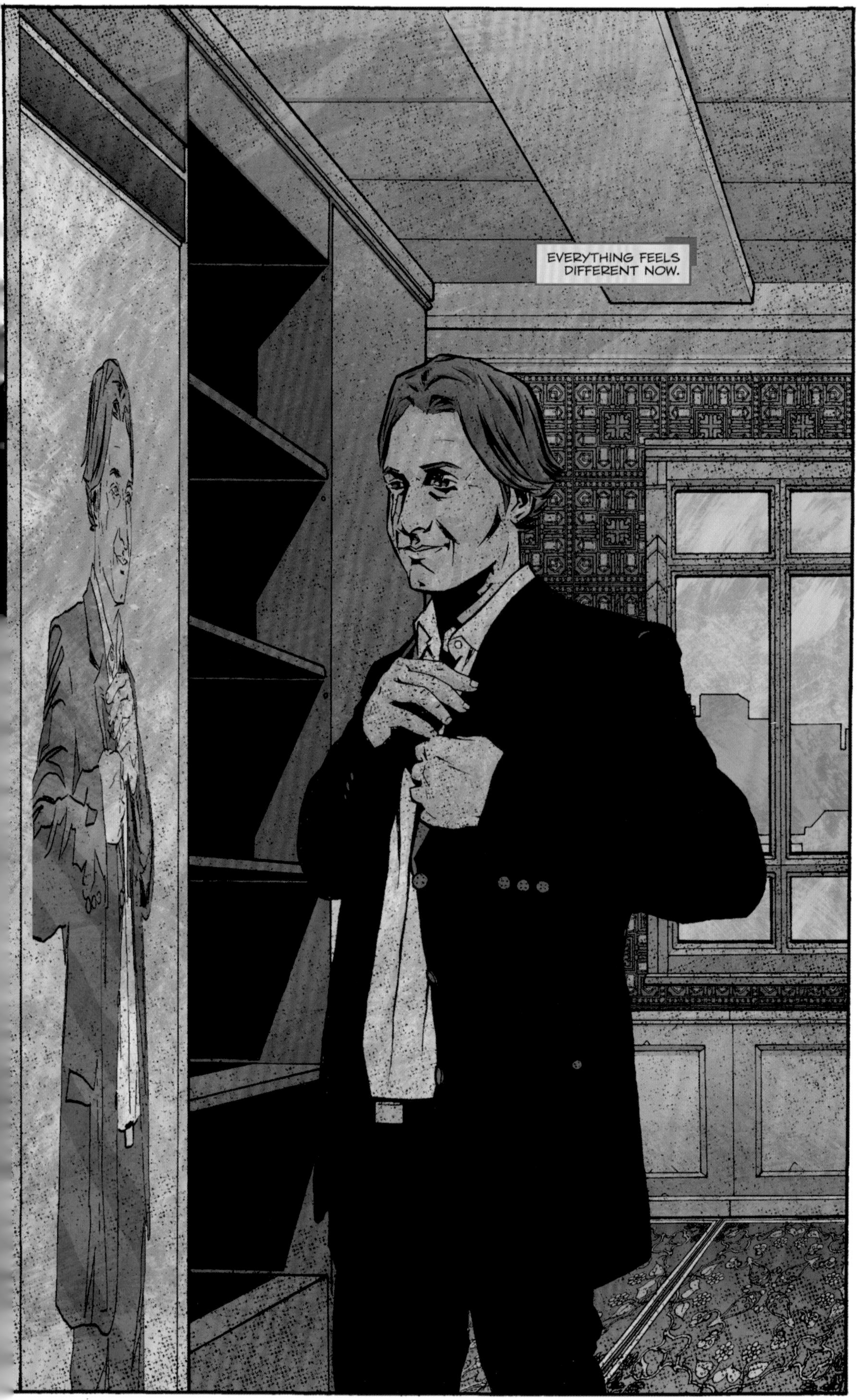
EVERYTHING FEELS DIFFERENT NOW.

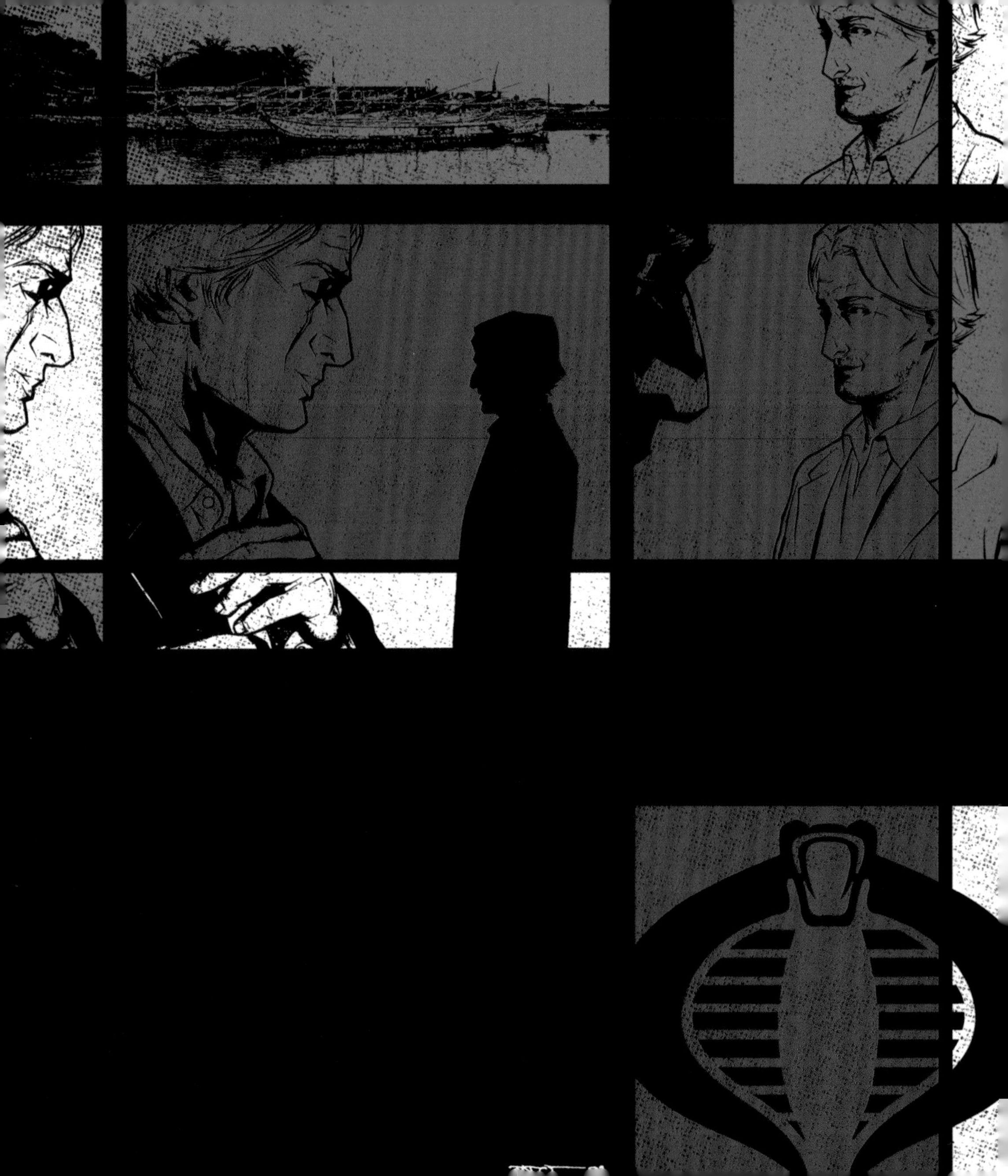

Art by Antonio Fuso

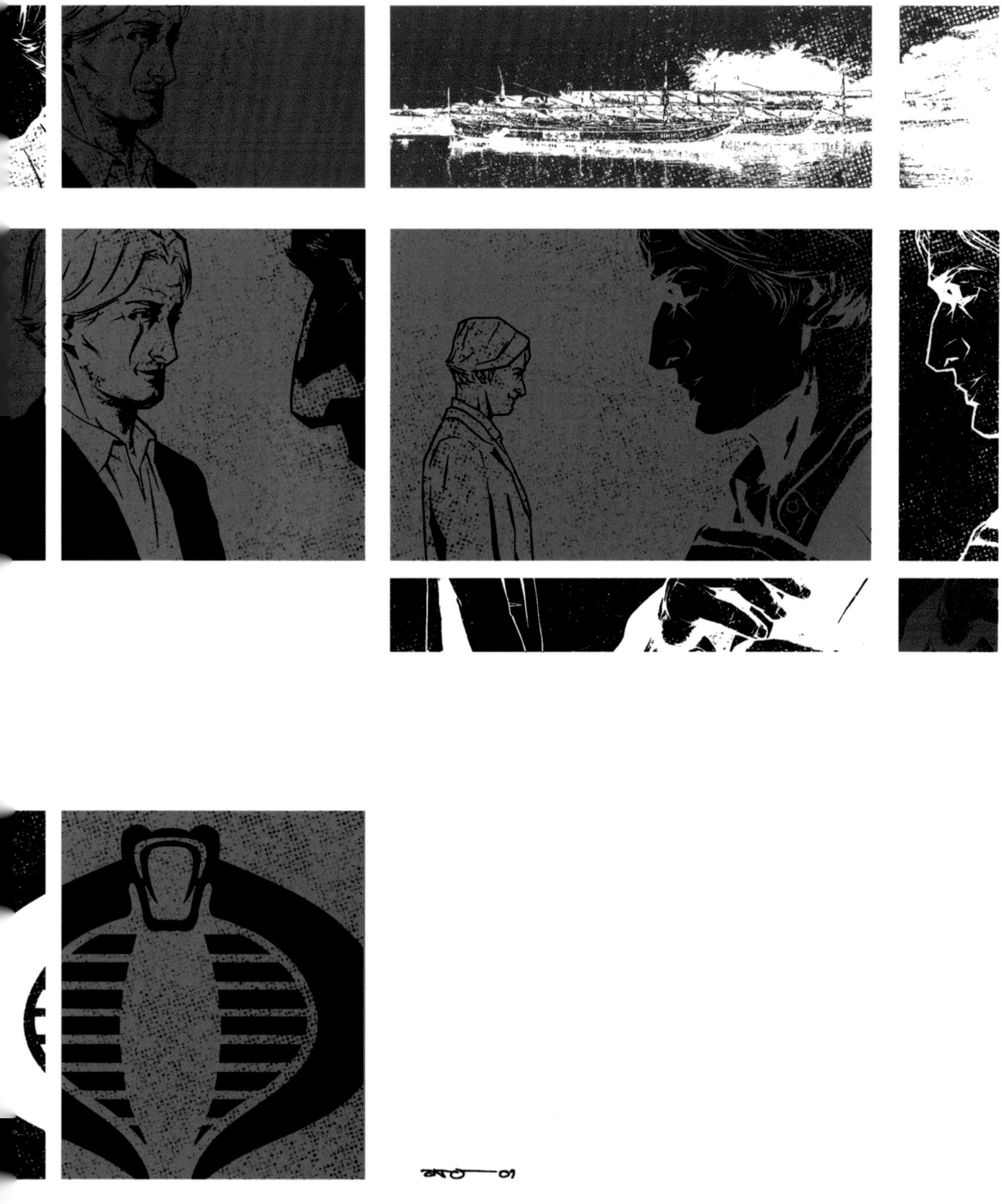

# CRIMSON GUARD

In addition to a new look at COBRA, the elite members of the Crimson Guard also got a makeover. Here are a few concept designs for the new guard uniform. Note that the helmet, while different, still retains some similar themes.

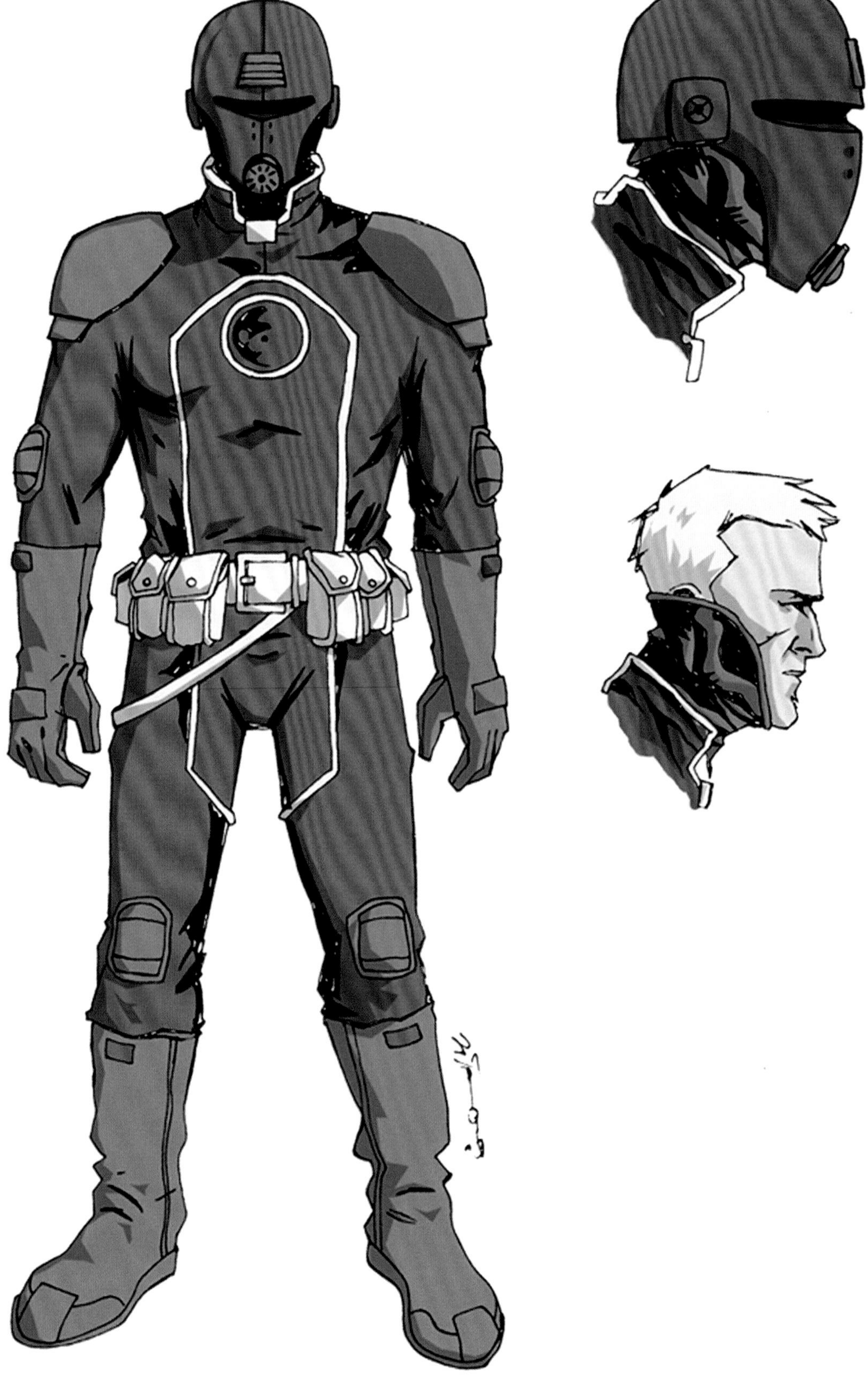

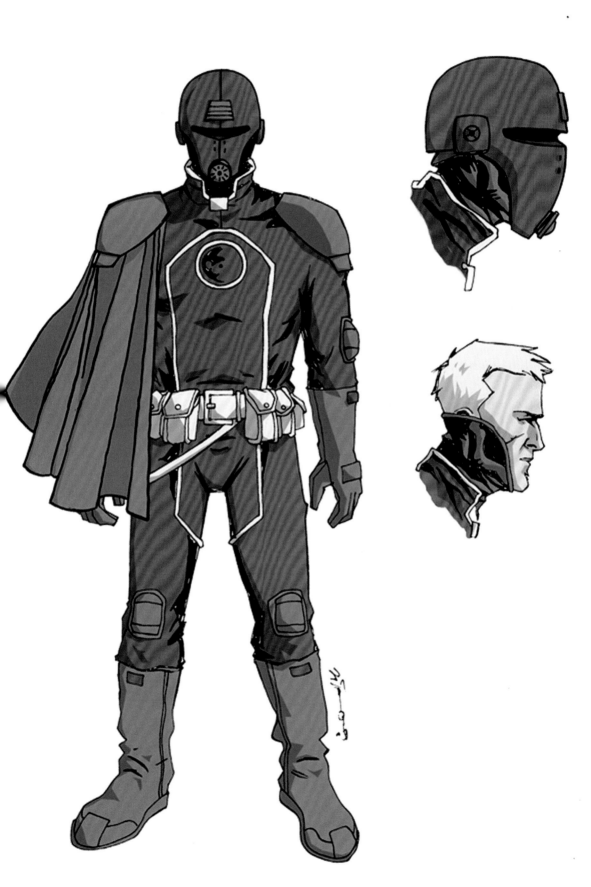

# THE DESIGN OF TOMAX & XAMOT

Expanding upon the mirrored appearance of the book's main characters, here's a look at the reflected pages of the *G.I. JOE: COBRA SPECIAL—TOMAX AND XAMOT.*

MY NAME IS TOMAX PAOLI, AND THERE IS SOMETHING I'VE LEARNED...
...SLAVERY IS FREEDOM.

MY NAME IS XAMOT PAOLI, AND I WOULD FORGET EVERYTHING...
...FOR FREEDOM FROM BEING A SLAVE.

THIS IS THE GREAT TRUTH THAT SO MANY RUN FROM. THEY FEAR IT. BUT THE TRUTH IS TERRIFYING BECAUSE IT IS POWERFUL.
THE AWFUL LIE OF FREE WILL IS EXPOSED IN THE UNBREAKABLE CONNECTION BETWEEN MY BROTHER AND MYSELF. AND HOW WE BEGAN TO BUILD OUR WORLD WITH OUR FIRST FAMILY.

BUT THAT IS THE GREAT LIE I MUST EMBRACE TO REMAIN COMFORTABLE. BUT IT IS IN COMFORT THAT I AM MADE WEAK.
FOR THE AWFUL TRUTH IS THAT I FEEL VERY LITTLE CONNECTION TO MY BROTHER ANYMORE. AND THOUGH IT MAY END MY WORLD, I WOULD LEAVE THE LAST OF MY FAMILY.

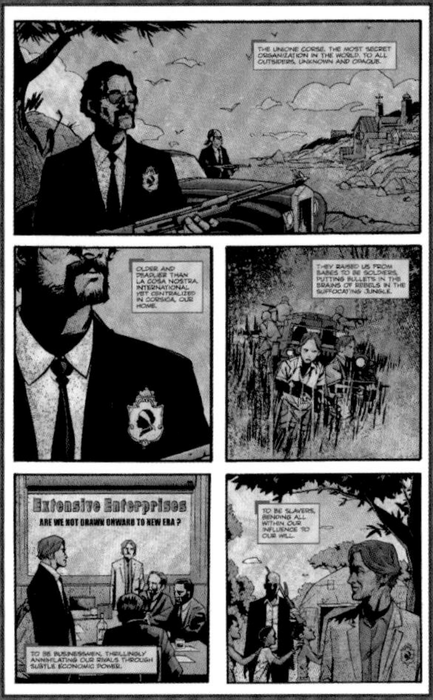
THE UNIONE CORSE. THE MOST SECRET ORGANIZATION IN THE WORLD. TO ALL OUTSIDERS, UNKNOWN AND OPAQUE.
OLDER AND DEADLIER THAN LA COSA NOSTRA. INTERNATIONAL YET CENTRALIZED IN CORSICA, OUR HOME.
THEY RAISED US FROM BABES TO BE SOLDIERS, PUTTING BULLETS IN THE BRAINS OF REBELS IN THE SUFFOCATING JUNGLE.
Extensive Enterprises
ARE WE NOT DRAWN ONWARD TO NEW ERA ?
TO BE BUSINESSMEN, THRILLINGLY ANNIHILATING OUR RIVALS THROUGH SUBTLE ECONOMIC POWER.
TO BE SLAVERS, BENDING ALL WITHIN OUR INFLUENCE TO OUR WILL.

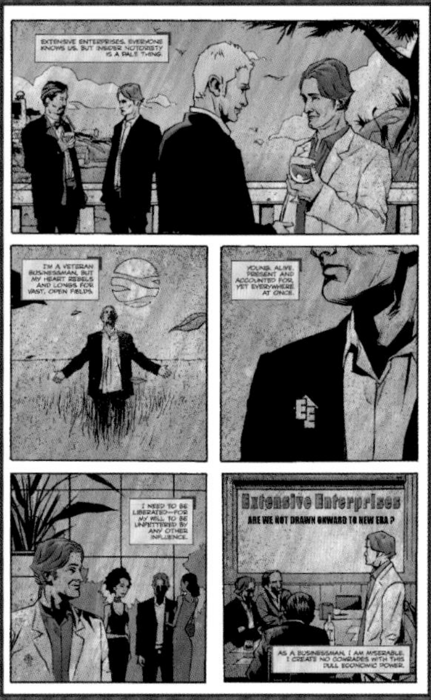
EXTENSIVE ENTERPRISES. EVERYONE KNOWS US. BUT INSIDER NOTORIETY IS A PALE THING.
I'M A VETERAN BUSINESSMAN, BUT MY HEART REBELS AND LONGS FOR VAST, OPEN FIELDS.
YOUNG. ALIVE. PRESENT AND ACCOUNTED FOR, YET EVERYWHERE AT ONCE.
I NEED TO BE LIBERATED—FOR MY WILL TO BE UNFETTERED BY ANY OTHER INFLUENCE.
Extensive Enterprises
ARE WE NOT DRAWN ONWARD TO NEW ERA ?
AS A BUSINESSMAN, I AM MISERABLE. I CREATE NO COMRADES WITH THIS DULL ECONOMIC POWER.

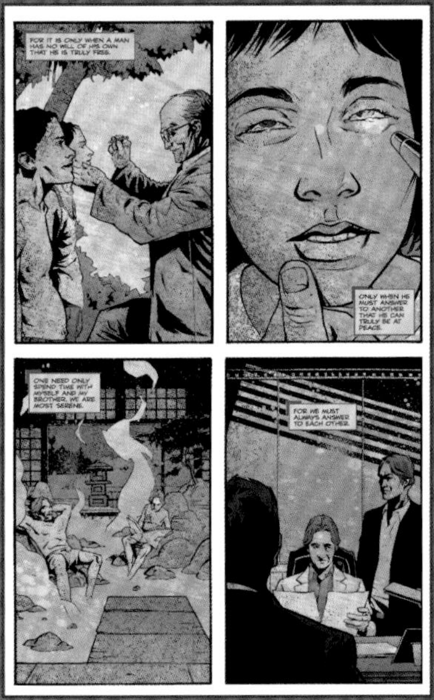
FOR IT IS ONLY WHEN A MAN HAS NO WILL OF HIS OWN THAT HE IS TRULY FREE.
ONLY WHEN HE MUST ANSWER TO ANOTHER THAT HE CAN TRULY BE AT PEACE.
ONE NEED ONLY SPEND TIME WITH MYSELF AND MY BROTHER. WE ARE MOST SERENE.
FOR WE MUST ALWAYS ANSWER TO EACH OTHER.

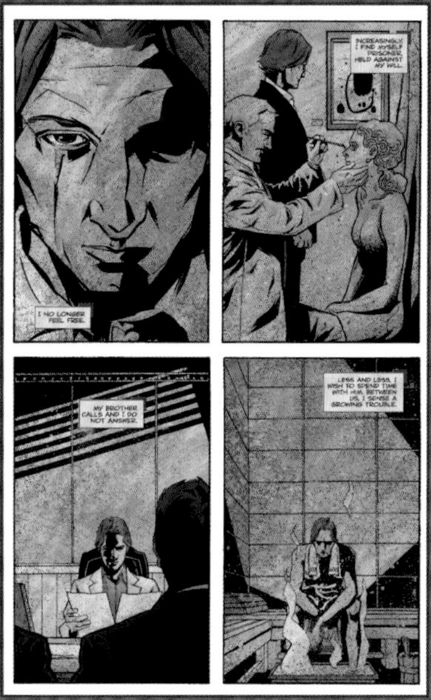
I NO LONGER FEEL FREE.
INCREASINGLY, I FIND MYSELF PRISONER, HELD AGAINST MY WILL.
MY BROTHER CALLS AND I DO NOT ANSWER.
LESS AND LESS, I WISH TO SPEND TIME WITH HIM. BETWEEN US, I SENSE A GROWING TROUBLE.

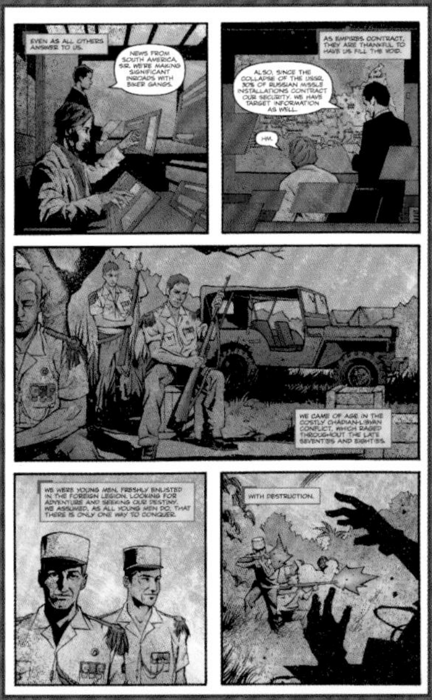
EVEN AS ALL OTHERS ANSWER TO US.
NEWS FROM SOUTH AMERICA, SIR. WE'RE MAKING SIGNIFICANT INROADS WITH BIKER GANGS.
AS EMPIRES CONTRACT, THEY ARE THANKFUL TO HAVE US FILL THE VOID.
ALSO, SINCE THE COLLAPSE OF THE USSR, 30% OF RUSSIAN MISSLE INSTALLATIONS CONTRACT OUR SECURITY. WE HAVE TARGET INFORMATION AS WELL.
HM.
WE CAME OF AGE IN THE COSTLY CHADIAN-LIBYAN CONFLICT, WHICH RAGED THROUGHOUT THE LATE SEVENTIES AND EIGHTIES.
WE WERE YOUNG MEN, FRESHLY ENLISTED IN THE FOREIGN LEGION, LOOKING FOR ADVENTURE AND SEEKING OUR DESTINY. WE ASSUMED, AS ALL YOUNG MEN DO, THAT THERE IS ONLY ONE WAY TO CONQUER.
WITH DESTRUCTION.

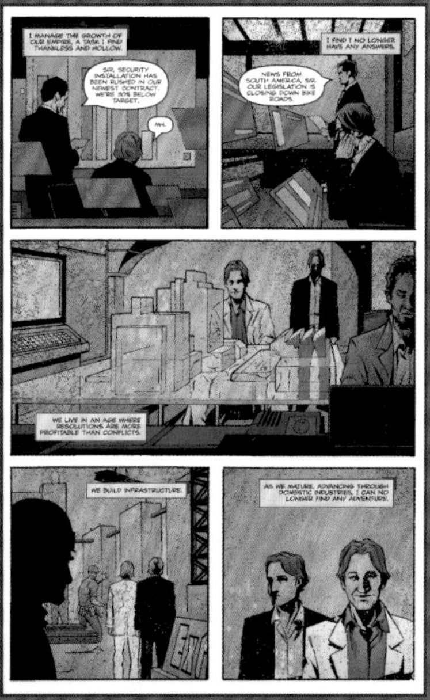
I MANAGE THE GROWTH OF OUR EMPIRE, A TASK I FIND THANKLESS AND HOLLOW.
SIR, SECURITY INSTALLATION HAS BEEN RUSHED IN OUR NEWEST CONTRACT. WE'RE 30% BELOW TARGET.
MH.
I FIND I NO LONGER HAVE ANY ANSWERS.
NEWS FROM SOUTH AMERICA, SIR. OUR LEGISLATION IS CLOSING DOWN BIKE ROADS.
WE LIVE IN AN AGE WHERE RESOLUTIONS ARE MORE PROFITABLE THAN CONFLICTS.
WE BUILD INFRASTRUCTURE.
AS WE MATURE, ADVANCING THROUGH DOMESTIC INDUSTRIES, I CAN NO LONGER FIND ANY ADVENTURE.

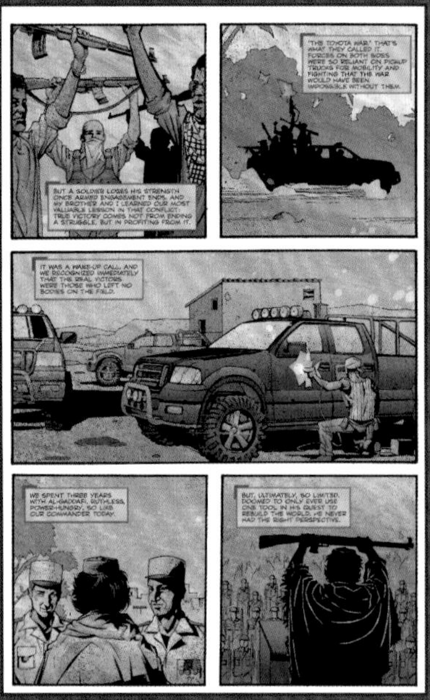
BUT A SOLDIER LOSES HIS STRENGTH ONCE ARMED ENGAGEMENT ENDS, AND MY BROTHER AND I LEARNED OUR MOST VALUABLE LESSON IN THAT CONFLICT: TRUE VICTORY COMES NOT FROM ENDING A STRUGGLE, BUT IN PROFITING FROM IT.
"THE TOYOTA WAR," THAT'S WHAT THEY CALLED IT. FORCES ON BOTH SIDES WERE SO RELIANT ON PICKUP TRUCKS FOR MOBILITY AND FIGHTING THAT THE WAR WOULD HAVE BEEN IMPOSSIBLE WITHOUT THEM.
IT WAS A WAKE-UP CALL, AND WE RECOGNIZED IMMEDIATELY THAT THE REAL VICTORS WERE THOSE WHO LEFT NO BODIES ON THE FIELD.
WE SPENT THREE YEARS WITH AL-QADDAFI. RUTHLESS, POWER-HUNGRY, SO LIKE OUR COMMANDER TODAY.
BUT, ULTIMATELY, SO LIMITED. DOOMED TO ONLY EVER USE ONE TOOL IN HIS QUEST TO REBUILD THE WORLD. HE NEVER HAD THE RIGHT PERSPECTIVE.

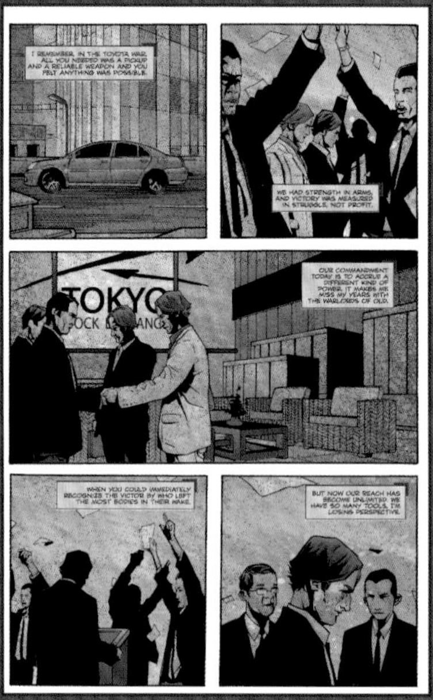
I REMEMBER, IN THE TOYOTA WAR, ALL YOU NEEDED WAS A PICKUP AND A RELIABLE WEAPON AND YOU FELT ANYTHING WAS POSSIBLE.
WE HAD STRENGTH IN ARMS, AND VICTORY WAS MEASURED IN STRUGGLE, NOT PROFIT.
OUR COMMANDMENT TODAY IS TO ACCRUE A DIFFERENT KIND OF POWER. IT MAKES ME MISS MY YEARS WITH THE WARLORDS OF OLD.
WHEN YOU COULD IMMEDIATELY RECOGNIZE THE VICTOR BY WHO LEFT THE MOST BODIES IN THEIR WAKE.
BUT NOW OUR REACH HAS BECOME UNLIMITED. WE HAVE SO MANY TOOLS, I'M LOSING PERSPECTIVE.

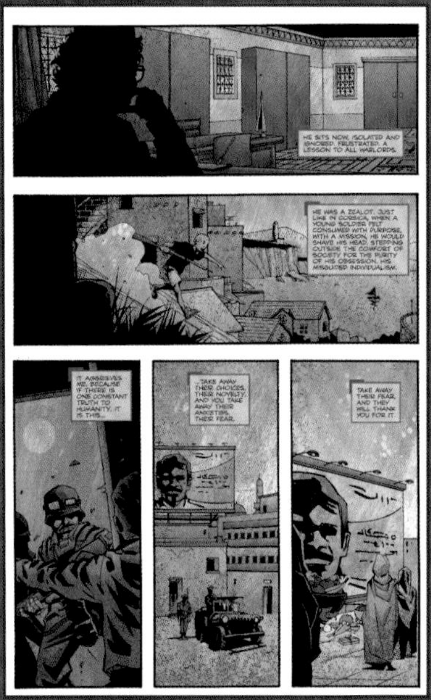
HE SITS NOW, ISOLATED AND IGNORED. FRUSTRATED. A LESSON TO ALL WARLORDS.
HE WAS A ZEALOT. JUST LIKE IN CORSICA, WHEN A YOUNG SOLDIER FELT CONSUMED WITH PURPOSE, WITH A MISSION, HE WOULD SHAVE HIS HEAD, STEPPING OUTSIDE THE COMFORT OF SOCIETY FOR THE PURITY OF HIS OBSESSION. HIS MISGUIDED INDIVIDUALISM.
IT AGGRIEVES ME, BECAUSE IF THERE IS ONE CONSTANT TRUTH TO HUMANITY, IT IS THIS...
...TAKE AWAY THEIR CHOICES, THEIR NOVELTY, AND YOU TAKE AWAY THEIR ANXIETIES, THEIR FEAR.
TAKE AWAY THEIR FEAR, AND THEY WILL THANK YOU FOR IT.

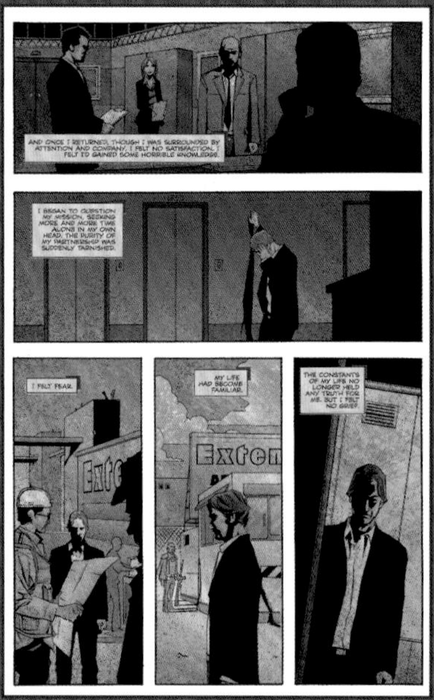
AND ONCE I RETURNED, THOUGH I WAS SURROUNDED BY ATTENTION AND COMPANY, I FELT NO SATISFACTION. I FELT I'D GAINED SOME HORRIBLE KNOWLEDGE.
I BEGAN TO QUESTION MY MISSION, SEEKING MORE AND MORE TIME ALONE IN MY OWN HEAD. THE PURITY OF MY PARTNERSHIP WAS SUDDENLY TARNISHED.
I FELT FEAR.
MY LIFE HAD BECOME FAMILIAR.
THE CONSTANTS OF MY LIFE NO LONGER HELD ANY TRUTH FOR ME. BUT I FELT NO GRIEF.

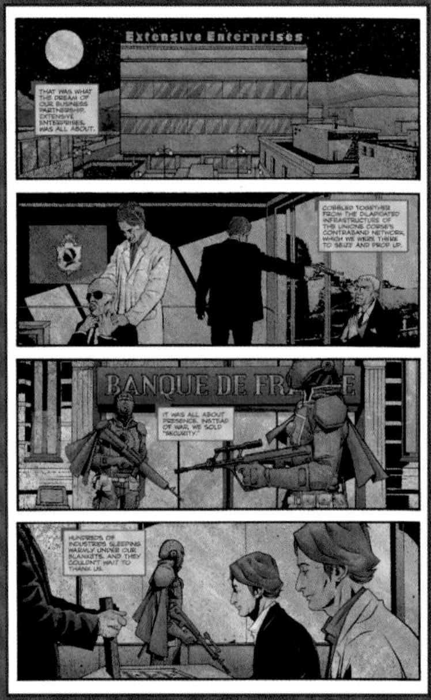
Extensive Enterprises
THAT WAS WHAT THE DREAM OF OUR BUSINESS PARTNERSHIP, EXTENSIVE ENTERPRISES, WAS ALL ABOUT.
COBBLED TOGETHER FROM THE DILAPIDATED INFRASTRUCTURE OF THE UNIONE CORSE'S CONTRABAND NETWORK, WHICH WE WERE THERE TO SEIZE AND PROP UP.
IT WAS ALL ABOUT PRESENCE. INSTEAD OF WAR, WE SOLD "SECURITY."
HUNDREDS OF INDUSTRIES SLEEPING WARMLY UNDER OUR BLANKETS. AND THEY COULDN'T WAIT TO THANK US.

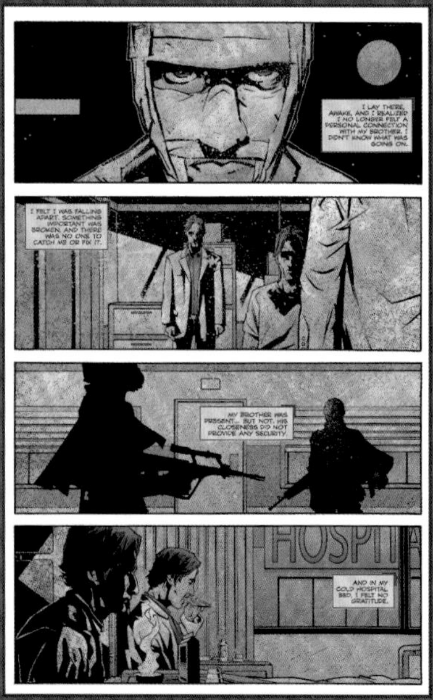
I LAY THERE, AWAKE, AND I REALIZED I NO LONGER FELT A PERSONAL CONNECTION WITH MY BROTHER. I DIDN'T KNOW WHAT WAS GOING ON.
I FELT I WAS FALLING APART. SOMETHING IMPORTANT HAS BROKEN, AND THERE WAS NO ONE TO CATCH ME OR FIX IT.
MY BROTHER WAS PRESENT... BUT NOT. HIS CLOSENESS DID NOT PROVIDE ANY SECURITY.
AND IN MY COLD HOSPITAL BED, I FELT NO GRATITUDE.

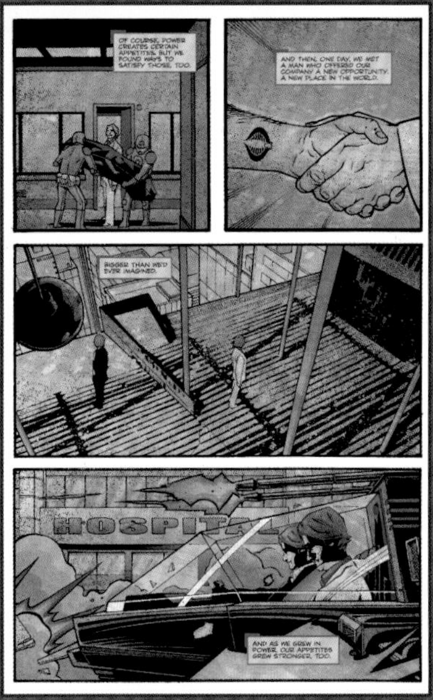
OF COURSE, POWER CREATES CERTAIN APPETITES. BUT WE FOUND WAYS TO SATISFY THOSE, TOO.
AND THEN, ONE DAY, WE MET A MAN WHO OFFERED OUR COMPANY A NEW OPPORTUNITY. A NEW PLACE IN THE WORLD.
BIGGER THAN WE'D EVER IMAGINED.
HOSPITAL
AND AS WE GREW IN POWER, OUR APPETITES GREW STRONGER, TOO.

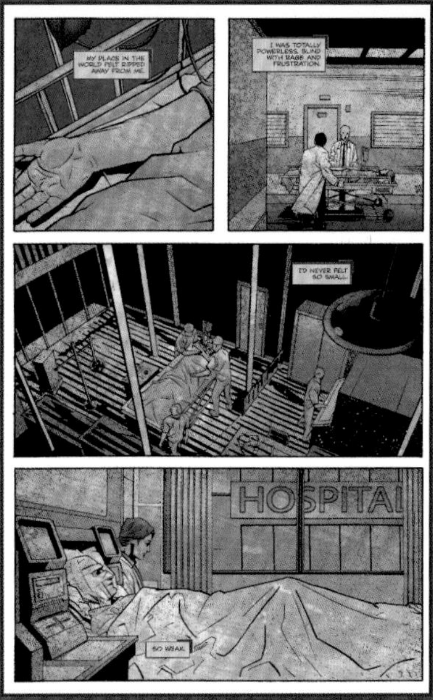
MY PLACE IN THE WORLD FELT RIPPED AWAY FROM ME.
I WAS TOTALLY POWERLESS. BLIND WITH RAGE AND FRUSTRATION.
I'D NEVER FELT SO SMALL.
HOSPITAL
SO WEAK.

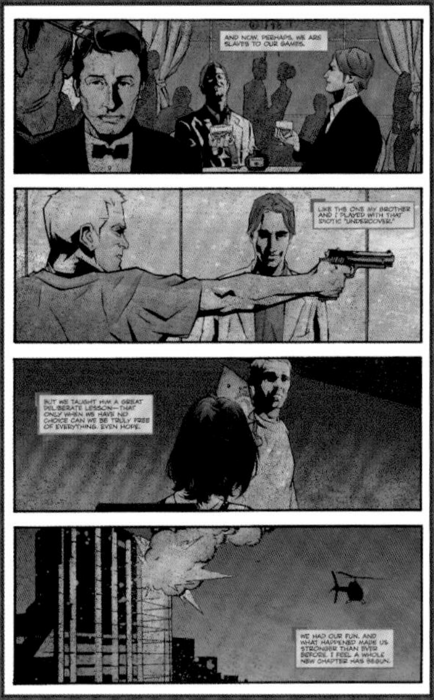
AND NOW, PERHAPS, WE ARE SLAVES TO OUR GAMES.
LIKE THE ONE MY BROTHER AND I PLAYED WITH THAT IDIOTIC "UNDERCOVER."
BUT WE TAUGHT HIM A GREAT DELIBERATE LESSON—THAT ONLY WHEN WE HAVE NO CHOICE CAN WE BE TRULY FREE OF EVERYTHING. EVEN HOPE.
WE HAD OUR FUN. AND WHAT HAPPENED MADE US STRONGER THAN EVER BEFORE. I FEEL A WHOLE NEW CHAPTER HAS BEGUN.

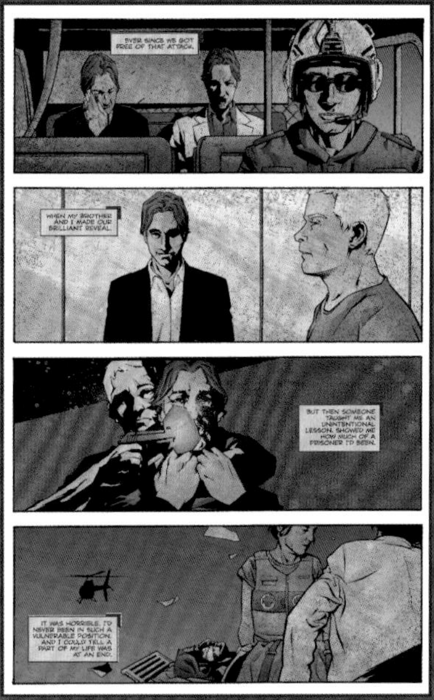
EVER SINCE WE GOT FREE OF THAT ATTACK.
WHEN MY BROTHER AND I MADE OUR BRILLIANT REVEAL.
BUT THEN SOMEONE TAUGHT ME AN UNINTENTIONAL LESSON. SHOWED ME HOW MUCH OF A PRISONER I'D BEEN.
IT WAS HORRIBLE. I'D NEVER BEEN IN SUCH A VULNERABLE POSITION. AND I COULD TELL A PART OF MY LIFE WAS AT AN END.

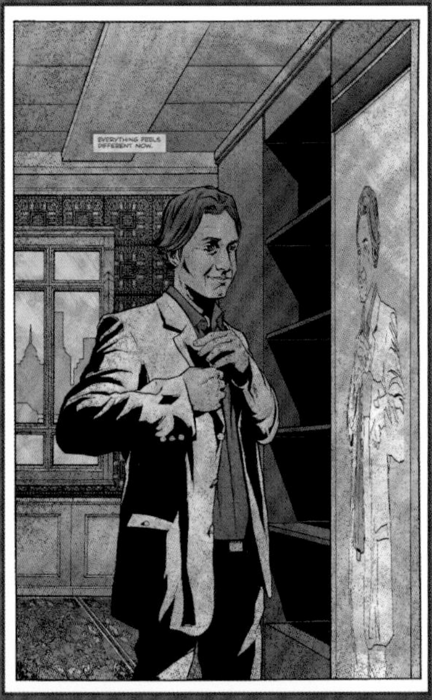
EVERYTHING FEELS DIFFERENT NOW.

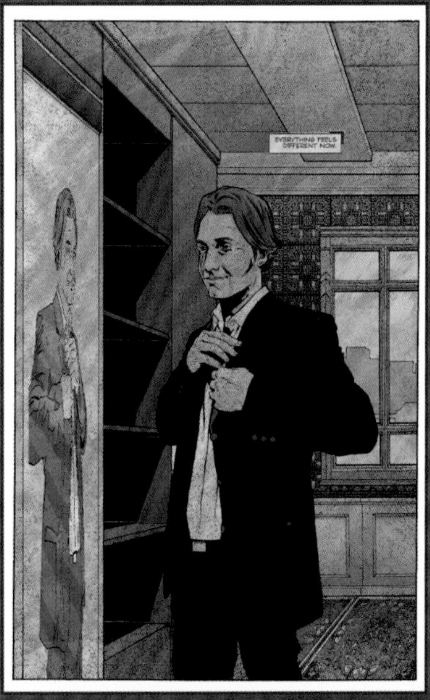
EVERYTHING FEELS DIFFERENT NOW.